T0246274

ALL MY EYES SEE

ALL MY EYES SEE

The Artistic Vocation of Fr. William Hart McNichols

Christopher Pramuk
and
William Hart McNichols

ORBIS BOOKS
Maryknoll, New York 10545

Founded in 1970, Orbis Books endeavors to publish works that enlighten the mind, nourish the spirit, and challenge the conscience. The publishing arm of the Maryknoll Fathers and Brothers, Orbis seeks to explore the global dimensions of the Christian faith and mission, to invite dialogue with diverse cultures and religious traditions, and to serve the cause of reconciliation and peace. The books published reflect the views of their authors and do not represent the official position of the Maryknoll Society. To learn more about Maryknoll and Orbis Books, please visit our website at www.orbis books.com.

Library of Congress Cataloging-in-Publication Data

Names: Pramuk, Christopher, author. | McNichols, William Hart, author.
Title: All my eyes see : the artistic vocation of Fr. William Hart
   McNichols / Christopher Pramuk and William Hart McNichols.
Description: Maryknoll, NY : Orbis Books, [2024] | Includes bibliographical
   references.
Identifiers: LCCN 2023044288 (print) | LCCN 2023044289 (ebook) | ISBN
   9781626985704 (print) | ISBN 9798888660263 (epub)
Subjects: LCSH: McNichols, William Hart. | Spiritual biography—United
   States. | Icon painters—United States—Biography.
Classification: LCC BX4705.M47658 P73 2024 (print) | LCC BX4705.M47658
   (ebook) | DDC 282.092 [B]—dc23/eng/20231122
LC record available at https://lccn.loc.gov/2023044288
LC ebook record available at https://lccn.loc.gov/2023044289

These drawings, illustrations, paintings, images, and icons are the work of one person's lifetime. I always appreciate it when an artist allows room for the viewer to see things even they could not see.

In this book I've attempted to discuss them with my dear friend Chris. But I don't want my words to close off your experience, but hopefully enhance it. What I mean is, very often, when I've shared these images in a presentation or slide show, people would come up with the most unusual insights, and it would enable me also to see what I'd been given, as if the work was not mine alone.

Since my childhood, I've always felt that God was in everything, but I struggled greatly with how to express that feeling in words. So I unconsciously took to art, to express the inexpressible. I really do "trust my art" as an honest expression, but words around it can be very awkward and fallible. As you see, even here, I'm tripping up already, trying to explain.

At age nineteen, the spirituality of St. Ignatius forever confirmed that early spiritual intuition of God in everything, and gave me the freedom to fly.

This is why my dedication is to my Holy Father St. Ignatius and the Society of Jesus.

And to my siblings, Stephen, Robert, Mary Elizabeth, and Marjory.

And for Robert Kerr and Kenn Ashe.

—Fr. William Hart McNichols

It is a great mystery to me that my own vocation "contains multitudes." I offer my part in this book to Lauri, my dearest companion of almost thirty-five years; to Isabell and Grace, whose gifts for "seeing" and fiercely loving—not least loving their Papa—never cease to astonish me; and to Henry and Sophia, may you always know how beautifully you shine, and never forget to "show 'em your sparkle!"

To Rob and Jenne Harris, artists in life and in friendship, whom I cherish beyond all words. And to my friends and colleagues at Regis University, especially Fr. Kevin Burke, to whom Lauri and I owe so much of our spiritual journey together.

Above all, for anyone who finds themselves on the outside, misunderstood, feared, unwelcome in society and church. May you find in Fr. Bill's art and life's journey a reflection of your own precious worth, reassurance that you are not alone, and that you are beloved by God.

May "all our eyes" see, come to know, and be set free in this truth.

—Christopher Pramuk

CONTENTS

PART III
ICONOGRAPHER: FRIEND OF PROPHETS,
PILGRIMS, AND SAINTS
109

POSTSCRIPT
Apocalypsis and *Veronike*: Art as Participation
in the Work of God the Creator
William Hart McNichols

AFTERWORD
The Iconography of William Hart McNichols
Robert Lentz, OFM

DAYS IN THE LIFE OF
WILLIAM HART MCNICHOLS

BIBLIOGRAPHY / ADDITIONAL READING

NOTES

FOREWORD

Our whole business in this life is to restore to health the eyes of the heart, whereby God may be seen.
—St. Augustine

This book begins with Fr. Bill's account of a nearly fatal "heart collapse," which he suffered in 2012. For two weeks, as he lay in a coma, his life hung in the balance. I remember that incident well. Some days after hearing the news, I called Bill's number, just to hear his voice on the answering machine. In leaving a message, I proposed that if he ever heard my words, it would mean our prayers had been answered and that "like Lazarus" he had returned to us.

Thankfully, that prayer was answered. But for Fr. Bill, it raised questions. For what purpose had he been spared? Was there some further work he was meant to accomplish?

This book is, in some ways, an answer to that question and to Fr. Bill's feeling that he had not yet fully shared his body of work with the world. Many readers are familiar with his status as one of the great iconographers of our time. But that work, following his apprenticeship with Br. Robert Lentz, came well into a long journey in which he sought, in various ways, to integrate his dual vocation as priest and artist. There was much that came before—not just a body of work, but the spiritual path that prepared him for the kind of artist he would become.

From early childhood, as we learn, Bill sensed that all reality was embraced by the love of God. That love took flesh in a helpless baby, lying in a manger in Bethlehem. But from the beginning that child was stalked by dark forces that sought to suppress its light. In one of Bill's earliest drawings, at the age of five, he depicted the baby Jesus, already bearing the wounds of his later passion. The facets of complexity within that image would contain the seeds of Bill's own ministry and artistic work.

From his early schooling by Catholic Sisters of the Precious Blood, Bill acquired a lifelong devotion to the saints, responding in particular to the stories of child saints and martyrs, who, in their innocence, confronted the cruel powers of the world. Even without training, he was compelled to draw, to bear witness to all that his eyes saw. At the same time, he felt an irresistible call to the priesthood.

During his subsequent formation as a Jesuit priest, he was fortunate to find support in cultivating his artistic talents—even though, as one priest who conducted his entrance interviews in 1967 said, "We [Jesuits] don't really have people who do art." His first professional commissions were for illustrating children's books. But then urgent pastoral duties called. During the AIDS crisis in New York, he became one of the priests on the frontlines, ministering to countless young men who were dying under miserable circumstances, their suffering compounded by the stigma associated with the disease, and all too often by a sense of abandonment by their church.

Following in the footsteps of saints like Aloysius Gonzaga, Damien of Moloka'i, and Francis of Assisi, Bill became the face of mercy and love for all of these precious children of God. And it was in this time that his priestly ministry directly converged with his artistic vocation. In such works as his AIDS-inspired *Stations of the Cross* or the *AIDS Crucifixion*, he created devotional works that spoke directly with "arrows into the heart of the church," drawing the connection between the passion of Christ and those suffering the pain, scorn, and ignominy associated with AIDS.

It was after this period that Bill turned to the study and writing of icons, the work for which he is best known. To many Catholics, the Byzantine world of icons is mysterious and hard to understand. Icons are not intended to serve as religious decoration, nor to be realistic portraits of their subjects. They are meant to serve as a portal to prayer and contemplation, a window into deeper spiritual realities. To understand them properly requires cultivating a new way of seeing, with the eyes of the heart—a capacity we might then extend to our encounters with other human beings and all of creation.

The story that Fr. Bill relates in this book is marked deeply by two important identities. One comes from his formation in the spirituality of St. Ignatius Loyola, founder of the Jesuits. Even after his departure from the Society of Jesus, that deep Ignatian identity remains strong, from his ceaseless depiction of Jesuit saints, to his identification with Christ's ongoing passion in the world, and his determination to "find God in all things." But another deep theme in the book comes from his identity as a gay man, a story he shares with poignant honesty and courage. In an identity that has long been subject to scorn, persecution, and shame, Fr. Bill describes a long journey to self-acceptance and safe-harbor in the love of God. He finds in his identity a distinctive angle of vision, a point of identification with others on the margins, including so many mystics, artists, and spiritual explorers who don't fit easily into the pre-established mold.

It is doubtful that Fr. Bill would have been able to share this story without the help and encouragement of his friend Chris Pramuk, whose empathetic listening and discerning questions and comments make him the ideal guide and companion. Through the conversations recorded here we come to know the heart of a great spiritual master, a heart that remains deeply vulnerable to the wounds of the world, while pointing toward glimpses of that Beauty, which Dostoevsky said will save the world. Dorothy Day loved to quote that famous line. For her it did not mean the world would be saved by pretty things. It referred to the capacity to see reality in its ultimate dimension, where Beauty is another name for what is Good and True.

In one of my own meetings with Chris and Fr. Bill I used the phrase "terrible beauty" to describe Bill's preoccupations. It is a phrase from a poem by Yeats, and I smiled to see Chris and Bill refer to it here in their conversations. The beauty that Bill depicts is the vulnerability of a poor child born in a stable, worshiped by shepherds, while soldiers of the king seek to do him violence; a savior born to die on a cross, who even after his resurrection bears the wounds of his passion. All that his eyes see includes the cruelty, violence, and darkness of our world, but also a window into another world transfigured by love, a dimension of joy and beauty that death and darkness are powerless to suppress. "What you gaze upon you become," Fr. Bill says, and so it is all the more important that we train our gaze on witnesses who embody the moral and spiritual beauty that will save the world.

For his own sake, and for my selfish reasons, I am grateful that Fr. Bill was allowed to return from the other side of his "heart collapse." Yes, he had more work to do and more work to share with the world. But with this book, I feel strongly that he has accomplished one of his most important, outstanding tasks: to share with the world the gift of himself.

ROBERT ELLSBERG
Publisher, Orbis Books

INTRODUCTION

Opening the Eyes of the Heart

Father William Hart McNichols (Fr. Bill) is widely known, admired, and sometimes scorned, as one of the world's most gifted living religious artists and iconographers. The icons of Fr. Bill, a former Jesuit and student of the famed Franciscan iconographer Br. Robert Lentz, have been honored with exhibitions in major U.S. cities, featured in many books, and the subject of a full-length documentary by filmmaker Christopher Summa. More recently, his years of ministry to the dying during the AIDS crisis in New York City in the 1980s were the focus of a podcast, and later a book, by journalist Michael O'Laughlin.[1] In letters published between author Robert Ellsberg and the late Sr. Wendy Beckett, the beloved British nun and art historian who hosted TV programs on religious art for many years, Sr. Wendy confesses that Fr. Bill's icons are "profoundly full of the presence of God for me. . . . When I look at [them] I fall into prayer, and that's it. . . . They're not 'works of art' in the worldly sense but functional, living theology, uniting us to Our Lord as we look at them."[2] In all of this, it is fair to conclude, as one Jesuit commentator noted several years ago, "At last, the art of Rev. William Hart McNichols is enjoying the treatment it deserves."[3]

What has not yet received sustained attention is the story of Bill's artistic journey in the decades prior to his work as an iconographer, when drawing was his primary means of expression as a young, gay man, coming into his identity while growing up in a prominent political family—his father served as governor of Colorado from 1957 to 1963, and his uncle was mayor of Denver from 1968 to 1983. From the age of five, through his teenage years and during his AIDS ministry as a young Jesuit in the 1980s, Bill created hundreds of drawings and paintings that convey a vision of Christ-like compassion for the marginalized; many do so, arguably, in a more intimate and personal key than the icons for which he would become famous decades later. His drawings of the Holy Family, for example, often created for children's books, portray the "hidden years" of Jesus in tenderly familiar, down-to-earth scenes; the "AIDS drawings," by contrast, can still shock in their portrayal of Christ crucified, naked on the cross, covered in Kaposi sarcoma lesions.

These latter drawings still speak quite powerfully into our present-day social, political, and ecclesial atmosphere, where unspeakable suffering continues to afflict the most marginalized of God's people—including queer persons, who still face widespread isolation and discrimination in the church—and not only human beings, but the animals, waters, and trees, the suffering Earth itself. In Fr. Bill's art across some five decades, human beings and the natural world share a fluid, inextricable relationship, reflecting the "integral ecology" to which Pope Francis calls us in his teaching, and which the Pueblo Indians of the American Southwest, Bill's longtime spiritual home, have always embodied in their communal beliefs and religious practices. In Catholic art, the creativity of the artist is a response in faith to the overflowing creativity of God, who seeks to birth fresh possibility into landscapes of chaos and evident hopelessness. As Fr. Bill has written, "Art is praise of God with every stroke and movement."[4]

This book represents the fruition of a friendship with Fr. Bill and innumerable conversations that reach back some fifteen years. What previous explorations of Bill's life and work lack in biographical detail, this book offers in his own voice, prompted by my questionings, though the picture that emerges here does not claim to be complete.[5] It is not a biography, autobiography, or memoir. If it were so, many more people close to Bill—family, close friends, and critical "life savers" along the way, people who came up often in our conversations—would have to be included. Fr. Bill and I dare to hope for something more modest: that through his art and in the natural dance of our conversations, something creative and perhaps unexpected will stir in the imagination of fellow pilgrims of all kinds—laypeople and religious, spiritual seekers, artists and scholars alike—anyone receptive to art's power to sustain the journey of faith, especially when the road descends into loneliness and hardship. This book seeks to give voice to experiences and insights that have gestated in Fr. Bill over a lifetime, while inviting the reader to contemplate a remarkable legacy of illustrations, paintings, and icons, some published here for the first time.

In an essay titled "Art as Witness" by the famous illustrator Fritz Eichenberg, whose striking wood engravings graced the pages of the *Catholic Worker* newspaper, Eichenberg writes, "Creativity is potentially dormant in every human mind," yet creativity "needs nourishment and care."[6] Just as Eichenberg's images have nourished the lives of countless pilgrims in a vision of faith that seeks justice, so have Fr. Bill's illustrations and icons. They do so

even more potently when contemplated against the backdrop of his life's story. "If we could only learn to approach everything we do with love . . . ," says Eichenberg, "realize the joy of creating beauty in ourselves and around us, open our eyes to the grand design in all things living, we would be rewarded immeasurably." Few persons that I know have lived out this creed more faithfully over the course of a lifetime than Fr. Bill McNichols.

Yet I share with those who know Fr. Bill personally a certain reluctance, or inability, to claim that I truly know him. Of him it might fairly be said what one of Abraham Lincoln's numerous biographers said about his enigmatic subject. "The more fully Lincoln's varied career is traced . . . the more his genius grows and passes beyond each interpretation."[7] One of Lincoln's contemporaries put it more succinctly: "He still smiles and remains impenetrable."[8] Fr. Bill has been described as a mystic, and even a saint, by those whose lives he has touched. He has also been the object of public scorn from a vocal minority of Catholics who have denigrated his art as "profane," or who find the very thought of an uncloseted gay priest to be scandalous. Though Bill would never think to apply the term "saint" to himself—he resists even the title of "mystic"—Michael O'Laughlin in his book quotes one young man who regularly attended Fr. Bill's "Healing Masses for People with AIDS" in New York City. He said simply that Bill "is the most Christ-like man I have ever met."[9] When a cynical editorial writer accused Lincoln's biographers of being "hagiographers," that is, "saint worshipers," one reader responded, "We could use a few real saints in this country now."[10] Is this not also painfully true today?

During his Jesuit formation, Bill recalls one of his Jesuit theology professors saying bluntly to the class, "If you seek ordination, get ready for chaos. Your very brief life in the church will be a lonely journey. You will sow the seeds for the new church but you won't live to see it. If you can accept this, then get ordained. If not, it would be very wise not to." An all-encompassing "Ignatian caution," as he describes it, "was drilled into us about false claims to vainglory." My aim in this introduction is not to lift Fr. Bill onto a pedestal. Rather, both as his friend and as a theologian, I have come to see Bill's art as a luminous thread in a vast and ancient tapestry, weaving together Eastern and Western spiritualities, and, as we shall see, the American Southwest, a lineage almost too wondrous, too mysterious, to write about. In what follows, my aim is to situate Fr. Bill's artistic vocation not in isolation (the lone artist-priest-hero-saint), but far more humbly, as he does: as one in a very long lineage who has been called to "take instruction" from the Spirit, regardless of personal cost, out of loving fidelity to a new church, a new creation, he will never live to see. As a friend and fellow pilgrim, I also wish to say a word about how our relationship has changed me.

Biographical and Spiritual Roots of McNichols's Artistic Vocation

As noted above, the atmosphere of Bill's childhood was thick with politics and religion. Born in Denver to Marjory Hart and Stephen McNichols on July 10, 1949, his father was elected governor of Colorado in 1957. Thus, in 1960, he and his four siblings (Steve, Bob, Mary, and Margie) found themselves living in the Governor's Mansion.[11] Five years later, his uncle, William Henry McNichols Jr., was elected mayor of Denver. His grandfather, William Henry McNichols Sr., was Denver city auditor for nearly twenty-five years. These were no small accomplishments in a state rife with anti-Catholic sentiment. For much of the first half of the century, Colorado politics was controlled by the Ku Klux Klan, which frequently targeted Catholics and Catholic institutions. It was an often-hostile climate that undoubtedly still shapes the way Fr. Bill moves in the world as artist, gay man, and priest, now "out" for almost fifty years. While that particular choice has made many uncomfortable, including some of his fellow religious, it has also and always been a

tremendous struggle for Bill. "Some people want to be subversive," he once said to me. "They try to be subversive. For gay people, just being born, just being alive, is already subversive. I've spent my whole life trying not to be subversive, trying to fit in."

As a child, Bill's love of art was nourished by a Catholic parochial school education in Denver. He credits the Sisters of the Precious Blood with encouraging his artistic gifts and infusing his elementary school years with a deep spirituality. "In my own life, especially in childhood, art was the primary way I was introduced to the two thousand years of Christianity."[12] Though he endured years of bullying through grade school and high school, art and humor became ways to express, and mask, his suffering. It was during his teenage years, among the Jesuits at Regis High School in Denver, that Bill would find his lifelong home and refuge in the atmosphere of Ignatian spirituality.

> From the age of nineteen I was brought into the life of the Spiritual Exercises of St. Ignatius of Loyola, which consist of four weeks of prayer and meditation on the life of Christ. The retreat culminates with a glorious burst of light, which launches the retreatant into a life of ministry of "finding God in all things." Once these words settle in your heart, they never leave you. They become the way you live in the world with its great variety of people, as well as the creation, both damaged and abundant.[13]

Here is the key to Fr. Bill's twin vocation as an artist and priest, and perhaps the golden thread that unites our wide-ranging conversations below. In life and in art, he seems most at home in the darkly liminal passage between the Third and Fourth Weeks of the Spiritual Exercises of Ignatius. Though people continue to be crucified across the world (the Christ whose passion is the focus of the First and Third Week meditations), an Ignatian sensibility perceives that *another world is possible* because God, in Christ, has planted in history the seeds of all creation's transformation in love, in resurrection hope, our joyful participation in the very life of God (the risen Christ of the Fourth Week). Activating all the senses and powers of imagination through the Four Weeks of the Exercises, the humanity of Jesus whom we encounter in the Gospels (Week Two) refracts that same glorious "burst of light" in all of us.

Imbibing the inner dynamism of Ignatian spirituality, Fr. Bill sums up his philosophy of art in six words: "What you gaze upon, you become." "You gaze on the icon," he says, "but it gazes on you too. We need to gaze on truly conversational, truly loving images, images that will return our love."[14] Implicit here is a call to fully participate in the co-creative labor of beloved community, God's dream for the world. We are not beholden to "reality" as mediated by the prevailing culture. Like a pebble thrown into a pond, the pattern of Jesus's life, death, and resurrection continues to birth an amazing "cloud of witnesses," saints both ordinary and extraordinary, from whom we can learn what it means to be fully human. Indeed, much like the art of his teacher Robert Lentz, the sheer diversity of subjects across Bill's corpus is staggering.[15] It proclaims that there are no cookie-cutter saints; there is no single, perfect way to be authentically human, to be holy, to embody the divine.

To gaze on "images that return our love," then, far from binding us to some dead thing of the past called "the church," is for many believers a subversive spiritual practice, a disciplined "spiritual exercise" that aims to get the heart into its best, most divine–human, shape. Each must discover our own particular gifts, and for every pilgrim and every community the path will be unique. The sacred image or icon, in other words, always turns back upon the viewer. If images tell stories, and those stories attach themselves to our hearts, *what kind of images and life stories do we choose to inhabit*? Are they helping us become the persons and community God calls us to be?

To Reinforce or Resist the Prevailing Order

Nearly a hundred years ago, the philosophers of the Frankfurt School drew a critical distinction between authentic art and art refracted through popular, political, and mass culture, or what they (derisively) called the "culture industry."[16] What happens to art, they famously asked, when it is suddenly produced on a mass scale for the consumption of everybody?[17] The question takes on heightened urgency in the age of the Internet, the smartphone, and artificial intelligence, as we find ourselves awash in a chaos of images. How does one distinguish what is good, true, and beautiful from the barrage of messages that aim solely to provoke, to stimulate, to sell us something? In simplified terms, for the critical theorists of the Frankfurt School, authentic art is something that's elevating and challenges the existing social, political, and economic order, whereas mass culture does precisely the opposite. "Culture, or the culture industry, uses art in a conservative way, which is to say it uses art to uphold the existing order."[18] In this context, I wish to suggest, Fr. Bill's art is prophetically Christian, authentically Catholic, and frequently subversive, or interruptive of mass culture, in the best sense of these terms.

In ways resonant with the teaching and pastoral witness of Pope Francis, Fr. Bill's interpretation of the biblical and Christian mystical tradition reflects a "mysticism of open eyes,"[19] reminding the viewer that contemplation of the Gospels and the lives of the martyrs and saints is no aesthetic or disembodied escape from reality. To paraphrase German theologian Johann Baptist Metz, the stories Bill tells through his images are "subversive" and "dangerous" insofar as they seek to make visible "all invisible and inconvenient suffering," and, convenient or not, to pay attention to it and take responsibility for it, "for the sake of a God who is a friend to human beings."[20] No doubt the creation of such images can be threatening to the prevailing powers of society and church, and at once a vital source of hope for the "little," the poor and marginalized across the world.[21] The 1960s folk singer Phil Ochs, a fierce critic of American hubris, once said of his music, "Ah, but in such an ugly time, the true protest is beauty."[22] Fr. Bill's protest, we might say, is the good news, the truth, the beauty, of the gospel itself, and in lives of holiness across the ages.

In sum, if being subversive means to threaten or tear down the tradition, then Fr. Bill's art can hardly be described as subversive. As even a cursory glance across his body of work makes clear, the artist himself disappears behind the illuminated faces of the prophets, saints, and martyrs of the Christian tradition and well beyond. While his subjects are not always Christian, his vocation is profoundly "traditional," even theologically conservative, at the meeting point between Western and Eastern Christianity. If by subversive, on the other hand, we mean radical (as in "returning to the roots"), challenging in the way that the prophets and saints shatter our complacency, then his work is rightly called subversive—though Bill himself shudders at the word. The more fitting term may be *anima ecclesia*. Fr. Bill is a *church soul*, though his vision of "church" cannot be confined to a building. Though the "precious blood" is everywhere in his work, so is the "burst of light" that characterizes the joy of the gospel: the call to live and labor together as resurrected beings.

Bringing Nativity into the Apocalypse

"The Kingdom of God," says Russian Orthodox theologian Paul Evdokimov, writing in Paris under the shadow of World War II, "is accessible only through the chaos of this world. It is not an alien transplant, but rather the revelation of the hidden depth of this very world."[23] In a world that despairs of God, the artist's vocation, says Evdokimov, is both priestly and prophetic: she "creates the transcendental and attests to its presence." "A little dust of this world, a board, a

few colors, a few lines—and there is beauty . . . *a vision of things which cannot be seen.*" Likewise, the poet, "attuned to the beginning of things," helps us remember that "beauty is the fulfillment of truth, and that moment when 'all is fulfilled' is always marked by glory."[24] To say it more soberly, as was once said of a young Abraham Joshua Heschel, the poet, the theologian, the artist "must speak for a silent God."[25]

Growing up as a Roman Catholic in the United States, I am far more accustomed to sacred spaces filled with sculptures and stained glass than with icons, which are often described as "windows to the sacred." Much later in my life I would experience this mystagogical sense of iconography, but as a younger man, I would have found it difficult to pray before icons. The faces gazing back at me from their gold-leafed surfaces seemed to me strange and exotic, somewhat rigid, not quite people; to my eyes they were otherworldly, not "realistic," seeming to come, as it were, from the other side. Later I would understand that this visual dissonance is precisely the point, that by their very nature icons attempt to do what is logically impossible: to unite at once the unportrayability and portrayability of God, whose presence is both hidden and manifest in the world, shining, as it were, from within all things.[26]

To say it in terms of eschatology, that realm of Christian faith and theology most saturated with paradox, icons presume that another world is possible because the seeds of transformation, of divinization, of participation in the divine Energy, which is Love, are *already present in this world*, in history, if painfully hidden.[27] Much more than a painting, then, the icon is best described as *a theology* laid down in lines and colors. Thus, icons are not said to be "painted" but "written," and the art of writing icons is passed down methodically and prayerfully from teacher to student. As Henri Nouwen writes in his classic meditation on the Russian tradition, icons are not easy to "see" because they "speak more to our inner than to our outer senses. They speak to the heart that searches for God."[28] Prayer before the icon facilitates the re-centering of subjectivity from oneself to the divine, no longer related to as an object of self-fulfillment, but rather related to as a Person and Presence.[29]

Still, the dissonance I felt in viewing icons as a younger Catholic was not so much cognitive or theological as it was cultural and aesthetic. Accustomed to the more "realistic" style of Western religious art, iconography to my eyes seemed to *paint over* the messiness of life as it really is in favor of highly idealized representations of the human world and of the church. It smelled to me of Gnosticism, a suspicion of matter and the flesh, an escape from history, rather than its illumination.[30] Thanks in no small part to Fr. Bill's work, I have since come to see that I was mistaken, that my reticence before icons was misplaced. The dilemma could only be resolved when I began to see them not through my own culturally conditioned eyes but rather as they are meant to be seen, as "the presencing of the divine in and through the material form."[31] This required a fundamental shift in my default manner of seeing, a pedagogy, as it were, of seeing through the eyes of the heart. And to effect this shift I needed a teacher. Fr. Bill has been that teacher.

In her meditation on his iconography, spiritual writer Mirabai Starr underscores the "apocalyptic" or revelatory power of Bill's work to open urgently, if gently, the eyes of the heart.

> In the book of Revelation, Fr. Bill points out, the dragon goes after the pregnant woman to eat her child. We are all her children, he says. And, in the lineage of the prophets, *we are bringing nativity into the apocalypse. . . .* Fr. Bill's icons are beacons in the darkness, beckoning us home to love.[32]

To "engage with Fr. Bill's offerings is a subversive act," Starr concludes. "It quietly overthrows the patriarchy and gently reinstates the feminine values of mercy and connection."[33] Theologian John Dadosky recalls that when he first began to explore Bill's art, he "was struck by how much of his work was devoted to the divine feminine. I became convinced that much of Western Chris-

tianity suffers from this lack." Dadosky describes the feminine aspect of God as "a gaping wound" and "one of the most neglected dimensions" of Western religious life, even while many Christians remain "unaware of the ramifications of its absence in our collective psyche."[34]

While feminist theologians have long sought to restore the divine feminine in Christian spirituality, Bill's work has done so as well, if from a very different direction. He has, as it were, "put a face" on the divine feminine with his icons of Mary, and with his explicitly "sophianic icons," or images of Divine Sophia and the Shekhinah— in the rabbinic tradition, the divine Presence who accompanies and sustains her people in exile.[35] We are seeing "the last gasp of the dark side of masculinity," he says. "We are moving beyond viewing the struggle strictly as between the masculine and the feminine, to seeing the struggle as between light and darkness. Both sexes can be equally light or dark."[36] The point recalls for me the poet Rainer Maria Rilke, who speaks of a "great motherhood over all, as common longing," and who observes that "even in the man there is motherhood."[37] And as well, the writings of Thomas Merton, whose remembrance of God as Father and Mother, as Child and Sister, as Proverb and Wisdom-Sophia, has done perhaps as much as any Western spiritual writer to reclaim an experiential, felt knowledge of the living God in a feminine key.[38]

The task of the poet, the prophet, the contemplative, says Rowan Williams, is to interrogate the repetition of "old words for God, safe words for God, lazy words for God, useful words for God."[39] In like manner, the vocation of the prophetic *visual artist* is to interrogate the complacent repetition of old images, safe images, lazy images, useful images, of God. Theologian Wendy Wright beautifully drives the point home on the role of images and imagination in Christian spirituality down through the ages:

> [Images] are not only the products of our imagination but they give form and content to our imaginations. Repeated focus, as in

practices of meditation or contemplative gazing on religious images, facilitates this transformative process. The visual contemplative or meditative arts cultivated in the great religious traditions are vastly different from ordinary sight. Indeed, they are uniquely designed to deconstruct habituated imaginative constructs and allow visual imagery to reconstruct *a new imaginative lens through which reality is interpreted and possible worlds perceived.*[40]

Perhaps this is what it means to "bring nativity into the apocalypse." Both in life and through his art, Fr. Bill stands quietly at the threshold—often in the midst of evident chaos, as during the AIDS hospice ministry—midwifing our encounter with "possible worlds" that both do and do not yet exist. Though I was initially resistant to icons, the eyes of my heart have been opened by Fr. Bill's work to the illumination of the world—"finding God in all things"—and of human beings as ever-potential sacraments of the living God.

But how, exactly? In a passage I have long treasured, Rabbi Abraham Joshua Heschel speaks of the "powerlessness" that we often feel in prayer, the gap between our desire to pray and the means to express what we yearn to say. "Should we feel ashamed," he asks, "by our inability to utter what we bear in our hearts?" No, he says, we should not feel ashamed. "God loves what is left over at the bottom of the heart and cannot be expressed in words. . . . The unutterable surplus of what we feel, the sentiments that we are unable to put into words are our payment in kind to God."[41] What I, like so many others, have discovered in Fr. Bill's images and icons is that sacred images, much like music or liturgy, can help us bridge the distance we feel between ourselves and God. Both in his life and in his art—these, we shall see, are quite inseparable—Bill reminds me that it is possible to be a human being and to strive each day to be a follower of Christ: that is, to hold the fragility of the world and of our own lives with loving tenderness, and therein to discover, perhaps to our great surprise, that the world, charged everywhere with ineffable mystery, is loving us back.

As Heschel encourages me, so does Fr. Bill. When we bring our poverty back to prayer, God affirms our longing and our inability and mysteriously fills the gap. Jesus encouraged his followers to pray, to pray *boldly*, for the Reign of God to come "on earth as it is in heaven." Perhaps the distance is far smaller than we could ever imagine.

"All My Eyes See": On Nurturing the Spiritual Senses

In his classic study of 1923, *The Art Spirit*, the American painter Robert Henri offered an assessment of Western society that seems to me highly prescient of the present-day climate in America—and the hyperpolarized U.S. Catholic Church—now a hundred years later.

> We are living in a strange civilization. Our minds and souls are so overlaid with fear, with artificiality, that often we do not even recognize beauty. It is this fear, this lack of direct vision of truth that brings about all the disaster the world holds, and how little opportunity we give any people for casting off fear, for living simply and naturally. When they do, first of all we fear them, then we condemn them. It is only if they are great enough to outlive our condemnation that we accept them.[42]

Now nearing the end of my sixth decade, I've learned to pay attention especially to those religious thinkers, artists, and writers who get attacked or dismissed by the "defenders of orthodoxy," whether because they are perceived as too naïve or childish or because they seem to live from a posture of love and mercy that others suspect is too profane, too open, too vulnerable to the world's manifold diversity. Or perhaps, for lack of empirical evidence of the sacred realm they labor to defend, we simply deem them "impenetrable."

Like a great many intellectuals, artists, and visionaries in the history of the church, the categorical labels that would fix a person on one side of an absolutized binary (e.g., liberal/conservative; progressive/traditional) do not hold in the case of Fr. Bill. His work "contains multitudes,"[43] equally at home with the mystical theologies of Hans Urs von Balthasar and Adrienne von Speyr, the prophetic voices of Gustavo Gutiérrez and Daniel Berrigan, and a growing litany of unsung witnesses both within and beyond the boundaries of Christianity. Thus Fr. Bill stands both within and outside the margins of an institution that hasn't always welcomed him, giving new form and new content to the radical capaciousness of Catholicism, and vital expressions of Christian faith from East to West. Today you can often find him wearing a black T-shirt emblazoned with "Glory to Ukraine" in the language of that country, and in the bright yellow and blue colors of its flag. To a fault, some might say, his heart is torn open again and again by the pain of the world.

Initially unsettled by the "strangeness" of certain pieces of Fr. Bill's work, I learned to open myself to these images especially. I learned to trust the revelatory nature of our long, often meandering conversations about life's difficulties; the question of God's presence amid terrible suffering and violence on the world stage; or simply as one of us was yearning for hints of grace in situations of prolonged personal difficulty. (We've shared a great deal of laughter and silliness, too, not easily transferable to the page.) I've incorporated his art into my classes, alongside others not "at home" in the dominant culture, especially African American writers and artists. Their testimony, like Fr. Bill's, often gestures to the presence of the divine, not in some distant heaven but immanently, often painfully, "in the valley of the shadow of death." And like these others, I find Bill's work not only compelling in its piercing honesty, but trustworthy. Why? Because he has lingered in that valley much of his life, accompanying others in hope against hope, witnessing to God's concern for the least.

"There are moments in our lives, there are moments in a day," says Henri, "when we seem to see beyond the usual. Such are the moments of our greatest happiness. Such are the moments of our greatest wisdom. If one could but recall [this] vision by some sort of sign. It was in this hope that the arts were invented. Sign-posts on the way to what may be. Sign-posts toward greater knowledge."[44] New Testament scholar N. T. Wright puts the question of art and its relationship to hope in more explicitly Christian language: "When art comes to terms with both the wounds of the world and the promise of resurrection, and learns how to express and respond to both at once, we will be on the way to a fresh vision, a fresh mission."[45] Following what he calls the "slender threads," letting himself be led by the Spirit—"to hear, to find, to take instruction"—Bill's work bears us through the world's wounds and toward the gospel promise of resurrection.[46] In bursts of light and sometimes in terrible shadows, he shows the way to a fresh vision, a fresh mission.

It is in this spirit of promise—the vision of the Fourth Week—that we have taken our title, *All My Eyes See*, from a poem by the great English Jesuit poet, Gerard Manley Hopkins—"Not of all my eyes see, wandering on the world," writes Hopkins.[47] Bill has described Hopkins's meaning to me in terms of intuition, a sixth sense, a capacity to see and feel beneath the surface of things. "We don't always see the suffering in people, the beauty in people, but as you grow near to God that sensibility opens up. As a hospice chaplain, *a lot of my eyes opened up. And they never shut down, that's the problem!"* There's a profound vulnerability, in other words, along with inexplicable joy, intensity, and depth, that comes with opening all of one's senses to the world. "In New York, on the subway, you learn that you've got to pay attention to everything, heighten your antennae, your sense for who and what's happening around you." More positively, he says, "It's like the communion of saints, this palpable knowing that those who have died are really present to us. You try to talk about it and people think you're crazy. But it's a way of talking about a deep truth of human experience that's difficult to explain. We didn't just make up this stuff."

For me, the notion of perceiving with "all my eyes" shares something of Eichenberg's wonder that creativity "is potentially dormant in every human mind." In the language of the Christian mystical tradition, we all bear innate "spiritual senses," dormant "seeds of contemplation," *more than just two physical eyes*, by virtue of our source and destiny in God.[48] Yet these seeds of awareness, the bud of creativity, as Eichenberg observes, require "nourishment and care." Robert Henri calls this inner sensibility "the art spirit," and like Eichenberg—like Hopkins, like Fr. Bill—Henri insists that this capacity for sensing the holy, the beautiful, the sacred in all things is "the province of every human being." It "is not an outside, extra thing. When the artist is alive in any person, whatever his kind of work may be, he becomes an inventive, searching, daring, self-expressive creature."[49]

However you might define it, whatever your experience of this heightened sensibility may be, it is our fervent wish that this book will nourish your own art spirit, your innate spiritual senses. "Let those who have eyes to see, see," says Jesus. It is the image that leads to insight, and the artist who opens the door to such a faith.

An Unexpected Friendship

This introduction would be incomplete without a brief recounting of my friendship with Fr. Bill, the backstory for our conversations in these chapters. It was almost fifteen years ago, some months after my first book on Thomas Merton was published, that I received a handwritten letter bearing a name and address I didn't recognize: Fr. Bill McNichols, Taos, New Mexico. The sender described himself as someone who "did not like Thomas Merton very much" until he had read my book; that to his great surprise, I had helped him "discover a side of Merton completely unknown to me," namely, Merton's encounter

with Wisdom-Sophia, the divine feminine, and his translation of her voice into the West. He went on to explain that he had first encountered the divine feminine some forty years ago in the liturgy and iconography of the Christian East, and that he had portrayed her in several of his works as an iconographer. He concluded, rather matter-of-factly, that one of the drawings in my book had inspired him to create a new icon of Sophia, and would I be interested in seeing it?

Little could I have imagined that the person who wrote this kind letter would become a dear friend. It was the first of several written exchanges that merged into phone calls and eventually several pilgrimages I would make to Fr. Bill's studio in Taos. The first of these I undertook with our eldest daughter, Isabell, then fifteen, who was keen to meet him, and who I secretly hoped would fall in love with the high desert landscape that I had come to love decades earlier. (A hike through the Chama River Canyon to Christ in the Desert Monastery near Abiquiu sealed her own bond with this sacred geography.) The second involved our whole family traveling to Taos to visit with Fr. Bill. Our daughter Grace, a budding artist, watched in wonder and utter delight in Bill's studio as he showed her how to apply gold-leaf to an unfinished icon. We shared many meals, Mass around a small coffee table, and a back-entrance journey into Taos Pueblo, where he introduced me to several artist friends from the Native American community. Since his move to Albuquerque in 2013, I have visited him there several times, and he has stayed with us when visiting with his siblings or passing through the Denver area. In short, Fr. Bill has become a beloved part of our family.

Bill and I share an obsessive love of music, perhaps nobody more than Stevie Wonder and Joni Mitchell, who, in her wondrous renaissance of recent years, is a frequent topic of conversation. I have stacks of CDs in my study that he has sent me, from Barbra Streisand and k. d. lang to Bach, Pergolesi, and Gershwin, with scribbled notes about each for my edification. I receive almost daily texts and emails from Bill with links to

Write What You See and Send It to the Seven Churches:
The Apocalypse 1:11
WHM, 1982

YouTube interviews or performances by various artists, both popular and obscure. Of course, it is impossible to sum up a friendship in a few lines. I can only hope that hints of Bill's personal qualities come through in our conversations below: his eye for beauty, both childlike and sophisticated; his lively sense of humor and quickness to laugh; a deep love for his parents and each of his four siblings, for the Jesuits, his Jesuit mentors, and enduring friends in the Society of Jesus; and perhaps above all, his vulnerability and sensitivity to others, including his insecurities, oft-repeated to me, about revealing so much of himself in this book.

In light of the latter, it has been a tremendous privilege and grace to "listen in" and try as best I can to convey to the reader something of the gift that Fr. Bill has been to so many. In the language of St. Ignatius, Bill is a "helper of souls," not least because the "pilot light" of his faith, as he calls it, an early gift from the church and its artistic riches, burns so fiercely in his heart, through periods of loneliness, joy, and trial, warming others in its glow. I know that Bill's wish for this book is that the flame of your faith may be kindled by his art.

⸎

In preparing this book for publication, Bill and I recorded weekly phone conversations for the better part of a year to talk about his life, his art, and his ministry. Our conversations were then edited into manuscript form, alongside a wide range of drawings, paintings, and icons laid out in such a way as to facilitate contemplation. The twelve chapters are grouped into three major periods of Bill's life: Part I: Childhood and Jesuit Beginnings; Part II: Illustrator, Hospice Minister, and Priest; and Part III: Iconographer: Friend of Prophets, Pilgrims, and Saints. As a Postscript, we've included a meditation on the vocation of the artist that Bill wrote during his AIDS ministry; as an Afterword, a tribute to Fr. Bill penned by his teacher, the master iconographer Br. Robert Lentz, after Bill had completed his studies.

Though he is no longer a Jesuit, a story we touch on below, Ignatian spirituality remains Fr. Bill's spiritual homeland while he lives and serves as a Catholic priest in Albuquerque. He continues to write icons under commission from patrons across the country and world, including many Jesuit institutions. His icon *Our Sister Thea Bowman*, for example, a subject of chapter 11 and a constant presence to us both as he was painting her, now resides in a chapel that bears her name at Georgetown University. A number of Bill's original artworks reside very happily at Regis University in Denver, where I teach, and where Bill served as artist-in-residence during his early formation as a Jesuit.

For their expert help in providing high quality images of Fr. Bill's art and numerous photographs, we are indebted to Bill's sister, artist Marjory McNichols Wilson of Castle Rock, Colorado, photographer Sarah McIntyre of Albuquerque, and everyone at Barry Norris Photography Studio in Taos, New Mexico.

We are deeply grateful to Robert Ellsberg and Orbis Books, to Robert's wife, Monica, to my wife, Lauri, and to so many other dear friends and colleagues who have believed in and supported this project enthusiastically from the beginning. In what follows, Dear Reader, we invite you to gaze patiently and listen receptively with the eyes and ears of your heart. *Let those who have eyes to see, see.* Perhaps above all, I pray that this book brings you into the presence of a Love and Mercy beyond all names, yet nearer still than we are to ourselves.

CHRISTOPHER PRAMUK
Regis University
Denver, Colorado

PART I

Childhood and Jesuit Beginnings

My friend, I'm going to tell you the story of my life, as you wish; and if it were only the story of my life I think I would not tell it; for what is one man that he should make much of his winters, even when they bend him like a heavy snow?

So many other men have lived and shall live that story, to be grass upon the hills. It is the story of all life that is holy and is good to tell, and of us two-leggeds sharing in it with the four-leggeds and the wings of the air and all green things; for these are children of one mother and their father is one Spirit. . . .

—Nicholas Black Elk to John Neihardt,
1932, *Black Elk Speaks*

And if I had
that warmth to share,
if the Fire had seared
five shrines
in my side
and hollowed limbs,
I too would be
bound
to uncover that light
to unearth that treasure
and set fires
this very day
in all the souls
I see cold
and aching for God.
—William Hart McNichols,
"The Transitus"

CHAPTER 1

A Vision to Share

We begin this conversation with Fr. Bill's recollection of a nearly fatal incident that marked a dramatic turning point in his life. This leads us to a recollection of key moments in his early childhood and the first stirrings of his artistic vocation. From the beginning, Bill's drawings were connected to a deep grasp of the sacred, which endured even in the wake of an early traumatic experience at age five, and the initial dawning of his sexual identity as a young gay boy in the Catholic Church of the 1950s. We conclude with a nod to one of Bill's favorite poets, the nineteenth-century English Jesuit Gerard Manley Hopkins, and Bill's connection to Hopkins's poetic figure, and prayer, that "all my eyes" might see.

Chris: Fr. Bill, you've told me that your desire to share your work more widely, including the drawings and illustrations, goes back to your heart collapse when you nearly died. What happened?

Fr. Bill: On April 27, 2012, I was walking in the mountains with my friend Warren, and his daughter, Kailey, who was five at the time. I had this terrible out-of-breath feeling, and I said to Warren, "I have to sit down. I'm suddenly out of breath." He said, "I hope it's your breath and not your ticker." And I said, "It is my ticker." I could tell that it wasn't something really sudden, like a heart attack; rather it was like I was going out really slowly. Warren went running down to his car, which got stuck in the mud, and he was swearing. Kailey sat next to me and said, "It's going to be all right, Fr. Bill; it's going to be all right."

Kailey helped me walk down to the car, and the next thing I remember a helicopter was flying in. I remember they gave me a shot and put me into the helicopter. . . . When it landed at the hospital, the EMTs came running out and gave me another shot. That was April 27, and I woke up May 11.

When I woke up, I did not know that I had been in a coma that long. I later learned that they tried to take me out of the induced coma, several times. Finally, the doctor said he was going to try one more time, and if it didn't work, they would have to accept that that was it. It worked, and I woke up on May 11. It was the day after Pope Benedict had canonized Hildegard of Bingen, May 10, 2012.

When I woke up, my sister Mary was sitting there, and my brother Bob, too. Mary told me that when I awoke, I said to them, "Did you see Hildegard, she was just here?" And the nurses looked at each other, like "Uh oh, we shouldn't have brought him back." Evidently I also said, "Did you see Padre Pio?"

Later on, when I found out how long I had been under, I was praying about it, and I said, "God, why did I come back? It would have been a perfect time to die." I had this feeling, there must be some reason I'm back; there must be something I haven't done yet.

And the first thing that came to my mind was, "You haven't given your work to the world yet. There's so many

Fr. Bill two years before his heart collapse

things that people have not seen." That was it. Number two was, "These things don't belong to you. I gave them to you." I suppose this could have gone two ways: the work could come out after I die, or, if God wanted me to do it, I would come back and keep working.

I thought it was just the icons. But then I looked at all of the drawings and thought, "These are really different from the icons; does God want me to get these out?" When I was up in Taos where all the work is photographed and stored, and looking at everything, I wondered, "Is this material important, too?"

In the opening pages of *Black Elk Speaks*, Nicolas Black Elk asks, "What is the life of one man? Why should he share it?" He knows that he's nobody special, yet because he was given a vision to share, he is obedient to it, and opens up. As you know, I go back and forth about sharing. Since you had written about some of the work long before my heart collapse, and you've shown not only an understanding of what I'm doing,

but you like it, you see something in it, I think you see that this work might be from the Holy Spirit. If that's true, then I have a responsibility to give it to the world.

We're All Born with a Brilliant Light

Many people have come to know you as I did, through your icons. Your image of Matthew Shepard is the one that so struck me and first introduced me to your work. Most still know you today as an iconographer.[1] But after the heart collapse, you say you had a strong conviction that God wanted you also to bring forward the drawings and the illustrations, some of which go back to your childhood and early career as an illustrator.

What did you find in drawing or in creating art as a child? And what is significant for you about this body of drawings from childhood and then the beginnings of your artistic vocation as an illustrator?

In kindergarten and first and second grade, we were given these black-and-white drawings to color in. There were illustrations of Mary as a little girl, and her mom and dad, Joachim and Anna, and there was the baby Jesus. Recently I found one of these drawings I had colored in of the baby Jesus. I had given the baby Jesus the wounds, and on top of his chest I had put a sacred heart with a knife in it.

When I saw the wounds, I was shocked. I thought, "Oh my God, *what is going on* in that little five-year-old boy's head that he put the wounds in the baby?" I realized it was kind of a self-portrait. It was me looking at the baby and

Baby Bill and Mom

Bill as child and Father

Childhood portrait of Bill

Happy baby Bill

Bill as child at Christmas

saying, "This child is wounded." Uncovering it was like uncovering a photograph of myself as a five-year-old.

It brought back something that happened to me at the age of five, when I was abused in some way, sexually abused, though I don't remember who it was. The abuse changed me. My dad used to say, "You are the fastest runner in kindergarten!" There was a little hill that I just loved to run up and down. After this incident, I remember being sick and then not wanting to go outside anymore, not wanting to run. It was kind of like the heart collapse. And when I came out of it, I was a different child.

I remember seeing this dark shadow in the doorway of my bedroom, and me being a little

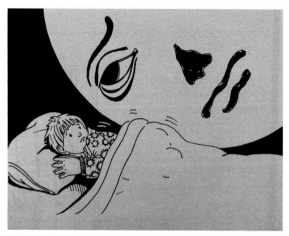

Illustration from *The Hurt*, 1983

five-year-old in bed. The feeling I got from this person, the clear intent of the dark shadow, was to put out the light that was in me. I have a picture of me at age three that is really full of light. Later I came to see that this is the intention of all abuse: to put out the light. And we're all born with a brilliant light inside of us.

After that I began to unconsciously draw pictures. The Sisters of the Precious Blood from Dayton, Ohio, were teachers at my school, and they encouraged me to draw. One of the first pictures I drew on my own was a crucifixion scene—again, kind of unusual for a five-year-old. There is Mount Calvary, blood running down the mountain, Mary crying, and Mary Magdalene on the ground beneath the cross. I didn't yet know about John, the beloved disciple, so in the picture I put St. Francis next to the cross.

At age five or six, I had been given four little books called *Little Lives of the Saints*, by Fr. Daniel Lord, SJ. I would look at them all the time. I began to know the saints through those four little books, and it encouraged me to draw them, too. In fact, many years later, the day I entered the Jesuit novitiate, September 1, 1968, I noticed a cemetery right outside the building, and I asked someone, "Is Daniel Lord buried out there?" And they said, "Oh yes, he is." The next day I went out and found his grave and said, "You know, the reason I'm here is largely because of you." And I thanked him.

So, at age five or six I began to do my own drawings. Later I realized that the theme of blood, the wounds that I had put on the Child, came to me partly through the spirituality of the Precious Blood Sisters, and also because of the incident of abuse. Jesus's suffering came to me really strongly. And then I became attracted to the child martyrs: St. Agnes, St. Pancratius, St. Tarcisius, St. Philomena. As a child, I was living spiritually in the church of the first martyrs. And somehow the Holy Spirit was also important to me. I did this drawing of a Christmas tree ornament, for example, with the Spirit on the ornament.

My Aunt Dolores had this book called *Fabiola: The Church of the Catacombs*, written by Cardinal

Holy Spirit Christmas Ornament,
early childhood drawing

Wiseman in the 1890s. On the cover of that book was St. Pancratius, who was looking up at the emperor Diocletian. The emperor was looking very imperious, of course, and behind Pancratius was a tiger lurking. It was a novel about the child martyrs, so I was caught up in that whole world.

Meanwhile, in the "real world," so to speak, we were living in 1950s America. In 1956, Elvis came on the radio with "You Ain't Nothin' but a Hound Dog." The world of music was extremely strong in my life, equal to the world of the church of Rome and the world around me, which was the political world.

During my childhood, Dad began to go from being a state legislator to a state senator to lieutenant governor and finally to governor of Colorado. When we moved into the Governor's Mansion, there was a huge, ancient baptismal font that the Boettcher family had gotten in Rome and was used for large palms and plants. All of these worlds were interacting, and I felt like I was living in another century, or a giant art museum.

Bearing the Wounds through Art

I want to come back to your father and mother and what it was like growing up in such a political family. But let's linger for a moment with these earliest drawings, when you described putting the wounds on the child Jesus, and you linked that with the crucifixion scene that you drew at age five, and the Sisters of the Precious Blood, and your experience of being abused by someone whose intention, as you understood it even then, was to put out your light.

One of the things about your work that has always struck me is this theme of the blood, of being wounded, of being targeted, even. I'm thinking of the Matthew Shepard image, or Sr. Dianna Ortiz, who also, of course, experienced terrible sexual violence.[2] Someone who is unfamiliar with your life and work might ask, "Why this preoccupation with the blood? What is sacred or precious about it?" For people outside of Catholicism, outside of the art world, or people who haven't had the kinds of experiences you're describing, such images might seem morbid. How has this theme of the blood and wounds in your art not been re-traumatizing, as it were, but somehow healing or salvific?

When I saw this shadowy figure in the door who was backlit—I couldn't tell who it was, and I don't remember, but I know it was a man—I could feel, even as a five-year-old, that this figure was filled with jealously, filled with anger toward the light. That has stayed with me forever.

In our church there are so many people that have been abused by the church, by church people, whether they're women or men doing the abuse. My road to recovery—although as a five-year-old, you don't know that's what you're doing, you're just trying to find the light again— well, part of my light was put out. You might say I was made into an introvert at that moment. I did not want to go outside anymore, to be with other people. This picture I'm looking at right now of me at age three, two years before the abuse, I was just glowing as a little boy. I can see the light in

St. Joseph and the Holy Child, for AIDS Healing Mass, 1988

the picture. I really was lit up. My way of dealing with that loss was to draw it.

You may have seen this show on TV about a special police investigative unit in New York, and sometimes they have an episode about a child who has been abused. The investigator will take the little girl or little boy into a room and have them draw, and they'll end up drawing what happened to them. Nobody did that with me. But the Sisters encouraged us to draw, so I identified with Jesus very young, because they gave us pictures of him. Somebody at the time should have said, "Wow, we gave you a picture of this happy little Christ Child and then you put the wounds on him. What's going on with this child?" That should have been a red flag. In those days it wasn't. Nobody would have ever asked me that as a child in the early 1950s.

Much later on in my career as an iconographer, I found this icon of Mary holding the baby with the wounds. When I wrote the icon

of Rutilio Grande, I put that child on the lap of Rutilio because in El Salvador—"*el salvador,*" the "savior"—the baby is wounded in that country. To have Fr. Grande in Mary's place, and to have him holding the bleeding child, for me it was the perfect icon.

Throughout my life I've been sensitive to those who have been wounded, in the way that Henri Nouwen famously wrote about in *The Wounded Healer.* I've seen that the wounds can be very powerful, if you can manage to find a way to use your wounds to relate to other people. My way as a child was to draw and read. I read a lot and I drew a lot.

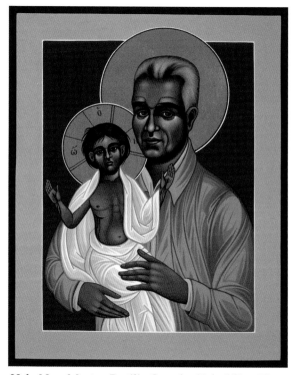

Holy New Martyr Rutilio Grande, SJ, holding El Salvador/The Savior

The Symbols Were Inside of Me

Did your parents, your siblings, recognize a budding young artist in their midst? Did they encourage you?

Everybody just knew that's what I did. But I wasn't a child prodigy, like your daughter Grace.

Precious Blood Crucifixion, age five

I wasn't really good at drawing. I just really liked to draw. I was compelled to draw.

In *Letters to a Young Poet*, the young poet writes to Rilke and he asks, "Do you think I should do poetry? Should I keep writing?" And Rilke says, "If you have to ask the question, probably not. You write because you have to write." It's the same with me. During my Jesuit novitiate, when I was twenty, Fr. Walsh gave me *Letters to a Young Poet*, and I think that's the same age the young poet wrote to Rilke, at twenty.

I always felt compelled to try to be an artist, to work out the wounds in that way. Once I became aware that I was different, that I was gay, well, that was another wound. It was a further impulse to stay inside, to turn inward.

When did the awareness of being gay come to you?

Early. Probably nine or ten. I began to gain weight when I was ten. I remember taking an eye test, and I lied on the exam so I could get glasses. I didn't know this consciously, of course, but unconsciously; I gained weight, and I got glasses to protect myself. Being a chubby little boy with big black glasses, it created a bit of a wall around me. That lasted until eighth grade.

At the end of sixth grade, when we moved into the Governor's Mansion, the kids at the new school were a lot nicer. I began to shed some of the weight and I began to feel safe. Now those two years at St. John's were also with the Sisters of Loretto. It was really wonderful for me. Just to be accepted was amazing.

I had two women lay teachers for both of those years. Mrs. McGuire, my teacher in eighth grade, knew I was an artist, and she said to me, "You know, Billy, Vatican II is starting. I need you to draw a picture of the church as a ship for the bulletin board." I had never heard of the church as a ship. But I was recognized as the kid who could draw and was asked to do these sorts of things.

Believe it or not, we had a teacher who taught dancing. She taught us all to do the polka, and the twist, and ballroom dancing. Because we were living in the Governor's Mansion, I invited the whole class over, and we danced the polka all through the place. Those two years at St. John's were really happy for me. The school was ethnically much more diverse, more accepting, a nicer group of people. From there, after eighth grade, I would try to get into Regis High School.

Let's stay with these early years a moment longer. I'd like to go back to the crucifixion drawing at age five, one of your first. I'm looking at it now. There is Francis of Assisi, who stands in for John the Beloved Disciple, and Mary Magdalene, and, of course, Mary, the Mother of Jesus. And there are angels on either side of the cross, and above the cross is a crown, which looks like it is glowing and in motion. It seems that as a five-year-old there was already in you an awareness of being part of a reality that extends beyond what we can see—a fluidity, as you said earlier, between the visible and the invisible world. Where do you think this sensibility came from? How would you describe it?

First, let me say that in the *Little Lives of the Saints* by Daniel Lord there was a picture of Francis holding onto Christ as Christ reached down to him from the cross, which was a take-off on the famous Murillo painting. So that's what I thought had happened, that Francis was with Christ on the cross. In Daniel Lord's book there wasn't a picture of John under the cross.

In my drawing there's also a cloud—the Shekhinah, I would later learn—and there's a voice coming from the side, which Hildegard called "the voice of the living light." Of course, these are things that I learned about later. And behind Christ is this blazing sun, which is not morbid. There's a balance in the drawing, I think, and a balance in the child who did this drawing, a balance of *the wounds* and of *the resurrection*. The angels are dipped in blood, rising up to glory, from red to yellow. The crown is going from red to yellow. From the blood comes the glory; the yellow, the glory of the sun.

As I looked at it later, I thought, "What on earth was this kid thinking?" Obviously, it wasn't me. The symbols were inside of me. I was putting them out without knowing what they were. It would be years before I would find out the cloud had a name, the Shekhinah, the feminine presence of God. I had never heard of God as the "living light" until I met Hildegard, who said, "The living light spoke to me." All of this, I think, was planted inside of me.

When I was very young my mom told me a story that affected me my whole life. When I was born, my grandmother, Mimi Hart, told my mom she should name me William Hart, after my mother's family. And then she said to my mom, "Don't get too close to this one, he belongs to God."

I don't know when my mom told me this story, but at the age of two, I had had an experience of God, of the real God, I believe. From then on, I knew that God was everywhere. I was aware of God just as I was aware of the Colorado landscape around me. In the creed we say we believe in the "seen and the unseen." From age two, because of this experience, I was aware of the unseen.

Many Waters Cannot Quench Love, from *Through the Loneliness,* 1987

Always Reaching for Something

I can remember a number of vivid moments in my childhood when I was "aware of the unseen," as you put it, struck with wonder by a sense of presence around me, even when I was alone. Your description of your crucifixion drawing reminds me of St. Ignatius's experience of God at the Cardoner River. He's careful to say that it wasn't a physical vision that came to him. He says, rather, "It was given to me to see these things," and then he describes a mystical experience that was quite profound. This is how I've heard you describe the process of creating icons. You open yourself in prayer, and it is given to you to see and to know, as it were, how to proceed. Sometimes it is only much later that you begin to understand what was given to you, and even then, perhaps, only partially.

Yes... A lot of people will say "I was born to perform," or "I was born to act." Lately I've been listening to books about the lives of composers, Mozart, for example, when he was very young. Where did all that musical ability come from? How could it be, when he was so young? And with Bach, the same thing. And then there are people who really have to work at it. The images were inside of me, but I really had to work to get them out. Fortunately, later in my life I was able to take art classes and get better at it. You can tell when a child has a natural ability to be an athlete, or an artist, or a musician. I don't consider myself to be in that category. Your daughter Grace has that kind of natural ability. In comparison to her paintings, my drawings at age sixteen are very primitive.

I like that I had to work at it. There's something in all of my work that has remained inquisitive, that is *always reaching for something.* It's always there. It creates a kind of childlikeness within me, because I'm always reaching, I'm always looking . . . and that something can stop me in my tracks, completely.

The cover of Adrienne von Speyr's book *The Boundless God*, for example, completely stopped me. I had it enlarged and put it on my wall. I can barely get through the book itself, but the cover is a meditation, a contemplation for me. And that image is affecting the "Rothko-esque" background of the icon of Sr. Thea Bowman that I'm doing right now. When I'm working, everything becomes connected for me.

It seems to me that this boundary between the seen and the unseen worlds that we've been talking about, a sensibility that came alive in you very early as a child, gets to the heart of what Gerard Manley Hopkins calls the "inscape" of reality. What do you hear in Hopkins's poetry, and in this image from one of his poems—"all my eyes see"—that has captured both of us?

"His lovescape crucified . . ."—this is how Hopkins describes St. Francis in "The Wreck of the Deutschland."

In freshman year in high school we had a truly brilliant Jesuit scholastic teacher who taught English, Ron Miller, who introduced us to poetry, Shakespeare, and enigmatic short stories I'll never forget. And because he was such a natural-born teacher, we were able to understand it all. He had us memorize Hopkins's "Pied Beauty." In my Jesuit life I was able to continue to live in Hopkins's spiritual world and learn that he is considered "the father of modern poetry." I believe his art saved him, kept him going, even though he only had one poem published. Like Van Gogh, he gave everything to the world through his art, with no recognition.

In my large image with icons *Viriditas: Finding God in All Things*, for Loyola University of Chi-

cago, I dedicated a panel to Hopkins, the panel with rocks as jewels. In his life he was continually stopped in his tracks by something beautiful. A Jesuit Brother once saw him standing in the rain looking down at the rocks and pebbles lining the way up to the Jesuit residence. He was transfixed by the beauty of the way rocks change color and are transformed by water. In 1979 I also painted four panels of the four seasons in a chapel for Regis High School in honor of Hopkins's love of nature and "the wild."

I could go on forever about the way he and two other deep Jesuit loves of mine, St. Robert Southwell and Pierre Teilhard de Chardin, had to create a language of their own to express the inexpressible. It's not difficult to say of them, "All My Eyes See." My prayer to these three men is, "Open all my eyes, too."

I'd like to pause here, take a deep breath, and thank you for all that you've shared of your childhood and the early drawings. It opens up for me not only the crucifixion drawing from age five, but really the whole body of your work as shaped by some of the early experiences that you've shared. Thank you for trusting me with these parts of your story. Are there any final thoughts you'd like to add?

This conversation is very good for me. I hope it is for you, too. In the past, when I've been too open, when I've been interviewed for articles, for instance, it has caused a lot of commotion, and I got into trouble. So, I'm a little squeamish. I've taken to asking Ignatius to guide me.

The Holy Spirit really comes when you're in conversation, when "two or three are gathered together." This is what I've been praying for with our conversations, that they would be alive, that they would be moving, that they would be searching, like my whole life has been, and your whole life has been.

We're always searching. We're always moving.

CHAPTER 2

The Unseen World Is Real

I open the conversation by asking Fr. Bill to share some of his earliest childhood experiences of God and of the saints as real, tangible presences in his life, which leads him to reflect further on his grandmother's words to his mother, "this one belongs to God," and first intimations of being called to the priesthood. His early awareness of being different, of not conforming to cultural norms around boyhood and masculinity in the 1950s, led to some painful, and poignant, moments with his mother and father. Further on, Bill recalls with gratitude and pride his parents' respective strengths: his mother's faith, his father's many gifts as a politician. The dominance of the Klan in Colorado politics cast a shadow over the climate of Bill's childhood, even while the church and the religious sisters who taught him in elementary school provided a refuge. Looking back over the arc of his relationship with his parents, Fr. Bill recalls, finally, what it was like to preside at his father's funeral.

Chris: You've spoken about "the wounds," some of the painful early experiences that drove you into drawing. This included the realization that you were gay, around age nine or ten, and an earlier experience at age five of being abused. Creating art and drawing your own pictures was a way of "carrying the wounds," you suggested, of "working through them." You've also talked with me about periods much later in your journey as an artist, as a Jesuit and priest, when you've felt on the outside not really "part of the club."

Fr. Bill: I have a dear Franciscan friend who once said to me, "This is the way it's going to be. You're going to be on the outside. Let it go, quit trying to fight it." When I am able to go with that, it takes me back to the work. I carry the wounds into the work, and it makes the work more powerful. I'm

bringing this to my work on Sr. Thea right now, who was also excluded, in her way, like other Black Catholics.[1] Maybe I relate to those on the margins in a way that I couldn't relate if I were in the Catholic "mainstream."

You also spoke of your grandmother's words to your mother, "Don't get too close to this one, he belongs to God." That's a remarkable thing to say to a mother about her child. Do you mind sharing the experience you mentioned at age two, when you said you came to be aware of the reality of God, of the unseen, and not only of God's presence, but the saints as well, who were quite real to you?

It has taken some time for me to be able to talk about these things. I guess I'm old enough now to do so for the right reasons. Even as a young Jesuit, I wasn't really ready to share these experiences with others.

When I was a little boy we lived on 732 Cherry Street, by Christ the King Church, near Eighth Avenue. When I was two or three, everyday I used to take a nap. All three of us, Steve and Bob and I, slept in the same room. There was a single bed and a bunk bed. My mom asked me where I wanted to sleep, and, of course, I wanted to sleep on the top bunk, where the big boys slept. I remember Mom closing the wooden venetian blinds, and all along the floor were these stripes of light, and then they vanished.

Bill, Bob, and Steve as young brothers

She closed the door and I fell asleep. I had this dream that I had fallen out of the bed, and that angels had caught me and carried me down and laid me on the floor, unhurt. When I woke up, I was lying on the floor. Immediately, I knew who God was, I knew who angels were, and many things you don't know at that age. I felt the presence of God in the room. It's something that I'll never forget.

Around age five, as I mentioned, I got the illustrated books by Daniel Lord, *Little Lives of the Saints*, and devoured them. Somehow, I understood that these were people who were close to God, little and big people who understood. So,

I knew from childhood that the unseen world is real, absolutely real.

And benevolent.

Yes, caring for me. But I never talked about it to anybody. I was sure they would say, "Well that was just a dream, that's silly." But I knew it was not a dream. I've had several experiences like that in my life, not many, but these experiences also caused me to think that God was asking something from me, that God wanted me to belong to him. When my grandmother said to my mom, "Don't get too close to this one," I think it scared my mom, and she did exactly the opposite. She felt she had to protect me, so she hovered over me a bit. It could also be the reason why the person who abused me knew that I was a golden child, a bright child, a light child.

Evil is always jealous of the light. As I said before, when I saw this man in the doorway, his shadow backlit, all I could feel from him was rage and anger, anger about the light. Having had that earlier very powerful experience of God as a two-

Cover illustration, *Through Loneliness*, 1987

Illustration from *The Hurt*, 1983

or three-year-old, I was lit up like 150 watts. And that sense of light has never really dimmed, even though, as I said, the abuse changed me.

Whenever I'm close to God, whether I'm giving a homily or presiding at Mass, most of the time I feel that same sense of God's presence, though I'm not always capable of showing it. The Mass is so important to me. I love it so much.

The Communion of Saints

As you describe the impact of the Little Lives of the Saints *books on you as a child, I can't help but think again of St. Ignatius, recovering on his bed from his battle wounds at Loyola. He's reading the lives of the saints, and his imagination is getting totally lit up by it. "What if I could be like St. Francis or St. Dominic?" You spoke of getting this feeling, even as a very young child, that God was asking something of you. Of course, Ignatius was much older when he was overcome by that feeling—much more than a fleeting emotion—a deep, life-altering conviction.*

I felt wrapped like a blanket by God all around me. I can only imagine that my little being emanated the joy that I had. Later on, when Mom told me what my grandmother had said—"this one belongs to God"—I began to wonder if it was the mark of Cain rather than a good thing. I thought, Oh, does "being chosen" mean I can never be with another person, never have any human love? I knew it meant that I was supposed to serve God, and I knew I wanted to be a priest at that age, even though I thought, "How could I ever do that, they're lonelier than I could ever dream."

Bill's niece Melissa as infant Jesus

You thought about being a priest as early as age five or six?

I didn't think about being a priest. I knew that *I was one*. It's like: you know that you're gay. You know that you like to color and draw. You know that you're a priest. I *am* a priest, like it or not. This is it. But I kept looking at the priests around me, thinking, "How will I ever do that?"

I remember my favorite priest, Fr. Leyden, and the others—they wore cassocks in those days—and you'd see them walk across the playground to their house, and open the door and close it.

27

Of course, there was a housekeeper, a cook who lived with them. But I wondered, "Why do they have to be so alone?" It didn't seem joyful to me.

Sometime after getting those books on the saints, my parents went to San Francisco, and Mom brought back a statue of St. Francis for me. That began my desire to collect statues of all these people. There were two Catholic stores in Denver. Whenever I'd get any money, I'd ask my mom to bring me. I'd walk in, and it was like, Oh my God, there's St. Clare. I got one of Santo Niño, with no idea that it was the Child Jesus. People started giving me statues as gifts, and I ended up with about eighty of them. St. Philomena was huge for me. My mom went to that church, and she used to take me there. There was a beautiful statue of Philomena on a plaster sconce on the side wall of the church, and Mom really loved her.

About that time, I saw the movie *Miracle of Marcelino*, and it reaffirmed for me that God is real. In the movie this little boy goes up to the attic in the house where these friars live, and there's this lifelike cross and it talks to him. It becomes real. So, I go to St. Philomena's, and I'm kneeling in front of the cross, trying to get it to talk. But I really didn't need it to talk, because I knew it was all real.

The Church as Ship, 1981

And then, in 1961 or 1962, Philomena got thrown off the list of official saints, and they demolished that church. That was the dark side that came out of Vatican II, the iconoclasm, the saints that got lost. A lot of them got bumped off, because they were legends. That was very upsetting for me, because I thought of them as friends. What? Where did they go?

I guess they're all hanging out in Limbo, because that's also gone away.

I know. We so much believed in Limbo, all those babies that never got baptized.

You've Got to Have Armor

It's clear you were very close to your mother, and you speak of her care for you. You've also spoken of your father with genuine warmth, but I wonder if you can say more about your relationship with him. In our previous conversation, you said that when your family moved into the Governor's Mansion "all these different worlds were interacting": the world of the Roman catacombs, the world of American music in the 1950s, and Elvis singing "Hound Dog"; and now the political world, with your father as governor.

When I was little, I remember Dad really well, and being involved with us. He wasn't that busy yet. I remember my brothers and me getting marionettes for Christmas. Being so little, I'd always get the strings mixed up. I was constantly asking him, "Daddy, can you please undo the strings?" He was very sweet and patient, and would undo the strings for me.

When I was in second grade, when he first ran for governor, everything started to change. On the night of the election, the black-and-white TV was on, and they had the numbers on the screen, and I tried to stay awake, but I just couldn't. I fell asleep. In the middle of the night, I went into Mom and Dad's room, and they were sleeping. Dad woke up and said, "What do you want, Billy?" And I said, "Daddy, did you win?" He said, "Yes, I did, now go back to sleep." So, I went back to sleep.

The next day at school, everybody was like, "Oh my God, you're the governor's son!" I went home, and I said, "Daddy, *what exactly are you governor of?*" We took out the map and he showed me, and I said, "Oh, *it's only Colorado?*" I went back to school and I said, "Don't worry, it's only Colorado." I felt a lot better that he wasn't so big that I would be excluded forever from human community.

But it did exclude us. We were pointed out. We were not able to be regular kids. My older brothers were told, "You better not get into trouble, because it will reflect on Dad."

When I was ten, I began to gain weight. As I mentioned earlier, I lied on the eye test so that I could get glasses. I didn't think anyone could hit me if I had glasses. I was getting bullied a lot. My mom took me to the doctor, who first met with me alone, then he met with my mom alone. She came out furious, and took my hand, and we just left. Later she told me that the doctor had told her that I was a homosexual. In those days, to be told you were a homosexual was to be told that you were a pedophile, or a serial killer, and you would not change. You could not change. She told Dad about it, but not the other kids.

I've never seen her so angry. She put me in the car, and said something about what the doctor had said to her, but at age ten, I didn't know what the

The McNichols family in front of the Governor's Mansion

words meant. Much later, when I was in seventh or eighth grade, *Life* magazine had an issue featuring "photos of homosexuals." There were all these pictures of biker guys with mustaches and leather. I thought, "Oh, *thank God*, I must not be a homosexual," because I looked nothing like those guys in the pictures.

I did not get along with Dad. I realized later that he was afraid for me, as any father would be at that time, or even today. He was trying to mold me to fit in, and I knew I would never fit in. I would not learn to be a regular boy, not talk the way they did, follow the way they did. I refused to pretend and try to be like other boys. I just said, "Nope, I don't know *what* I am, but I'm not like them, and I'm not going to try."

We're talking about the late 1950s and early 1960s, when culturally the popular image of the American family, the American boy . . .

It was *Leave It to Beaver, American Bandstand.*

Yes, and you're refusing to conform to that model.

Mom would take me for a haircut, and there were these regular guys with crew cuts, and they'd use this stuff called butch wax to make your flat top stand up. The barber shop had men's magazines on the tables and a TV showing sports, a very old fashioned, all-male barbershop, with the

School picture of Billy, age eight

candy-cane, striped barber pole and everything. After they cut my hair off and put that stuff in it, I walked out into the street and pressed my hair down. I didn't want it standing up straight. I had left something in the shop, and walked back in to get it, and they all burst out laughing, because they could see that I had pressed my hair down. I'm sure they knew, because, as I said, I wasn't hiding anything.

I envied girls at that time, because they didn't seem to get bullied, though that wasn't really true. My friend Stephanie, who was from Ireland, got bullied a lot, so we became very good friends.

I realized much later that Dad and I didn't get along because he was terrified for me. He knew that I wasn't hiding. He was trying to toughen me up. He was trying to say, *"You've got to have armor. You're walking around naked."* He was really worried that I was going to get demolished.

In fact, he worried about me until many years later when he came to visit me in New York. He saw me living in an apartment in Brooklyn, in a semidangerous neighborhood, and working with people with AIDS. He said, "Oh my God, Billy, I can't believe you're doing this." For so long he thought that I was the most vulnerable of all the kids, and I ended up in situations that nobody in my family would believe—on the subway late at night, and all that.

He was scared for you.

Yes, he was.

---

*For the Sisters of the Precious Blood
(In Dayton, Ohio and Denver)*

There was an obvious shame for him at
   school,
and a palpable wish-in-the-air,
that he was more a boy . . . but
Sister gave out a veritable jewel box of
sixteen Crayolas and wheat colored paper
   every Friday.
All he could color and draw then was the
Crucified King and His Court of abused
   children . . .
Tarcisius, Pancratius, Agnes, Philomena, all
   reigning in
the Church Triumphant.
Right along with the little gay boy, the Sisters
seemed to know something too of
being no one here below
and having
nowhere to go but up.
They taught him a Secret of the Kingdom;
to see the blood of Christ . . . everywhere,
   and the fine art of
enduring the desert solitude of the out-cast.
This ex-communication slowly, slowly, slowly
became an oasis where he could always seek
and find again, the Church Above.
A Church where he would never be judged
   or shamed,
inside or out,
and this has been
the actual means of his survival, and I
thank them.

WHM, October 1993

After that experience of God and the angels at age two, when I fell out of bed and woke up on the floor, maybe a day or two later, I remember seeing on the wall, right near the bed, the face of the devil. I didn't know what the devil was, but feeling this presence, and realizing, "Okay, this is the enemy. Somebody doesn't want you to survive, somebody is going to be in the way." It was like, "Okay, you've had the good experience, but you're also going to have to face the other side."

We would travel with Dad all over the state. As governor he had to go to everything—4H festivals, Indian powwows, throwing out the first pitch at baseball games. There are so many stories about him that I am so proud of. Did I tell you that he rode a bucking bronco?

Wait, what? No, you didn't.

During the election, in the southern part of the state that was wildly Republican, they dared him to ride a bucking bronco. I have no idea how he did it, but he did. And he stayed on. *He stayed on.* And he swept that part of the state. They all voted for him, because it was a show of his masculinity. At that time, there were what they called "range wars," sheep and cattle ranchers fighting over land and water. It was very dangerous. Dale, my dad's driver, drove him down to the southern part of the state in the government Cadillac. He had Dale park far way, and then got out and walked. My dad was wearing his cowboy hat. He walked right up to the guys and discussed it with them. That's how he was.

There were many, many instances like that. Even though we didn't get along, I was so proud of him. I thought, he is *so good* at what he does. He is *really good.* When he ran again for governor and lost, I told him, Dad, someday I'm going to stand up and tell everybody what they've lost. He was very depressed for about ten years after he lost, very angry, and we all went through a very rough period.

When it came time for his funeral, which I was asked to do, and as I was planning the homily, I was going to say things I had always wanted

to say about him: how he had stood up for the outcast; how he had changed the mental health institution in Pueblo, Colorado—I remember he called it "medieval" after he visited. He did so much good for people. He built the highways in Colorado, and as soon as he built them, he said he knew that they were inadequate.

I came to see him in Denver as he was dying. It was November 25, 1997. He died that night. The next day his obituary appeared in the *Denver Post*, and it was everything I had wanted to say. And I realized: people really do know who you are. They're just not going to say it until you're dead.

St. Joseph the Worker with the Young Child Jesus, from *The People's Christmas,* 1984

That obituary was so beautiful. When I stood up at the funeral to speak about him, I said, This is exactly what I was going to say, because I felt that Dad was never really understood. But they did know him after all. People understood all the good things he did. And still they didn't vote for him.

A Looming Presence

Like my mom and dad, your parents seemed to have very different, almost opposite personalities. Of course, culturally, the expectations for women and men during the 1950s and '60s—the constrictions placed on people by virtue of gender or sex—were very different than they are today. What would you say you learned from your mother and father?

Both my mom and dad were very strong people. You couldn't say one was stronger than the other. It caused a lot of friction because neither would give in. I learned from both their strengths. From Mom, I learned emotional intelligence, what we used to call the "language of the feminine, of women," which, as you say, was very different in those days. Dad would say all these corny 1950s men things: "I don't know what women want." "I don't like small talk." "I don't understand your mother." But I'd been listening to my mom, and I'd think, *I know exactly what she wants.* I knew exactly what she's talking about.

I also learned her prayer. She was always saying, "Dear Lord, please help so and so." Always "Dear Lord," which is an Irish thing. Mom never said too much about Mary, but I knew she loved her as a mother. There's a saying that goes something like, "Religious devotion is best caught rather than taught." Every May she'd quietly make a shrine for Mary at the end of the hallway, and I'd go outside and get lilacs. Mom didn't talk about Mary; she showed me her love for her, so I was never oppressed with her devotion.

From Dad I learned so much, by osmosis, about politics. He was an extraordinarily natural leader. And for me personally, I can't speak for my siblings, one of the most important things he taught me was how to fail royally, and still go on. How to lose everything, and continue on. Dad was skeptical about religion, but he still would go to church. Dad remains a looming presence in my life. Everything that happened between him and me was completely healed when I moved to Brooklyn and he came to visit me.

Burning Crosses on Your Lawn

I'm wondering if there is a connection between your dad's experience as a Catholic politician, when the Klan was such a presence in Colorado—that sense of being on the outside, even threatened—and his relationship with you as you got older? Was there something in his experience of breaking into politics as an outsider that may have helped him, at some point, to

recognize your own vulnerability as a gay person? As a gay priest?

First, I would say that because he was a politician, he knew that some priests and bishops were also like politicians. The priests would always come over to the mansion and so would the bishop. They all wanted to come. I think he felt some kinship with them, having to live so much in the public eye. But about your question, let me share a story that has never left me. On the day of my ordination, we were sitting at the bar in the basement. Some of my best friends were there, Jesuit classmates from novitiate, and Dad told us a story that I had never heard him tell. It was such a strong story; I could tell he was trying to say something to me about the priesthood, about *my* priesthood.

When he was a child, and his dad, my grandfather, first ran for Denver city auditor, the Klan came one night to their house, not far from the state capitol, and burned a cross in the front yard. My great grandmother was there at the house with all the kids. She brought all the children out of the house and onto the balcony, and said, loud enough for the men to hear, "Do you see those men? They are cowards. Don't ever be afraid of men who don't have the courage to show their faces."

I think my dad was saying to me, "Your whole life there are going to be people burning crosses on your lawn." I'm not sure why he told me this story, but it's gotten me through a lot.

In a letter he sent to me before he died, he said, You're not always going to be a Jesuit. He said, "Willy, follow the Holy Spirit. The Holy Spirit will guide you." I was still a Jesuit at the time, and I thought, this is the weirdest thing; why would he be saying this? He never spoke or wrote about such things. It was like he was channeling the Holy Spirit.

Given the political and religious climate of those times, I'm struck by your later realization that your father was scared for you, but he didn't know how to express it in a way that you could receive.

In my early years in the Jesuits, I learned about emotional intelligence, and how many men were not really trained in that way. I saw firsthand how adult Jesuit men—actually all religious men in different orders, and, eventually, diocesan priests—could be quite formidable intellectually, but would run from conflict or be passive aggressive and hurt people because of their own wounds. It made me realize that intelligence has many aspects, and emotional intelligence is as important as the others. In any case I was in no danger of becoming a high-powered intellectual. And I'm still capable of these same faults too; I'm still learning, and I want to keep learning always.

I think I learned a lot from Carl Jung's ideas of the *anima* and *animus*. Hopefully, we're all looking for that balance.

There were things that happened in those early years between Dad and me that really hurt us both. But the gradual healing that occurred later makes all that go away. Having lived through my fifties and sixties and early seventies I can now understand his anger, which was largely about injustice. I don't think about it anymore unless I'm consciously recalling those years, or seeing the blatant injustice all around us. I totally forgave him and he forgave me.

I Saw a Young Father

I saw a young father
with his child.
He was wheeling a stroller
through the airport
and made a great circle
on the red carpet at gate seventeen.
His face was stern and guarded,
the very mask of masculinity,
then the child reached for him,
tiny arms and hands up-like-prayer,
and the young man bent low,
mask fell,
the father became a child
and the circle closed.

CHAPTER 3

God in All Things

While the Jesuit apostolates in Denver are now part of the U.S. Central and Southern Province, at the time of Bill's entry into the Society of Jesus, Denver was part of the U.S. Missouri Province, with its leadership in St. Louis and the novitiate in Florissant, Missouri. In this conversation Bill describes his adolescent years at Regis High School, the shock of hearing God call him to become a Jesuit, his years under novice master Fr. Vince O'Flaherty—a period in which he and his Jesuit superiors were "coming to terms" with Bill's sexual identity—and his first contact with Jesuit communities in New England, when he was permitted to study art in Boston. Bill's love for Ignatius as his "spiritual father" was sealed especially when he read Ignatius's spiritual diary, where he discovered a more tender side of the Jesuit founder than is typically depicted in religious art. The late 1960s were years of great change in the church following Vatican II and in the Society under the leadership of Fr. General Pedro Arrupe; it was also a period of tremendous social and political tumult in the United States, all of which shaped Bill's formation as a young Jesuit.

Chris: Fr. Bill, you came into the orbit of the Jesuits for the first time when you attended Regis High School, at the time, an all-boys high school located in north Denver on the campus of Regis University. As you know, that's where I got my first job teaching theology, although by then, the high school campus had moved to the suburbs south of Denver. Thus, our paths in the Jesuit world converged long before we ever met.

You've mentioned how those high school years were often quite painful for you. The fact that you were gay, from a very public family, and now attending an all-boys Catholic high school in the mid-1960s—it's not hard for me to imagine that it was difficult. What do you remember most about those years, and what was happening for you artistically?

Fr. Bill: When we moved into the Governor's Mansion, I had just finished sixth grade and was now enrolled at St. John's, run by the Sisters of Loretto.[1] As I mentioned before, those two middle school years were very happy. At the end of eighth grade my parents wanted me to go to Regis High School because both of my older brothers went there. I took the test and couldn't pass anything that had to do with math. Nothing. So, I didn't get into Regis.

The truth is, I was happy because I wanted to go to Bishop Machebeuf High School, where my two cousins went, Maureen Batt and Kathy Hart. It was co-ed, and I knew that if I went to an all-boys school it would be bad. I think Mom and

Dad talked to Regis. I was put on a waiting list, and eventually they let me in. Of course, going to Regis would be the source of my Jesuit vocation. Had I gone to Machebeuf, I probably would have become a diocesan priest.

There were four divisions in the freshmen class: Freshmen 1 (smartest); Freshmen 2 (second smartest); Freshmen 3 (borderline); Freshmen 4 (lowest). I was at the back of Freshmen 4 with one other kid, and we became friends. We sat at the very back at the very end of the train.

Freshmen year I had Ron Miller for English, a young Jesuit scholastic. He was the kind of teacher you never forget. In those days the Jesuits wore cassocks, but the really cool young Jesuits wore loafers instead of tie shoes. He taught us to read Shakespeare and to read poetry: Emily Dickenson, Walt Whitman, E. E. Cummings, Gerard Manley Hopkins, in a way that we were understanding it. It was amazing. But there were no art classes. Art is like dessert, they told us. It's not really necessary.

Was there a Jesuit or Ignatian atmosphere—art, symbols, weekly Mass—that you began to absorb as a teenager?

There was a wooden statue in the chapel of St. John Francis Regis; you've probably seen it, it's literally "wooden" in every way. But in the back of the chapel there was a painting of John Francis Regis in France, surrounded by other people of his time, and I remember thinking, He's a real person. I don't remember them talking about the Jesuit saints or St. Ignatius very much— maybe a few of the North American martyrs, Isaac Jogues, Jean de Lalande, Noel Chabanel, and Jean de Brebeuf—but they did talk about Hopkins. I don't know if you're aware of this, but up until Fr. Arrupe became general of the Society, Jesuits did not make the full thirty-day Spiritual Exercises as they do now.[2] Some of the older Jesuits were quite bitter about a fixation on the saints and what they felt was a kind of toxic piety, because they had been formed in a semi-Jansenist spirituality—everything was

"no." If you love what you're doing, you have to be tested and be willing to give it up, for no logical reason.

As I saw it, this was a deep misunderstanding of Ignatian obedience. Ignatius might ask people to do something different, but always for a higher good. His approach was flexible. He insisted that the Exercises be adapted to how God was working with the individual. In any case, Fr. Arrupe brought back this flexibility and adaptability. We all thought he was a kind of "Ignatius reincarnated." He was even Basque, like Ignatius, and looked like him.

You Can't Do the Lockstep

I've gotten the sense from older Jesuits about what those years were like before Fr. Arrupe. It seems like many of them were thrilled with the changes, but for others, as you say, it really shook them. This is also when the changes of Vatican II were beginning to sweep through the church.

Vatican II happened when I was in seventh and eighth grade. We went from the Latin Mass, in which only the servers could respond, to allowing the people to respond in Latin to some things. Then English was slowly introduced, and the altar turned around. For the older priests, it was like the French Revolution. They were horrified. During high school, I saw how painful it was for those parish priests and Jesuits who had spent their lives celebrating Mass in one way, while some of the priests were overjoyed.

After the Mass changed, we went through a period of iconoclasm, throwing out the statues, the old vestments, the music. Partly I think it was a reaction against the spirituality of Jansenism. While I understood the need for the church to come fully into the present and much of the change was good, in some cases, I think, we threw the baby out with the bathwater. Partly I think some of the reactions were psychological: introverts like a quiet Mass and extroverts enjoy a more lively, communal atmosphere. It's a complicated period in the church, and there are still such strong feelings about it.

Pope Francis loves devotion, and shows it. He also wants to continue to implement Vatican II. Many of the people who now yearn for the Latin Mass never experienced it. It seems to me that what many are really asking for is for the priest to pray the Mass with respect and devotion, which doesn't depend on the language that the Mass is said in. I remember plenty of priests who would fly through the Latin Mass without either prayer or devotion. It's the same thing now with Mass in English.

Meanwhile those first two years of high school were a nightmare of bullying. It was so bad that I went into a kind of catatonic state, a severe depression. There were a couple of kids who would target me on the way to the bus, so I would get into after-school detention on purpose to avoid them. In junior year the main perpetrator went to a different high school, but the damage had been done.

Graduation with Mom

You've told me that humor became a defense mechanism for you, a way of dealing with the bullying.

I kept a lot in. I didn't tell my parents what was going on. But I also had a lot of friends from the girls' school, St. Mary's, that really liked me. The boys at Regis couldn't figure it out. Since Dad was governor, I could take them everywhere, to places like the Chinese Café, and my dates would be like, I've never had Chinese food before. We laughed a lot.

In sophomore year, I was sitting in geometry class and I heard God say to me, "You must become a Jesuit. You are going to become a Jesuit." I was so shocked that I just sat there. The bell rang and the next class came in, and I was trying to collect myself, staggering to the door, thinking, "What does this mean?" During the retreat later that year, I went for a walk with one of the Jesuits, and I said, "I think God wants me to be a Jesuit." He said, "Well, you should really think about it." They clearly weren't excited about me being a Jesuit.

Come senior year, I told my dad, "I'm going to be a Jesuit. God wants me to be a Jesuit." He said, "Oh, no. Billy, you're never going to make it. You can't do the lockstep."

That's . . . just classic.

He was just getting started. "This is the wrong order for you, they're going to cremate you. You won't last a week. I don't want you to become one of those close-minded Jesuits." But then he said, "I want you to go to college. And then, if you still want to be a Jesuit, I won't stop you." The problem was, because of math, I couldn't get into any colleges. None of them would admit me. It's a long story, but I was eventually admitted to Colorado State University in Fort Collins. I enrolled and took philosophy and art, all the classes that I loved, and did very well. But in the middle of the year, it came to me again, a clear message from God. "You've got to go now. You've got to go into the Jesuits."

New novices at Florissant. Bill is far left in front

Shake Hands Like a Man

During my application to the Jesuits I seemed to have passed all the psychological tests, and then I was interviewed by a Jesuit named Fr. Gough. When I told him of my interest in art, he said, Art? We don't really have people that do art. What would you do if you had to give it up? I said, Well, I haven't really started yet. Then he said, We don't usually take boys from famous families, but we'll give you a chance. I got my letter of acceptance on the Feast of the Annunciation, March 25, 1968.

On September 1, 1968, I boarded a plane that would take me from Denver to St. Louis. My dad was aware that there was this rift between us. I was sitting on the plane, and Dad boarded and came back to my seat to tell me he loved me. We both cried; he left, and the plane took off. I'll never forget it.

When we came into St. Louis it was pouring rain, just buckets. I walked into the novitiate in Florissant—"The Rock Building," they called it—and Fr. O'Flaherty, the novice master, made this grand entrance down the staircase. As you know, he had a big and blustery personality with a booming voice. I put out my hand to shake his and I was soaking wet, so I handed him this limp, wet hand. He said, "Oh I'm going to teach you

how to shake hands like a man!" And I thought, "Oh my God, here we go again."

Um, yes, I can imagine that encounter. Fr. O'Flaherty, as you know, was Fr. Vince to us. Lauri and I got to know him much later at Regis University, in the early 1990s. He was a big presence in our lives, and we were brokenhearted when he died. But he was from such a different generation of men, of American men, of Jesuits. It's not hard for me to imagine the two of you locking horns. Just as your dad warned you, "You can't do the lockstep." How right he was.

During that first year I was allowed to do some art, which helped me get all these feelings out. We had to meet with Fr. O'Flaherty about once a week, and before long retreat you had to make a general confession. The word "gay" wasn't out yet. The word people used was "homo" or "queer." I went to him and said, I think I'm a homo, or a queer, or something. He asked me if I would like to see a psychologist. I said, Yes, I would. He sent me to a psychologist at St. Louis University, a behaviorist, who told me, you can change if you want to. What you need is aversion therapy.

After several months of that—I'll spare you the details—I said to the doctor, I don't want to do this anymore. He said, Okay, we'll try shock therapy. I told Fr. O'Flaherty about it, and he said, I can't tell you whether or not to do it. Do you want to do it? I was nineteen. Well, I said, if God wants to change me, I'm open to doing it. I'll do it.

Jesus. I'm so sorry.

During the first session he gave me 75 shocks of 110 volts, not on my head but on my wrists and ankles. The next time he gave me 45 shocks within an hour. He said to me, you've got the strongest resistance to pain I've ever seen. By then I had taken first vows and had moved into the residence at St. Louis University. There was an older Jesuit, Fr. Walsh, who was helping out at the residence, and one day I told him everything that was happening. He was horrified. That's it, he said. You're never going back to that man. God made you the way you are, and you have to accept it and be happy.

That summer, a movie with Barbra Streisand had come out, *On a Clear Day*, with the song "What Did I Have That I Don't Have." It was so meaningful to me. The question she sings was my question. *What is wrong with me? Why doesn't he love me?* Of course, it was God I was asking about.

Because of the aversion therapy, for a whole summer I wasn't attracted to anybody. I thought, *Oh, good, it's gone.* I don't have to worry about it ever again. Later that summer—by this time I was 21—it came back. I was walking along the sidewalk and passed a really good-looking man. And I thought, *darn it*, it's back again. Because I was so happy being sexless, not having any of these feelings. You know Ignatius said something like, "As for chastity, men in the Society of Jesus should be like the angels." So, for one summer, I thought, I've finally got wings. But if you fly too high, you end up like Icarus.

I'm both humbled and horrified, Fr. Bill, by what you've shared, just trying to imagine myself at age 21 going through anything like these experiences.

To be honest it's healing to tell someone these stories, and I don't feel any shame when I talk to you. I've always been trying to put these con-

tradictory things together, because inside of me, *they are together*. But they're not together on the outside. It's a private thing between you and God, how you grow up in that way. But you're the right person to tell.

Daniel Berrigan, Gerard Manley Hopkins, and the Jesuits of the Northeast Province

Thank you, Fr. Bill. I'm struck by the realization of how many young Jesuits, how many diocesan seminarians or young men in other religious orders, were going through similar trials. While your story is utterly unique to you, it's also a window into an ecclesial culture that was, and still is, riven by impossible choices. Inhuman choices. I wonder what was happening for you artistically at this time. Was art helping you, as it did during your childhood, to get through these experiences?

I began studying with the artist-in-residence at St. Louis University, Tom Toner. He was a straight guy, a wild, realistic kind of artist who did paintings with demons and naked women and everything. I did a couple of oil paintings with him, and he let me paint at night in his studio. I was so scared to go into that studio, because it was full of all these paintings with the devil.

I was doing a large oil painting of the two angels sitting on the tomb of Jesus, and I asked my friends Steve and Jim Janda—everyone called him "JJ"—both Jesuits, to come and pose for me. They did, but the whole time they would throw insults at each other; they'd just laugh and laugh. JJ would say to me, "Billy, don't worry about Rogo!"—that was his name for the devil—and we'd put sheets over all the devil paintings when we were there.

This was 1968, 1969, 1970—I was four years old in 1968. My earliest political memory is of Richard Nixon and Watergate, 1972 or so. But during your novitiate and scholastic years at Regis High School, the country was going crazy. So much was happening politically. At what point, if at all, did you and your

Jesuit classmates get swept up in everything that was going on politically?

There was a young Jesuit from the California province named Jim who was kind of a revolutionary. His idol was Daniel Berrigan. He decided that a group of Jesuit scholastics, twenty-seven of us, would turn in their draft cards and renounce their 4D status, which we all had as divinity students. He wanted to see if the government would come back and make us all into 1A status. He came to me and said, Billy, out of all of us you're the most poetic. We want you to write the statement. He gave me a copy of Dan's book *No Bars to Manhood*. Fr. O'Flaherty had already given us some of Dan's writings, and I liked him, but I was terrified of him. I thought that he would have nothing to do with me if I ever met him.

I listened to Jim speak about all this, I read Dan's book, and then I wrote the statement. Meanwhile, my superiors had decided I should finish my undergraduate studies in Boston, with the New England Province, because there was no way I would pass all the math requirements at St. Louis University.

When I got to Boston, the very first night, one of the guys at the house said they were all going to the retreat house in Gloucester to read Hopkins. Do you want to go? I'll never forget that night. We're standing out on the rocks, and the waves are crashing, and he's reading "The Wreck of the Deutschland." I thought, Oh my God, I'm in heaven. This is it. I went back to St. Louis and told everybody that I was transferring to the New England Province, though I never did.

I enrolled at Boston College for liberal arts classes and at Boston University for art. I loved BU. At BC, most kids were not yet fully into the hippie-costume movement, and everything that went with it. But at BU the hippie movement was in full force, like in Boulder, Colorado. So naturally I gravitated to BU. All the art students looked like Pre-Raphaelite paintings.

It's clear you felt a sense of liberation among the Jesuits and in the culture of the Northeast, like you

Seal of Jesuits, the Society of Jesus

could finally begin to be yourself, in contrast to the Midwest and the Missouri Province.

Just try to be different or stand out in Boston or New York, it's pretty impossible! Among the Jesuits in New England, I was way under the radar. To them, I was an odd mix of conservative and radical—liberal was not yet used to demean people. But I really, really, felt loved by them, and the New England sense of humor is both joyfully irreverent and self-deprecating. I'll never forget one fellow Jesuit coming into my room one night and saying, "Billy, what the hell are you reading?" I was in my bed looking ghostly, like a figure from an Edvard Munch painting. Sheepishly, I answered, "Ummm . . . Kierkegaard's diary." And we both just burst out laughing!

I Could See That He Was a Real Person

Before we get into the Boston years, I want to step back a moment and ask about your introduction to the life of St. Ignatius and Ignatian spirituality. Earlier, you described hearing an almost direct command from God to enter the Jesuits. At what point did you feel confirmed that this path was really right for you, and how? I imagine it must have come during the novitiate, when you did the long retreat.

Yes. In fact, I did the Spiritual Exercises twice, during the first and second years of novitiate. Fr.

O'Flaherty and I got along well that second year, and he had gotten permission from Fr. General Arrupe for us to do the long retreat again. It was during that second retreat that I just fell in love with the Exercises. It was fall in Missouri, and the trees were just gorgeous, flaming yellow and red. And I was also helping with music, singing with Tim Manion and others who later would become the liturgical musical group The St. Louis Jesuits. Spiritually and musically it was an incredibly rich time.

I was really confirmed in my vocation during that second year. The novitiate in Florissant had such beautiful stained-glass windows and statues of Ignatius, Francis Xavier, and all these other Jesuit saints. I loved all of that. The rest of the novices made fun of me because, as I said, the church was going through this iconoclastic period after Vatican II. Above all, I loved Ignatius, his spiritual diary more than anything. I could see that he was a real person.

At the end of second year, Fr. O'Flaherty told me he wasn't sure that I should take first vows. He said to me, "You're pious, but not holy." And you know, the truth sometimes hurts. But he said

Bill in Boston, 1971

he would support me in taking first vows, and I really felt called to take them. I was a friend of John Foley, another member of The St. Louis Jesuits, and he came and sang his gorgeous song "Evening Sunrise"—the vows service was held at night, and it was really beautiful.

You said that the climate after Vatican II was "icono-clastic"—stripping down of a lot of the ornate, traditional symbols and devotional practices that were such a part of Catholic spirituality, some of it had been a reaction against the Protestant Reformation. Of course, Ignatius himself was steeped in devotion to Mary, his conversion prompted in part by reading the lives of the saints. In other words, his imagination was steeped in a very ornate, high-church Catholic piety. By contrast, it sounds like the post-Vatican II atmosphere when you came to Boston, at least among the younger Jesuits, was unapologetically low church, iconoclastic, politically activist.

Yes, when I got to Boston, in 1971, in Brighton, some of the Jesuit priests and scholastics were going through the dramatic cultural shifts taking place in the world. They didn't have a chapel in the house, and I thought maybe I could coax them into another shift by creating one. I asked, "Can I make one? We can make my room into a chapel. I'll move into one of the smaller rooms." And they let me do it.

I got three large sheets of plexiglass covered in contact paper, carved into each of them with a swivel-knife pen, sprayed them with white spray paint, and then tore off the contact paper. The three panels made a triptych, hanging from the ceiling. The centerpiece was the feet of Jesus on the cross; on the left was the famous picture of the Vietnamese woman with her dead baby fleeing the napalm bombing; on the right, the Buddhist monk who burned himself alive. The other Jesuits said, *This is the most depressing thing we've ever seen!* Where is the resurrection? You don't have anything about the resurrection. Then I realized I had to make or find the Risen Christ in some artistic way.

I got a large sheet of the same dark plexi-glass, took off all my clothes except for a sheet around me, changed the angel's face and body, leaned forward with an imploring hand, as if to ask, "Why are you looking here? He's not here." Then I took a Polaroid picture, and it became the final panel for the chapel. Because Salem is so notorious in American history, the background for the angel on the tomb was the cemetery in Salem. This was long before they built a stun-ningly beautiful memorial of stone benches with the names of the eighteen women and one man, which you can see today.

When I Give My Heart It Will Be Completely, watercolor and gouache, 1971

I'm just picturing you taking off all your clothes and posing as an angel to make that final panel. It's like your dad or Fr. Vince all over again. On the one hand, you're trying to fit into the Jesuit way of doing things; on other hand, you're blowing open all their catego-ries, from left to right. Isn't this also when you did the "Chapel of the Blood of Christ" for the Jesuit commu-nity in downtown Boston?

Yes, a year later, in Beacon Hill, I did a chapel dedicated to St. Robert Southwell, the English Jesuit poet and martyr who had become one of my favorite saints. Again, the chapel had a triptych, three painted wooden panels, each sig-nifying something of the Passover passage in Exodus 12: "The blood will be a sign for you, and I will see the sign and the plague will pass over you."

Each panel had a scene with blood running down from the panel and onto the matching red carpet: the first was wine spilling over from a chal-ice; the second was blood coming out from under a ghetto door; and the third was a sunrise land-scape with the blood of Christ coming through the trees. I was very much influenced by Lady Julian of Norwich's accounts of her near-death experience and apparitions. When I think of it now, it seems to me awfully prophetic, because it was about ten years before the beginning of the AIDS pandemic. As far as I know, none of those paintings have survived.

If You Belong to Him, You Don't Have to Talk about It

It brings me back to your earliest drawings, the cru-cifixion scene at age five, for example, and how art helped you to "bear the wounds" of childhood trauma. In that drawing you described a balance between the wounds and the resurrection. I have to say, the "Chapel of the Blood of Christ" sounds like it was all about the wounds, and not much resurrection. I wish those paintings had survived. I wonder if they're hid-den in a basement or attic somewhere in a Jesuit house in Boston. I'm also struck by this enduring tension in the church—and in your vocation—between left and right, progressive and traditional, and the impos-sibility, I think, of boxing your art into any of these categories.

When did Ignatius really become for you a kind of spiritual father, as I've heard you describe him?

It was during the second of the long retreats at Florissant, and then during my studies in Boston,

St. Ignatius Collapsing at the Altar, 1980

Our Lady and the Holy Child Jesus Visit St. Ignatius the Convalescent, 1983

when I had heard this Jesuit joke about an old Jesuit who is terrified on his deathbed. His fellow Jesuits do not understand why, and they say to him, "What are you so afraid of? You know God loves you!" And he says, "It's not God I'm afraid of, it's Ignatius." I was aware of all the depictions of a very stern Ignatius that you would see in every Jesuit house: Ignatius in a high-collared black cape and holding a book, looking demanding, uncompromising, and very severe. I was also aware of beautiful black-and-white drawings I'd seen in an edition of his autobiography, like the one of him in prison or the one where devils are beating on him in bed, images that hit

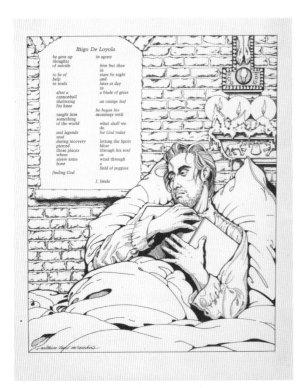

St. Ignatius the Convalescent, with poem
by Fr. Jim Janda, 1983

I know that Fr. Arrupe really emphasized the mystical or contemplative roots of Ignatian spirituality, notwithstanding the fact that most people seem to associate Arrupe with the activism and social justice turn of the Jesuits in the 1970s. I've been so moved to discover this side of Arrupe when I've taught him and have studied some of his lesser-known writings on Ignatius. As a younger Jesuit, what did you see in Ignatius that perhaps others in your generation overlooked or may have missed?

It was Fr. Walsh who really pushed this idea about Ignatius wanting us to find God in all things. And I loved that about him, because I was already doing that, secretly. I was finding God in the music of Laura Nyro and Stevie Wonder and in movies. Fr. Walsh really encouraged us in that. I discovered that Ignatius really is my spiritual father, that he doesn't care if I go to Hildegard,

me very hard. And the Reubens image, where he is in ecstasy during Mass, or the dramatic paintings of his vision at La Storta.

I thought, what can I do for my Holy Dad Ignatius, the Ignatius of the *Spiritual Diaries*? So often in his diary he'll say, "Abundant tears at Mass today," or "Uncontrollable sobbing at Mass today." During the first week of the Spiritual Exercises, he says, "Ask for tears." Any time he felt God communicating to him, he'd be sobbing. One of my first drawings of him, *Ignatius Collapsing at the Altar*, really emphasizes how the Mass affected him. Later I was commissioned by Archbishop Stafford of Denver to do a holy card for 1991, the "Ignatian Year," which shows Ignatius at prayer in Rome. He's filled with love and peacefulness, in the middle of a busy city and a very busy administrative life. Jim Martin has told me that this is his favorite picture of Ignatius. These are parts of his personality that we can share with him.

saint ignatius of loyola
1491 – 1991

For the greater glory of God

St. Ignatius at Prayer in Rome, 1991

or John of the Cross, because I'm his; I belong to him. I can go anywhere and I'll still be his. I could go to a Buddhist monastery for the rest of my life, and I'd still be one hundred percent Catholic, one hundred percent Jesuit. And there's no worry about it.

I drank in everything I could about Ignatius and the Jesuit saints that I loved. And then I was like, "Okay, you've got it now. It's in you." But I didn't talk about him all the time. It's like when Dad was governor. You don't run around saying, My dad's the governor, we're the best in the city. You don't do that. And I didn't do that with Ignatius or the Jesuits or Ignatian spirituality. I thought, If you belong to him, you don't have to talk about it. And yet I understand those whose vocation is to do that. I just tried to do it through art. But it was grievous for me when a few of my peers in positions of power could not see that. Or maybe they did see it, and still found major faults with me.

"If you belong to him, you don't have to talk about it." That's a beautiful insight. But clearly, it's tinged with some pain around the circumstances that would eventually lead to your leaving the Society.

In those early years with the Jesuits, it seems like Fr. Walsh provided an important balance for you and counterpoint to Fr. O'Flaherty as an older mentor. I gather that Fr. Walsh had some wisdom about normal and healthy human development that you and the other young Jesuits were experiencing, things

that were also part of secular culture, and he wasn't afraid of that. You're living in the world as an embodied human being with normal human desires and you shouldn't hide from it, is that right?

Yes. It's because he was a theater director before he was sent to the novitiate. That's a whole other story I won't go into. But you know, Fr. O'Flaherty once said to me, I've been the hardest on you because we are the hardest on people that most need to be pushed.

I'm thinking of the story that your dad told you on your ordination day about people burning crosses on your lawn, and the fact that even Fr. O'Flaherty, your novice master—and someone years later who would become so beloved to Lauri and me—that Fr. Vince would have been a source of struggle and self-doubt, that he would have allowed you to go through aversion and shock therapy. It saddens me, both for you and for him, the degree of ignorance and fear associated with being gay. Of course, I'm hearing your story half a century later, when things like shock therapy rightly horrify us.

It's a reminder for me of the messiness of our journeys through time, in families and cultures and religious communities that are inevitably broken, all of us stumbling and to some degree blind. For all our good intentions, our desire to follow Christ, to serve the gospel, we can't help but damage one another a little, sometimes a lot.

CHAPTER 4

The Zen of Seeing

This conversation covers a critical period in Jesuit formation from Bill's mid-twenties as an art teacher at Regis High School to his theology studies in Boston and ordination to the priesthood at age 29, after which he returned to Denver as artist-in-residence at Regis College. These were years of tremendous growth and experimentation for Bill as a painter, during which he was also coming out to his family, forging deep friendships in the Society, and hosting his first-ever art exhibit. This period also deepens his love affair with St. Francis of Assisi, St. Ignatius, Fr. Pedro Arrupe, the music of Joni Mitchell, Stevie Wonder, Joan Baez, Barbra Streisand, and many others who, half a century later, still anchor Bill's fascination with musical creativity—in later years, it will be Bach, Hildegard, and Pergolesi whose lives and music seize his imagination. As this final chapter of Part I draws to a close, Bill is poised to further his art studies at the prestigious Pratt Institute in Brooklyn.

Chris: At the end of your art studies in Boston, Fr. Bill, you were invited to come back to Denver to teach art at your alma mater, Regis High School, of all places.

Fr. Bill: Yes, I graduated from Boston College with a bachelor's in philosophy and a minor in art. Somehow the credits I earned from Boston University were accepted at BC for the art minor. Fr. Jerry Starrat, SJ, from the New England province, was principal at Regis High School and wanted me to start an art program there. Let me say that whenever I dream I'm still a Jesuit, I'm always in New England. I just loved the Jesuits there. As I mentioned, they were slightly irreverent, yet deeply spiritual at the same time.

I flew out to meet with Fr. Starrat, and I said, Jerry, you know, I don't have a lot of fond memories of this place. He laughed, but then he said, We really want you to come. If you're willing to

come, you can start the art department. I want every freshman here to take art class. You decide what you want to teach, and you can do an elective course for older students.

I went back to Boston and thought and prayed about it. I thought, Okay, maybe God is trying to heal my relationship with Colorado and with Regis High School. At the time, John Denver's song "Rocky Mountain High" had just blown up and really put Colorado on the map. Before John Denver, people out East were like, Where's Colorado? Isn't it somewhere near Ohio?

I Don't Have Any Talent; I Can't Do Art

It must have been quite a challenge not only to come back to Regis High but to be responsible for starting an art program from scratch. You were still so young.

Those three years at Regis were actually heaven for me. I loved the kids. I taught three classes every morning—all 180 freshmen had to take art. I had to figure out how to convince them that they could do art. So many of them hated it in grade school and would come in angry, saying, "I'm not doing art, I don't have any talent, I can't do art." I had them do the first project, and they were just shocked at themselves. Their parents would say, I cannot believe it, my son just loves your art class.

As they sat at tables doing their projects, I would read to them from *The Zen of Seeing: Seeing/Drawing as Meditation*, by Frederic Franck. The bell to end class would ring, and they'd say, "Oh no, already?!" I had a turntable in the classroom and sometimes would let them play records while they worked. I was 24, just ten years older than the freshmen, not much older than the seniors. After school, I'd go straight back to the Jesuit residence, and my students would ask, Why are you going home? Don't you want to get to know us? Not really, I said, I just want to go home and do my art!

This was the year that Stevie Wonder's *Talking Book* came out, the next year *Innervisions*, the next year *Fulfillingness' First Finale*, and I was also listening to Joni Mitchell and Phoebe Snow. Of course, the kids also introduced me to their favorite music. One time a bunch of the older students came to the Jesuit residence and knocked on the door. They said, Can we come in? We want to play you the new record by Traffic, "The Low Spark of High-Heeled Boys."

Classic. I'm just thinking about my freshmen theology class at Regis High School, where I began teaching in 1994—twenty years after your final year there. Almost from the beginning I made it a regular part of class to include music. And whether through music, poetry, drawing, or reading The Zen of Seeing, *as you did, it's trying to help them come alive to the world with all their senses, physical and spiritual, to offer a language for their yearnings, their questions, the sense of wonder and mystery.*

Yes, exactly.

I Come with Three Wounds

I think it was around this time that you painted what is, for me, one of your most arresting Jesuit-themed works, Llego Con Tres Heridas: I Come with Three Wounds, *which depicts Fr. General Pedro Arrupe taking the body of Jesus down from the cross. I saw it for the first time in the Jesuit residence at Regis University just a few years ago, and was stunned by it. The original hangs just outside a small chapel in the ground floor of the residence, and it's framed alongside a personal letter written to you by Fr. Arrupe, thanking you for the painting. When I saw it, I took a photograph and sent it to you right away, like, what is this? I can't believe what I'm seeing.*

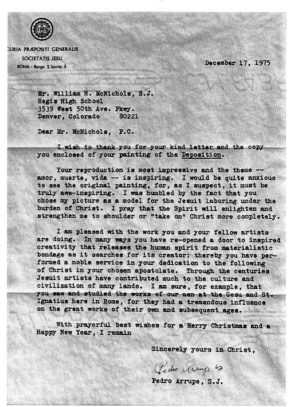

Pedro Arrupe letter to Fr. Bill

Near the end of my time at the high school I had to choose where to go next to study theology, and it sent me into a period of darkness. I think it was partly because I loved those years teaching, and I had begun to love Colorado, or at least to make peace with it. On weekends, Jerry would take me on drives into the mountains, like my family did when I was a kid, and it was really healing.

At the time Joan Baez had just released an album of folk songs in Spanish. It included a song by the famous Chilean composer Victor Jara, who was killed, you may remember, in the aftermath of the 1973 coup. There was another song by the Spanish musician Joan Manuel Serrat, "Llego Con Tres Heridas." The whole album was kind of enigmatic; I loved it. But that song in particular really moved me.

So, the darkness was there, and I wanted to do a painting about what it was like when Christ was dead, the hours immediately after he died. It's what you call a deposition painting—Christ being taken down from the cross—a very famous motif in art. Hundreds of artists have done deposition paintings down through the centuries. I wanted to include Fr. Arrupe in the painting. We all loved him so much, and he had written an important article for *Studies in the Spirituality of Jesuits* on the importance of being an artist, which meant so much to me. So, the idea for a deposition, with Arrupe taking Christ's body down from the cross, and the song title from Joan Baez, all came together in the painting.

I wanted to show Arrupe's legs bending under the weight of Christ, a total image of grief. "Oh my God, Jesus is dead." The striped shirt was meant to symbolize the Isaiah passage, "By his stripes we are healed." And above the body of Christ is an eclipsed sun, because, as the Gospels say, "The sun's light failed" when Jesus breathed his last. Christ's head is bent over resting on the top of Fr. Arrupe's head.

Years later I was showing the painting during a talk, and someone said to me, "But Father, didn't you notice that Jesus is kissing the head of Fr. Arrupe?" I looked at the painting again, and thought, "I never saw

Llego con Tres Heridas: I Come with Three Wounds

that before, but it's true." *Even in terrible darkness, Christ is there, consoling us.* That was the message for me when I painted it, though I never really got it until that moment.

So, I used the song title, printed the Spanish and English versions with a copy of the painting, and sent it to Fr. Arrupe. He wrote me back a letter, which I hadn't read for many years until you sent me the photo from Regis. I was really touched, almost shocked to reread it. I think they probably keep the painting there because of the letter. It's almost like a sacred relic of Arrupe for the Regis community.

Yes, but please don't underestimate the power of the painting itself and the contemplative intensity it brings to the residence. I can't speak for the Jesuit community, of course, but for me, both are quite powerful. Fr. Arrupe's letter reflects not just his gratitude for your artistic vocation but a prayer that he might live more fully into his own vocation, "to shoulder or 'take on' Christ more completely."

Self-Portrait: Symbols of Enduring Friendships

After finishing your regency in Denver, how did you decide where to go next to study theology?

There were openings at Berkeley, Chicago, Toronto, and Cambridge. Initially I applied to Toronto—it's a long story, but I didn't get in—and then I got a call from John Padberg, who at the time was the president at Weston School of Theology in Cambridge. I said, John, believe it or not, I got refused by Toronto. He said, *That's great, Billy, I want you to come to Weston.*

There was a joke among Jesuits: they called Berkeley "play school," they called Chicago "social justice school," and they called Weston "real school." I said to John, do you think I can handle real school? Because I wasn't brilliant like most of the guys going to Weston. John said, Yes, I think you'll do fine.

Bill Dobbels happened to be at Weston as a second-year theologian. As you know he would become one of my best friends. So, I went to Weston and I just loved it. I was twenty-seven, and was there for three years. Those were the years of Fleetwood Mac's "Rumours," Linda Ronstadt's "Facing Down the Wind," and Joni Mitchell's "Hejira"—the music was off the scales. We had a beautiful chapel in the residence, and the house was full of amazing Jesuits, guys who would go on to do great things.

This is around the time, I think, that you did your first self-portrait. It's quite striking, and quite different from the second one you did many years later. Can you tell me about it?

I had found these Russian illustrators who had made children's book covers with all these boxes filled with pictures—they were inspired by icons, but I didn't know it at the time—and I thought this would be a perfect way to do a self-portrait. I would put myself in the center, and the boxes around the perimeter would have symbols related to my life. I worked very hard on it. I did it as a profile, so the viewer would not see my eyes, like I was gazing toward something in the distance, perhaps something spiritual.

Bill Dobbels had given me a beautiful red vase from Czechoslovakia for my birthday—I still have that vase today—and the oak leaf is a symbol of enduring friendship. I put a red vase in one of the boxes with oak leaves to show our friendship. Years later, losing Bill and then losing Pat Arnold—they were both my best friends in the Jesuits. Both were "ones" on the Enneagram, and they loved to tease me mercilessly, as a "four."[1] Losing them was devastating to me. I still miss them terribly.

The thorns on the right and left are from Jesus's parable of the sower, where thorns grow up to choke the seed that falls on the soil. Worrying is my great temptation, so the thorns in the parable are what always threaten to choke my gifts. The hand with the rose is the Angel Gabriel offering me a rose, a symbol of my vocation. At the bottom is a poinsettia, because I love Advent and Christmas. On the right is a scallop shell, with a drop of blood, representing baptism with blood.

And again, with the blood.

Yes, I know! The seven candles at the bottom signify the seven rooms of Teresa of Avila's interior castle. At the top is the Colorado state flower, the columbine. At the upper-right corner is a poppy flower, from a trip to Paris when I saw these gorgeous fields of poppies, blowing in the wind, which just bowled me over. The wishbone was a symbol for me of hope from childhood—I always asked my dad for the wishbone at Thanksgiving. Finally, the pearl is the pearl of great price from the Gospel.

I Couldn't Hide It Even If I Tried

There are a few other illustrations from this period: By His Stripes We Are Healed, *and the drawing for your ordination to the priesthood,* Let the Flowers Bloom, *at age 29. Where were you in your self-identity at this moment? Were you fully out in the Jesuit community as a gay person?*

During Regency, age 24, 25, and 26, I had come out fully to myself, and everyone in the high school community knew, so I really wanted to tell Mom and Dad. One night I went over to their house for dinner. I think the word "gay" was not yet being used. During dinner, my knees were shaking under the table I was so terrified. I said to them, I'm pretty sure I'm a homosexual. The odd thing

Self-Portrait of the Artist, 1977

is, I expected Mom to fully accept it and my dad to object, but it was the other way around. At age ten, you remember, the doctor had told my mom that he suspected the same thing, and I had never seen her so angry. Maybe she had been in denial all those years, I don't know.

Mom said, Oh no, honey, you've always had girlfriends, you've always loved girls, and so on. Dad just sat there listening quietly. Finally, he said, maybe it's my fault, I've always had male friends. Anyway, it was all new for everyone, and they handled it as best as they could. They were both quite shaken, and I went home. The next day, Mom told me, "Honey, I hear you can get hormone shots at the Jewish community center?" I said, Mom, this isn't the flu, it's who I am. It's not going away.

A day later my dad called and asked me to come to his office to talk, which had never happened before. We sat down and he said, I just want to say to you, it must have been a terribly lonely life, you've had no one to talk with about this. It must have been really isolating. I said, Yes, Dad, you're right, it has been. He said, I also want to say, I've always been lonely. I have friends, but I don't let them in, I never talk to anybody. Really? I said, you're kidding. You don't talk to Mom? Your brother Bill? No, he said, not anybody. It turned out to be a beautiful conversation between my dad and me.

Jerry Starret at Regis had all of us teachers

Isaiah 53:5,
watercolor and gouache, 1977

"Let the wilderness bloom,"
ordination invitation, 1979

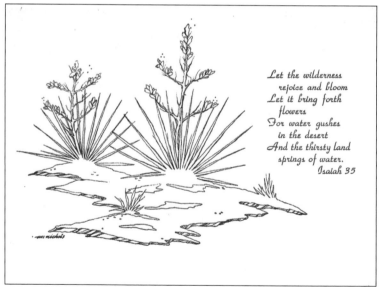

Let the wilderness
rejoice and bloom
Let it bring forth
flowers
For water gushes
in the desert
And the thirsty land
springs of water.
Isaiah 35

go through these Erhard Seminar Trainings, or EST, which were rooted in Zen practices of self-awareness. Going through those trainings with the other teachers, I clearly realized that I must come out; I had to accept myself. I couldn't hide it. I couldn't keep it secret even if I tried. So that's when I went to Mom and Dad. As they say, the rest is history.

Indeed, the rest is history. Thank you, Fr. Bill, for sharing this story.

Let's go back to your theology studies at Weston, which culminated with your ordination in 1979, and then, lo and behold, you went back to Regis College in Denver as artist-in-residence. Is there anything else from these years at Weston that would shape your vocation as an artist and priest?

50

Celebrating Mass in Medjugorje

We talked about the self-portrait and the Chapel of the Blood of Christ in Beacon Hill, but all of us Jesuits in theology were required to do some kind of outside work or ministry. People worked in parishes or shelters or other kinds of ministry. I worked on a suicide hotline called The Samaritans, founded in England and brought over to the United States, which Bill Dobbels had been working on.

You had to follow certain rules. You were allowed to use your first name, but not your last name. I was "Bill 249." People whom I had talked to would sometimes call again and ask for "Bill 249." While you could do everything possible to get them through a crisis, you couldn't take away their right to end their life, or call the police or an ambulance without their permission. The people I worked with were amazing, and some of them were hilarious. I remember working one Christmas Eve and the phone was ringing off the hook; it was such a lonely time for many people. Those years of listening and talking to people in crisis were a wonderful preparation for ministry, especially the AIDS ministry, which came a few years later. It taught me a lot.

There are other important things from those years that I'm reluctant to talk about.

As you put it earlier, there are parts of your life and who you are that are whole and integrated on the inside, where you can be open and free with yourself and with God, but impossible to show on the outside.

Some people want to be subversive; they try to be subversive. For gay people, just being born, just being alive, is already subversive. I've spent my whole life trying not to be subversive, trying to fit in.

Even to talk about it is like coming out as gay all over again, so I've kept all of these things shamefully hidden. I want to talk about it, and yet I don't think it's a good idea. People who don't like me or don't know me will say, *See*, he's always been a bad person. It's like a child who says something and they think it's okay, but then a parent responds, *Don't you ever say that again.*

In any case, I loved theology, everything about it, the studies, all the great theology coming out after Vatican II, life in the Jesuit community. My first day at Weston, all the other guys were dressed in topsider shoes and khakis, and I came in with my long hair and bell bottoms, and one of them says to me, "Are you trying out for *Godspell* or something?" I said, "Nope, I already got the part."

We would tease each other a lot, but it was

Bill, age 29, just before ordination

I Hold Out My Hand and My Heart Will Be in It, 1979

always in a loving way. We had these dinner parties, and they'd say, Billy, sing "Danny Boy." I had a better singing voice back then, and I would have them all in tears. I loved all those guys, and they loved me. John Padberg especially. Before he died, I wrote him a note and thanked him. I told him that if it wasn't for his belief in me I never would have gone to Weston, much less would I have passed the final exams.

I did pass and was so happy. I got one question wrong, about whether God suffered when Jesus was dying on the cross. I said, Yes, of course God suffered, his son is dying. They said, *No*, that would be *patripassionism*, and *that's a heresy*. You're kidding, I said. How can God love and not suffer? Anyway, despite botching that one, I got through it. That incident always reminds me of Psalm 131, "Neither do I exercise myself in great matters or things too high for me."

Oh my goodness, that's funny. Young Bill, the heretic, who dares to claim that God suffers. After you passed your exams, what happened next?

What a Fool Believes

After ordination, Mike Sheeran, who later became the president of Regis University, asked me if I wanted to come back to Regis College and be artist-in-residence for a year.[2] The only requirement was to do an exhibit at the end of the year. Of course, I said yes, so I could paint and be near my family again. It was a period of trying to find my style as an artist. I did all these paintings of mountains and meadows and trees. It was during that year that I did the four arched paintings for the Regis High School chapel, one for each of the four seasons, dedicated to Gerard Manley Hopkins.

Your painting of St. Francis, I Hold Out My Hand and My Heart Will Be in It, *was also in that chapel, wasn't it?*

Yes, and on a wall across from Francis, I had a large photo of a young Native American woman, based on a famous sepia photograph by Edward Curtis. On another wall, I had a picture of a hand holding out a rose, just like in my self-portrait, symbolizing the Angel Gabriel offering us our vocation. A few of my Jesuit housemates and I had found a huge striated rock up in the mountains. We had it brought down to Denver and had a tombstone cutter level the top off of it to use as an altar. A large print detail taken from Matthias Grünewald's famous crucifixion painting was suspended over the altar. Jesus's rib cage in the painting looked just like the jagged surface of the altar rock. The title of the St. Francis painting, *I Hold Out My Hand and My Heart Will Be in It,* came from the lyrics of a 1934 song, "For All We Know," recorded beautifully in 1979 by Joan Baez.

Of course, the marriage of Joan Baez and St. Francis, it makes perfect sense! Of all your paintings before you became an iconographer, the Francis painting is one of my favorites. It seems to anticipate some of the landscapes you did later at the Pratt Institute. The detail and depth of the scene is extraordinary, quite immersive, the emotional impact for me very strong, like the Arrupe deposition painting, very embodied, very human. I know your love for St. Francis goes back far and deep, and the stigmata especially—again, the wounds—and years later you became a Third Order Franciscan. But I wonder what inspired you to put St. Francis in a Jesuit chapel dedicated to Hopkins?

Well, this was long before Archbishop Stafford designated St. Francis as patron of Colorado, so maybe it was a spiritual premonition? The chapel never had an actual name, but the four painted panels of the seasons were pure Hopkins to me, above all, his love of the wilderness and his grief about the loss of the wild. The Native American

"What a Fool Believes" exhibit flyer

girl as Mary was a recognition of the Plains Indians, the original Coloradans.

At the end of your year as artist-in-residence you held an exhibit in the Regis College library. Was this your first formal art exhibit ever?

Yes, it was. I chose April Fool's Day for the opening, and titled it "What a Fool Believes." The Doobie Brothers had a song out with that title in 1979 that was a huge hit. I used the striped zebra—for me the zebra has always been a symbol of difference, of not quite fitting in—for the exhibit poster.

Earlier that year, Karl Laird, a Jesuit opera singer who was a few years older than me, came to visit and he put the fear of God in me. He said, Billy, you have to have a professional degree to

Fire Above / Water Below

The least little brothers
had this tale to tell,
how once he had
accepted the offer
of a prostitute,
if she would obey
the nature of brother fire
and lay down
with him
in the womb of the hearth
where all our desires
are purified.
And they recalled
this wonder too,
how one night
out of the heart
of the hearth he flew,
all engaged
in dazzling flames,
driven like Elijah
enroute Home.
He spun round and
round their waking dreams,
touching their
hopes and prayers
with tongues of fire.
And this most amazing miracle,
which made them weep
and run like rain
to remember;
how mercy had
always poured out
through him
because he used
all authority given
to him
to serve.

get any kind of respect, and I realized he was right. Initially I wanted to go to Rhode Island School of Design, but I knew I couldn't get into any school that required the SAT, because I would get a zero on the math. So that's how I ended up going to New York to study at The Pratt Institute in Brooklyn. Pratt accepted you based entirely on your art portfolio. I sent in a carousel of slides, and I got in.

Wow, what a journey. So, in 1980, at age 31, you moved to New York to study at Pratt, where you would create some of the most arresting drawings in your catalog.

Let me say, Fr. Bill, that your point about being able to share certain parts of your story without a sense of shame, things that are a normal part of being human, including your sexuality, to me, that is incredibly important, and I'm grateful for your trust. At the same time, I know there are things that you've chosen not to share, to protect yourself or others, given the often-dangerous, dehumanizing climate in the church for LGBTQ persons, and I respect that. I wouldn't ever ask you to do differently.

I think all priests today, as a result of the abuse crisis, are afraid to show too much love or basic human affection. It's terribly sad, if not demonic. What better tactic could the devil use than to make people afraid of priests, and priests afraid of laypeople? Now that I'm past 70, I'm really happy that I can love people freely without worrying that they'll take it wrong or misinterpret anything.

I've had to learn that shame comes from the outside; it's not from God. It was during the Pratt years that I was able to get some of these feelings out through my drawings.

PART II

Illustrator, Hospice Minister, Priest

Our lives are rarely as polished as blithesome youth once promised us. Jagged edges abound in even the best-lived lives, and we each have chapters of our lives that are better left unpublished. The arms of the past reach into the present. In the words of the American novelist William Faulkner, "The past is never dead. It's not even past."

Although we may not wish to revisit these jagged edges, these unpublished chapters, they serve a purpose: they let in light and love. They are a sign of being made real by love. But didn't we learn all this from the books that formed us as children?

—Martin Laird, *An Ocean of Light*

Things have meaning only to the extent that they lead to God, come from him, and can be placed at his service...

If a person seriously tries to locate all meaning in God, while he will become far more aware of his limitations, he will continually be meeting realities unfamiliar to ordinary life, things that have their life in God and cannot be reached by reasoning but only by prayer.

—Adrienne von Speyr, *The Mystery of Death*

The world was not created
under some kind of constraint . . .
rather, it was felt, it was
born of a wise liberty, of the
gay spontaneity of God's mind;
in a word, it came from the
hand of a child.

—Hugo Rahner, SJ

CHAPTER 5

Unless You Become Like a Child

As we venture into Part II, I ask Bill to share the backstory of two drawings that I find most riveting in his work: Illustration of a Faggot *and* The Akedah (Sacrifice of Isaac). *Both expose, rather shockingly, the interior struggle and vulnerability of a young gay Catholic who also happens to be in religious life and formation for the priesthood. From there we talk about his studies at Pratt Institute, during which he creates a series of incredibly beautiful watercolors set in Prospect Park, Brooklyn, begins to shop his drawings around New York City, lands his first book contract as an illustrator, and is soon spending his evenings creating drawings for children's books:* The Cathedral Book, The Hurt, The Story of Our Lady of Guadalupe, Encounters at Bethlehem, The Legend of the Holy Child of Atocha, *and many others.*

Reading about St. Damien of Moloka'i proves to be providential, drawing Bill into hospice ministry with men dying of HIV-AIDS—the "new lepers," some were calling them. The ministry effectively "outs" him as a gay Catholic priest, while the fear and ignorance around this frightening new "plague" become a source of tension in the Jesuit community. Yet what anchors this chapter is hopeful: the image of the Child and the sanctity of childhood in Bill's art, along with Jesuit saints like Aloysius Gonzaga. Working on children's books while "facing the very painful, very frightening deaths of young people," as Bill says, was an unexpected grace. "It was a great balance for me to go back to the Joy."

Chris: Fr. Bill, some of the most striking drawings in your work emerged during your study at the Pratt Institute in Brooklyn. A few of these are clearly autobiographical, like Illustration of a Faggot *and* The Akedah (Sacrifice of Isaac). *There are also a number of beautiful color pencil drawings, including Martin Luther King Jr.,* I Am Always a Drummer, *the* Flowering Crucifixion, *the cover of Jim Janda's one-woman play on Julian of Norwich, and* A Sower's Nightmare (Luke 8:5-15). *This period also includes the paintings of Prospect Park for your MFA exhibit.*

Fr. Bill: Yes, I did fourteen paintings for that exhibit in gouache and watercolor. For many

Prospect Park Stairway,
watercolor and gouache, 1982

painters, watercolor is very difficult. You have to be right there, on the spot, period. You can't paint over it or correct it the way you can with acrylic. For me, thankfully, it wasn't difficult, which is a real gift.

I'm looking at the Prospect Park Stairway *right now and the detail is just remarkable. As I mentioned before, for me it shares something with the painting of St. Francis,* I Hold Out My Hand.

I loved doing those paintings. I was living at America House at the time. Joe O'Hare and Vinny O'Keefe, who was Fr. Arrupe's personal assistant for many years, came down on the subway with me for my MFA exhibit.

As you've suggested, it would have been unusual for a young Jesuit to study art, rather than going further into theology or philosophy or some other professional field. But I have to imagine your Jesuit superiors must have supported you in the decision to do advanced studies at Pratt.

Park Slope Lamp, 1982

Lullwater Pond, Prospect Park, water and gouache, 1982

Prospect Park Tunnel Bricks, 1982

Prospect Park Azalea, 1982

Illustration of a Faggot (etching)

The Pain Body of Gay People

Yes, the summer before I entered Pratt Institute, my superior allowed me to find an apartment in Brooklyn. I found a place in the Park Slope area on the top floor of a brownstone. It had a fire escape right outside the kitchen window. I could climb out on the roof and look up into the sky and see a spectacular view of Manhattan. And I was just so happy. Not once did I feel lonely. I could finally hear myself, which I've always needed. I was kind of born to live alone, it seems, though I've not always been able to do it. I can be with people, but then I need to come back and listen to God, listen to myself, and ideas come.

I had read all these histories of gay people in the church that were published around this time: Fr. John McNeil's *The Church and the Homosexual*; John Fortunado's *Embracing the Exile*; John Boswell's *Christianity, Social Tolerance and Homosexuality*—all landmark works, and I had never been aware of a lot of this history. I learned that during medieval times, when they used to burn

people, they would take gay people, tie them up, and throw them on the fire, calling them "faggots," the term for scraps of wood. And that's how the word became associated with gay people. "Throw the 'faggot' on the fire."

I didn't know that.

Eckhardt Tolle has this notion of the "pain body." Every country, he says, has a pain body. When you step off the plane in Moscow, the pain body of Russia almost swallows you alive. Or Poland. Or Ireland. Or New Mexico. Women carry the pain body of women. Black people carry the pain body of Black people. I went into a period where I was deeply aware of and reacting to the pain body of gay people and reading what they had gone through. These drawings were just pouring out of me.

When I was 22, I took a class from the Jesuit scholar Robert Daly on "Christian Sacrifice." We learned all about the Akedah, the sacrifice of Isaac, and how that story would be linked to the sacrifice of Christ. Reading Fr. Daly's book *Christian Sacrifice* and taking the class as a 22-year-old was powerful for me. For my final project, I asked him if I could do drawings rather than a paper, and he let me do it. But I wasn't ready to reveal everything, about how the Akedah and the Christian sacrifice and the blood—everything that he writes about in his book—resonated so deeply with me, my own wounds.

As a result, the drawings I did for him were not very revealing, not really equal to what he wanted from the course. I think I got a B, which was a nice way of saying it should have been a C or a D! And even then, I was aware that I wasn't yet really capable of coming out, literally, or expressing my relationship to all these things, and how Fr. Daly had opened them up for me.

During that summer in Park Slope, all of these feelings began to pour out of me in these gay drawings, pouring my pain out. It was very cathartic. I was also reading G. B. Caird's commentary on the Gospel of Luke, and the two went together—the Akedah and the suffering of Jesus—because Caird calls Luke the "Gospel of the Outcast." Some of these drawings were technically good, and some were crude, cartoon-like. I was fluent in color pencil at the time, and they just got better and better. I had taken so many anatomy classes at Boston University and Pratt until they finally said, "Enough! You've taken this class four times, that's it!" But as an illustrator you've got to be able to draw the human figure. *Illustration of a Faggot* is actually a lithograph, where you etch into a plate, and have to do it backwards.

I'm looking at both Illustration of a Faggot *and* The Akedah, *in particular, where you are placing yourself fully inside a very disturbing biblical story of human sacrifice. Can you say more about coming into the realization, perhaps the inner freedom, of creating that very dark and intense drawing?*

The Akedah (Sacrifice of Isaac), color pencil, 1980

All through my Jesuit years, at Mass during Easter season, and every Holy Saturday, I just hated to hear that story of God telling Abraham to sacrifice Isaac. One year as a scholastic, in 1972, we were spending Easter weekend, the Paschal Triduum, at the Jesuit retreat house in Gloucester, Massachusetts. On Holy Saturday I couldn't go to the service because I just could not hear that story. Leonard Cohen wrote the song "Story of Isaac" with the same feelings of horror in it. I had heard the cover by Judy Collins. It frightened me and made me sick. When I entered Pratt in 1980, I started to ask myself, Why are you so upset by this story? What does it mean to you?

Originally, the story meant your own father would sacrifice you. Or the church fathers would sacrifice you. And having read all this church history and history of gay people, I knew that the church was responsible for burning "faggots," for burning people who were considered deformed or demonic. In Dante's *Inferno* the ninth circle of Hell is for gay people. In fact, there was a famous gay bar in the West Village on Christopher Street called the "Ninth Circle," right next to the Oscar Wilde Bookstore, where I got many of the books mentioned above, and others, like *The Men with the Pink Triangle: The True Life-and-Death Stories of Homosexuals in the Nazi Death Camps*, by Heinz Heger.

With all of that in the background, I thought, Okay, I'm going to do a picture of the Akedah. But *I'm also a Catholic priest now*, I've been ordained for a year, so I also bear responsibility for spreading this homophobia and these murderous thoughts. When I draw the Akedah, I'm going to be all three people: the young gay man, the priest who is trying to kill him, and the angel, trying to stop the whole thing. I'm going to represent myself as all three of them. That says it all. The lamb in the thicket symbolizes Christ in the drawing—the Christ figure is "barking," yelling, "Stop! Stop! Stop trying to kill yourself! Stop trying to deny who you are." Because I had been to New Mexico a number of times, I made a desert background, having no idea that I would ever live here. But even then, it felt like home to me.

That story is still hard for me to hear. In one interpretation, Abraham thinks God is telling him to sacrifice Isaac, but it isn't really God. I'm hoping that version is right, because I can't imagine a God like that. It's like the question I got wrong on my final oral examination after three years of theology. Did God suffer while Jesus was on the cross? Yes, of course he did, I said. But with my drawing *The Akedah*, I had to admit, the truth is, I'm doing this to myself because of my ingrained homophobia.

I'm the one trying to kill that part of myself.

I Didn't Realize It Was a Compliment

Were you still at some level in denial about your identity, or feeling like an outsider within the Jesuits or on the margins of the church?

People did not come out then. You had to keep quiet. Everybody knew you were gay, but nobody wanted you to say it. John Paul II came into the papacy in 1978. I was ordained in 1979. It was dangerous to say it. People didn't want you to be open about it.

I remember the first time Dignity, the organization for gay Catholics, called to ask if I would say Mass for them.[1] I talked to a Jesuit mentor, and he said, "I wouldn't do that if I were you. Then everybody will know." I was sort of isolated in Brooklyn. I didn't want to be alone all the time. I wanted to be with other gay people. So, I did accept and became one of the regulars to preside at the Dignity Mass, which they held every Saturday night. After Mass, they'd gather in the basement of St. Francis Xavier for coffee, and I got to know them. Eventually they would ask me to do the first Mass for people with AIDS.

As for the drawings, I was taking my portfolio to publishing companies throughout Manhattan. In those days you had to pound the pavement and show them your work. They'd always ask, "What books have you done?" I'd say, "None yet." "Okay," they'd say, "when you get a book, come back and see us." Every time I'd get turned away. Finally, I went all the way to New Jersey, to Paulist Press, in Mahwah, and showed them my work. Their reaction was like, "Um, this work is a little *strong*."

Really? I can't imagine why they said that!

And I didn't even show them *The Akedah* or any of the other more intense drawings. My teacher at Pratt said to me: "Do you know that everything you do is sensual?" I was so upset when he said that. "It is *not!*" I shot back, like an upset little kid, "It is not!" I didn't realize it was a compliment.

What he was saying is that everything you do has *élan vital*, it has a life force in it. It's sensual because—anybody, like Princess Diana, President Kennedy, Martin Luther King Jr.—anyone who has this *élan vital* pouring out of them—you can feel it when you meet them. He kept saying he saw that kind of force in my work, jumping off the page and grabbing people. But I *did not* take it as a compliment at the time. Anyway, Paulist said, "Don't call us, we'll call you."

A while later, thank goodness, they did call. They said they were having a contest to find an illustrator for a book called *The Cathedral Book*, and they asked me to submit a drawing. I submitted a drawing of a little child building a cathedral out of paper.

Child building church

I love that drawing.

Me too. I was so fluent in color pencil at the time, and the original was done in a kind of a red sepia. I was waiting every day at the mailbox for a letter, and my landlord was waiting too—he was kind of an Archie Bunker type, just wonderful. One day we both got to the mailbox at the same time, and I looked and there was a letter from Paulist Press. I opened it up, and I misread it to him on purpose, "We're sorry to inform you but. . . ." But then I said, "Oh my God. *I got it.* They said yes!" I just was so happy, and my landlord was so happy. They sent me the manuscript, and to be doing drawings of cathedrals, architecture drawings, for a first book was amazing.

I spent a long time doing that book, and that was the beginning. They kept sending me new projects, a few for older people but mostly children's books. And then other presses began to reach out, like the cover I did for Seabury Press for Jim Janda's play on Julian of Norwich.[2] I loved being an illustrator, like a duck in water. Tommie De Paola was one of my idols, like Maurice Sendak and so many others, and I went to meet him when he was signing books at the Met. I was doing all of these book illustrations while studying at Pratt, and eventually doing the paintings of Prospect Park for my MFA exhibit.

Notre Dame Cathedral, for *The Cathedral Book*, 1982

I had been living on my own for two years, but then my Jesuit superiors insisted that I move into a Jesuit residence. I was not expecting it, and it was pretty heartbreaking. Joe O'Hare learned I was looking for a place, and, when he saw the illustrations he said, why not come live at America House, I could do illustrations for the magazine. I moved into America House in July of 1983, and, not long after, did my first cover for *America* magazine. In September, I did the Mass for people with AIDS.

Damien Was Preparing Me for a New Life

As I understand it, the Mass of Healing for people with AIDS was one of the first and only of its kind in New York City, or indeed in the whole country, and they would continue for some years. What happened to draw you into the hospice ministry?

When I was at Pratt, I remember feeling unsatisfied with my life, thinking, "I really want to do something," like, "Lord, use me." I found a book on St. Damien of Moloka'i at a Catholic book store, *Damien the Leper*, written by John Farrow, Mia Farrow's father.[3] Just as I finished reading

it, I got a call asking me to do the first Mass for people with AIDS. When I got that call, I knew it wasn't just a phone call. I knew that Damien was preparing me for something, for a new life.

In those days, there were articles that called people with AIDS "the new lepers." They didn't want to be called "AIDS victims," "lepers," or other dehumanizing things. They wanted to be called "people with HIV/AIDS." Later, when the first drugs came out that slowed down the process, they wanted to be called "people living with AIDs," or "living with HIV."

Cover for Fr. Jim Janda's play on Julian of Norwich, 1984

In my poem about Damien, I say that Damien turned Moloka'i into the Emerald Forest. What I mean is, it had been a place of shame, a place of horror; and, after he came, the world began to see Moloka'i differently. The people who were afflicted with Hansen's disease began to see themselves differently. People were so taken by his sacrifice that it changed attitudes toward leprosy. God can take something that is extremely dark and horrible and harsh and turn it into something that is like a paradise. All of this darkness, this tragedy hanging over the leper colony, Damien sanctified. He made it human.

To make something holy, you're suggesting, is to make it more human. He restored them to their human dignity.

Didn't St. Irenaeus say something like this?

Yes, "The glory of God is the human being fully alive." It's a beautiful view of the human vocation, if we can believe it, and so powerfully dramatized in Damien's impact on the people of Moloka'i.

Yes, exactly. The opposite view is Gnosticism, which Irenaeus fought against. It had never occurred to me to identify the far-right element of the church today under the worldview of Gnosticism, but Pope Francis has made this connection. The genius of it, for him to say to the right wing, You're more or less trying to create your own separate church, "purified" from the rest of us, the rest of humanity. To the contrary, Francis is always saying the church is like a "field hospital after battle," that he wants priests to "smell like the sheep." God is found in the messiness, in the wounds, among the lepers.

Yes, though I would add that the demand for "purity" can be pretty relentless from the secular and religious left, too. Right or left, it's what William Lynch called the "absolutizing instinct," which elevates the absolute rightness of one's own position or group while scapegoating everyone else.

You said that just before you were called into AIDS ministry, you were asking God to use you in some way, reading about Damien serving the lepers, and then you were asked to preside at Mass for people with AIDS. The connection to Fr. Damien in your life runs deep.

To be honest, he was the harbinger. I haven't shared the details too often. When I've talked in the past about what the ministry actually entailed, people have had a hard time hearing it. So much blood, buckets of diarrhea, people sprouting lesions. For some, the cytomegalovirus would affect their mind. One day they were right there; the next day they were talking nonsense,

St. Damien of Moloka'i

seeing phantoms flying around the room and things like that. The doctors didn't know how to treat any of that. When it got into the brain, you could no longer talk to them. It was such grief to see them go.

Some years later there was a man in Washington, DC, Louis Tesconi, who himself had AIDS and wanted to start Damien Ministries to serve the poorest people living with HIV and AIDS. He contacted me and asked if I would do an image of Damien for them to use as their logo. Though Fr. Damien wasn't yet a saint—that would come later under Pope Benedict XVI—he was a natural choice as a symbol of compassion and hope. Of course, he himself would contract and die of leprosy. So, there he is in the drawing that I did for them, with Moloka'i in the background.

Unless You Become Like a Child

In his beautiful book Hidden Mercy, *Michael O'Laughlin describes the emotional impact of your*

65

first days in the hospice ministry, seeing the devastating effects of the illness up close, wondering how and whether you'd be able to handle it, and what good could you really do as a Catholic priest.[4] You attended workshops run by the Gay Men's Health Crisis, and then you volunteered at Saint Vincent's Hospital in Greenwich Village, where you met Sr. Patrice Murphy. Michael describes her as "a fierce advocate of people with AIDS and a hero to many in the gay community." But she also "radiated love," had a great sense of humor, and set a mood at St. Vincent's of celebrating life "even in the midst of unrelenting death."[5] What strikes me is that you had a lot to learn yourself, and at the same time you were having to educate others about the disease, including some in the Jesuit community.

It was Michael Hirsch, the hilarious, mischievous, and fiercely dedicated AIDS activist who suggested I work for Sr. Patrice and the Hospice Supportive Care Program. Michael had started a newspaper called *Body Positive*, which provided news, updates, event notices, personal stories—anything related to the virus and support for the gay community. We had become friends, and after the first Healing Mass he told me that Sr. Patrice might need a chaplain. So, I made an appointment, and she hired me immediately, but told me they had no money to pay me. If I could accept that, I could start as soon as I wanted. This meeting would turn into seven years of ministry in the hospice.

Though I had been doing the Dignity Masses, this was entirely different. There were very few men working with people with AIDS in the beginning, unless they were doctors. All the male volunteers doing hospice ministry were gay. If you were a woman, a nurse, or a religious sister, it was different. Though I had worked on the suicide hotline, I had never done direct work with the dying, much less with AIDS.

Sr. Patrice was a beacon of sanity and courage. A completely professional registered nurse, she required all her staff to take the training given by Gay Men's Health Crisis, which armed you with facts and prepared you to go into any situation involving people who had contracted the virus. She modeled so many qualities for me of being a professional, while learning how to find some occasional modicum of joy in the midst of an ever-growing pandemic. I loved her very much and learned so much from her, as well as from Sr. Anne Tubman, a truly charismatic healer who lived in the Bronx. I apprenticed myself to Sr. Anne to learn how to pray over and for people, both in the hospital and during the monthly Healing Masses. Both these extraordinary women generously shared their gifts with me, and I'm still learning from them, even though they've both passed away.

After some time at America House, I'd walk in during drinks before dinner and people would scurry away. I wondered what was going on. One of the Jesuits, who had been a missionary in

McNichols in America House (wearing the Third Order Franciscan Tau Cross)

Africa and was so kind to me, said, "You know, people are afraid you are going to bring AIDS into the house. They don't know if you should be eating with us, if it can be picked up on the glasses,

Santo Niño visits a prisoner, from *Legend of the Holy Child of Atocha*, 1988

Santo Niño de Atocha, Christmas card illustration

Cover of *Appointments with the Little King*, 1988

Cover of *The Legend of St. Christopher*, 1987

or the silverware." I explained to everyone in the community: you're not going to get AIDS from a glass, or a towel; it's only blood to blood or bodily fluids. But a lot of people didn't believe it; they were still scared. Eventually, I had to move out of America House, and was invited to live at the Jesuit retreat center in Manhasset, which is where I did a lot of the children's books: *Santo Niño, St. Christopher, Appointments with the Little King*.[6]

So, here I was, in the daytime, facing the very painful, very frightening deaths of young people, and at night, I was working on these children's books. It was a great balance for me to go back to the Joy. Because of reading Caird's commentary on Luke, I realized there were significant places in Scripture where the child or children are mentioned, when Jesus says, for example, "Unless you become like a child" you won't enter the

Kingdom of heaven. For me to draw those books, I had to become like a child. There's a playfulness in the images. In several of the books, for example, in every drawing I hid a little mouse somewhere in the picture.

But then, the same thing happened at Manhasset that had happened at America House. People were afraid that I would bring AIDS into the retreat center, and I was told I needed to find another place to live, that my room was being turned into an AA meeting room. I was stunned. When I've experienced injustice—I know that everybody has gone through something—it's very painful, of course, but I try not to concentrate on that. It's easy to get stuck in blaming or bitterness, and then the creative imagination gets blocked. I try to see it as: there's an obstacle in my path and I have to go here now, rather than there.

And it can open up avenues of creativity that I wouldn't have discovered otherwise.

This was 1984. I found this vacant apartment on Bleecker Street in the West Village, right across from John's Pizza, and the cafes where Dylan and Joni would play when they were just beginning. That apartment was pretty rough, but it was in that neighborhood, not long after, that I met Dan Berrigan on the subway. He said to me, You know, Bill Lynch died, and we have an open apartment.[7] Why don't you come live with us? So, I moved from Bleecker Street to Ninety-Eighth Street.

Try Holding the Baby

It's a strange blend of realities. You're doing AIDS ministry by day and illustrating children's books at night. When I first began studying your drawings from this period, I was struck by the prevalence of images of the Child: Jesuits holding the Child Jesus, Santo Niño visiting the prisoner, Mary and the Child Jesus visiting the wounded Ignatius as he convalesces at Pamplona. In the children's book Encounters in Bethlehem, *you depict the Holy Family in a very human way, not highly idealized, but real. I know that each book and each image had a specific purpose, but is there a through-line for you that joins these images of the Child together?*

At different times in my life, there have been different guiding spirits. During the AIDS ministry, Jesus was one hundred percent present to me—and Aloysius, and Francis. You can see this in the book of poems I wrote during those years, *Fire Above, Water Below.* When I would visit people in the hospice, I saw at least ten patients each day. One day they had me scheduled to visit seventeen patients, and I just couldn't do it. Today they call it "compassion fatigue," but you get to a point where you can't even listen, and it's embarrassing. "I just can't do it; I'll come tomorrow." "But what if they're dying?" "Well, put them at the top of the list; I'll see them first thing tomorrow."

It was so horrifying; there was so much blood,

so much death, so much suffering that could not be stopped. And witnessing that every single day, it led me to the Child somehow. It gave balance.

When I was doing the AIDS ministry, they didn't know I was a priest at first. If I had been wearing clerics, even though I was their age, they would have stopped me at the door. "No, no, you can't come in." I wore a sport coat with a St. Anthony button on the lapel where he's holding the baby Jesus, so that I could get into the room. The gentleness of Anthony holding the baby was also a reminder for me. I knew I had to be gentle doing this work.

"I'm a chaplain. Can I come in?" I'd sit down, and we'd talk for a while. Eventually they'd ask, What kind of a chaplain are you? "A Catholic chaplain." Are you a priest? "Yes, I am." But because we had been talking for a while, they knew I wasn't scary. But if I'd mention Jesus, the reaction was, "No, no. Please don't talk about him. I can't pray to him." "Why not?" I'd ask. "Because I know he judges me."

I'd say, "Okay, try this. Try holding the baby. Pretend that Mary gives you the baby. He's not going to judge you. He might poop, or he might wet on you, but he won't do anything else." They'd laugh, thinking it was hilarious to even suggest such a thing. The next day I'd visit and they'd say, "Well, I did what you suggested. I tried holding the baby and talking to him." "What was it like?" *"It felt good."* I carried a card with me, with a famous painting of Jesus embracing a man as he comes into heaven. When someone who was dying would ask me, "What is going to happen to me?" I'd show them the card and say, "This is what's going to happen to you."

I'll never forget one man in the ICU; he was 35 or 36, and he couldn't talk. I went in and his eyes looked just terrified. I asked everyone else to leave the room. I said, "I know you're terrified." Just blink once for yes. If no, blink twice. He blinked once. "You're afraid that you've done too much and that God is not going to love you." He blinked once. I said, "Let's try going to confession. I'll mention some things that you might feel bad about, and you blink if that's the case." I

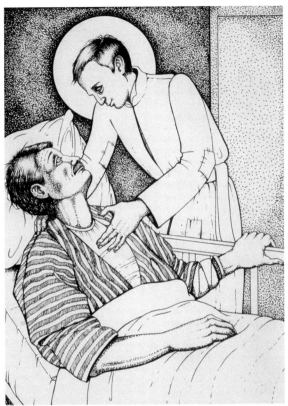

St. Aloysius Gonzaga, Patron of People with HIV-AIDS and Caregivers, 1987

went through the Ten Commandments, his relationships with family and other people, and I'd ask if I've covered everything. When I finally absolved him, I said, "Do you know what's going to happen to you when you go?" because he was very close to death. He blinked "no." I bent down and I put the card in his hand, and his eyes just flooded with tears.

I walked out of the room, very shaken. And very happy that *I was able to use those visual things to help.* That's why I began to use the image of the Child and Santo Niño in the books. I thought, I could give these books out to people when they were published.

What Kind of Power
Do You Have as a Child?

Some of your drawings during this period — AIDS Crucifixion, Stations of the Cross for People with AIDS *and* Francis 'Neath the Bitter Tree — *figure prominently in Michael's book. He also writes about your illustration of St. Aloysius Gonzaga at the bedside of an AIDS patient.[8] To your point about using artistic images to help people, Michael gives many powerful accounts of how your drawings brought real comfort to those who were sick and dying. It was because of your work, I think, that St. Aloysius Gonzaga would become the patron saint of people dying of AIDS.*

Yes, and it was a total revelation to me to come to that connection. "Oh my gosh, *of course, Aloysius.*" He had cared for people dying of the plague, and eventually he would die from it himself. The drawing first appeared in the *Missouri Province Jesuit Bulletin.* I began to make cards of the image, and would sell them at Dignity meetings.

The national Jesuit newspaper ran the image of Aloysius, so people became aware of him as a figure of hope for people with AIDS. Before that, people didn't really like Aloysius; they thought he was a prig, like "the good kid" at school whom everybody hates, the teacher's pet whom nobody wanted to be like. There were stories about his extreme modesty, for example, averting his eyes whenever a woman was in the room, or how he would run away whenever there was a dance with women, and stuff like that.

Around this time a new book came out about the history of the Gonzaga family, one of the most prominent and notorious families of the time. Women would come to these dances where the young Aloysius was serving at court, and some of the women, as a kind of entertainment, would target and molest little boys. All of a sudden it was clear to me: Aloysius had either been molested or was fearful that he would be molested. A lot of things began to make sense, for example, why he kept his eyes down when women were in the room.

The point is, *What kind of power do you have as a child?* None. I wrote an article about Aloysius, and suddenly people began to open up to him. The image of Aloysius caring for victims of the plague began to become more prominent than

Aloysius as the patron of purity, which turned many people away because they could not relate to someone so above them. In her book *Confession*, Adrienne von Speyr says, "When Aloysius sees his Jesuit brothers sinning, he doesn't judge them. He basically says, Well they don't love God enough, but then neither do I." So that's how my love for Aloysius began.

As I've mentioned, I was also trying to soften the image of Ignatius and place the Child and the Blessed Mother more prominently within the Jesuit order. When I was in Manhasset, they had me do Christmas cards for the community, and I wanted to do the Jesuits who had been associated with the Christ Child. Everybody knew that Stanislaus was associated with the Infant Jesus, and Robert Southwell had written a beautiful poem, "The Burning Babe," about an apparition, or a vision poetically imagined, of the Child Jesus on Christmas Day. But few knew about a real apparition of the Child to Bernardino Realino.[9]

Of course, Mary has always been a huge part of Jesuit devotion, but after Vatican II, not so much. People had to kind of make excuses as to why we still should love Mary, pray to the saints, and so on. While there was a concentration on Scripture and Ignatian studies that was all very good, the devotional part of Jesuit life was slipping away. That's because in my generation and the ones above me, the saints had been presented as perfect beings, and who could ever relate or live up to that perfection? It was again the harsh, and bitter, influence of Jansenism. I thought, How can I possibly balance this?

They're Not Mine to Keep

Of all your Jesuit-themed illustrations, one of my favorites is the color drawing of Mary and the Child Jesus at the bedside of Ignatius the Convalescent, *which really surfaces this more tender and vulnerable side of Ignatius at a moment of real crisis, after sustaining a devastating injury in battle. "My life is a mess. My body is broken. Everything that I thought would bring me happiness has left me empty and*

unfulfilled. Why am I here? For what purpose am I called to live?"

When you look today, Fr. Bill, at the children's books and illustrations, do they recede for you behind the significance or impact of the icons? Or in your mind and heart do you hold the drawings just as dear, just as significant theologically, if I could put it that way, albeit in a very different way?

I remember one guy saying to me, sometime during the AIDS ministry, "I love your books, but this isn't your art." "What do you mean?" I said, a bit taken aback. "I don't know," he said, "I just know this isn't your art. I know you have another art to do." I had no idea what he meant. I thought, that's odd, I really want to be an illustrator.

It's as if he had a premonition of your later work as an iconographer. And yet all of this earlier material—the children's book drawings, the Akedah, *the illustrations for various books, the Jesuit drawings—these have been largely hidden, not seen outside of the original books they appeared in. After your heart collapse in 2012, you said that you felt that God wanted you to get these out as well.*

Yes, I did, and I guess that answers your question. I do hold these drawings and illustrations very close to my heart. But more strongly, I feel they're not mine to keep for myself or keep hidden, and I needed to give them away—or allow them to be seen, along with the icons and other painted images. They belong to God, they belong to the church, they belong to the Jesuits and to anyone who might find in them an image of hope or healing.

As you know, even after about seven years of doing icons in the very traditional way, I wanted to expand into other kinds of images, and gave myself permission to do so. I could do somebody like Rachel Carson, or Matthew Shepard, or Elijah McClain. Strictly speaking, these paintings aren't icons, and I've had to be clear about the distinction between "icons" and "images." The trouble is, when you're an iconographer, everybody will call them "icons" anyway. They'll say,

"I really love your icon of Matthew Shepard." And I have to say, "Thank you, but technically it's not an icon."[10]

I would never have to say that if it weren't for the "icon police," who had already tried to censure my teacher, Friar Robert Lentz. I realized early on that just by having Robert as my teacher I was already canceled by those who had appointed themselves the "icon inquisition." There was a lot of jealousy around Robert because he was the one who almost single-handedly revived the love for icons in the Western churches. In my mind, Robert is the master, and I'm his student. And after being through seven years with people dying with AIDS, the criticism didn't seem very important.

CHAPTER 6

Arrows into the Heart of the Church

We begin with a transformational experience from Bill's early years in the Jesuits, when his hope had nearly extinguished and an older Jesuit threw him a lifeline. From there we return to the AIDS hospice years and a number of paintings and illustrations that Bill conceives of as "arrows into the heart of the church." St. Aloysius, St. Francis, St. Anthony, the Virgin of Guadalupe, and the image of the Child all figure prominently as sources of "hope against hope" in his ministry. The book of Revelation—especially chapter 12, in which the dragon is poised before the pregnant Woman Clothed with the Sun, ready to devour her child at the moment she gives birth—emerges as a key biblical image in Bill's spirituality and art, resonant with Fr. Daniel Berrigan's prophetic denunciation of society's "war against children."

What is the "arrow" that Fr. Bill's art aims to shoot into the heart of the church? It is the message of Jesus and St. Francis, of Damien of Moloka'i and Sr. Patrice Murphy, and of Fr. Dan Berrigan, who becomes a dear friend to Bill in these years: You must meet Christ in the wounded, in the afflicted, in the lepers. It is "not easy to turn the negative energy into grace," yet all around us, in kind people, in lives of holiness, in people who endure and struggle for justice, "the light is shining across the water."

Chris: Before we go further into your AIDS ministry and the art that emerges from the years in New York, I want to step back and ask you about an important spiritual experience that you've mentioned to me before, something that happened at Pine Ridge Indian Reservation in South Dakota, but you've never told me the details. It happened, I think, after the end of novitiate and taking first vows as a Jesuit but before you moved to Boston to complete your philosophy studies. Could I ask you to speak about it now? What happened, and why was it such an important moment in your spiritual journey?

Fr. Bill: What happened at Pine Ridge has been the guiding light of my life. Without it I couldn't have gone on the way I have. There are certain things you can make up and that come from you . . . and they don't help much! But when they come from God directly you can't deny them; they make an imprint on your soul. It's like we say about the sacraments, they make an almost physical imprint on the heart and soul.

It was the year that I had been through the shock therapy and conversion therapy. I was 22. One day I came home after the shock therapy and I put a sock on my door. In the Jesuit world, when you put a sock on your door, it means "Do Not Disturb." Do not knock, don't come in, don't even think about it, and everybody respects that. After one of the sessions, after being shocked like 45 times, I was just a mess. I put a sock on the door, and I slept for a very long time.

Tears of Overflowing Joy

One of the Jesuits, John Staudenmaier, who was probably ten or twelve years older than me, lived on the floor above me. He was straight and had a very strong personality, a big presence in the community, and he was just brilliant. One evening he knocked on my door and said, "I know something is going on with you." He sat in my room and began to coax out of me what was going on. I told him about everything, including the shock therapy and conversion therapy. His spiritual home was Pine Ridge, and he was giving retreats there that summer. He asked me if I wanted to make a retreat with him.

When the time came, a bunch of us younger Jesuits got into a van and drove to Pine Ridge. I had never been on the Indian reservation, so it felt like a kind of pilgrimage. We all stayed in a dorm with bunk beds, and I would lie on the bottom bunk and watch these bats darting around the room and flying over my bed. It didn't bother me at all. I mean, what's scary about bats after you've been through electric shock? I was a very young, melancholy, vulnerable young man. At 22, I had been through this thing that I was ashamed of and felt isolated. I wouldn't talk about it with anyone.

John was a brilliant retreat director, and he would give me a passage to read and send me off to pray with it. One day it was around one in the afternoon, and it was really hot. I went into the chapel and didn't feel anything. Just dead. I was so *not ready to pray*. Earlier I had gone out walking into a field, and an Indian boy came up to me and said, "Are you all right?" I said, "Yes, I'm all right." He said, "Well, you look really sad." I said, "Oh, I'll be okay." I remember telling John about this later, and he said, "That's very unusual. Native boys almost never talk with strangers." This boy must have been really sensitive. He really saw right through me.

So, I'm in this tiny chapel, just sitting there, hot and dead. And all of a sudden, this voice of God came into my cold soul, and said, "Hope." I said, "Hope? Hope what?" And the voice said, "Hope against hope." I knew it wasn't me, and now I was crying, because the voice was just flooding me. I said, "God if it's really you, then make this whole thing stop right now." And it did. It stopped. I said, "If it's really you, then come back." Again, I heard, "Hope against hope," and now I was really weeping.

The next prayer I had was something hopeless, something to do with the devil. John said, "Well, that makes perfect sense. You got a real confirmation, and then immediately, of course, you were attacked."

But honest to God, I don't think I've had more than a few instances where I felt the real presence of God so palpably as I did in that chapel, when I was in such despair. It really set the stage for any kind of hopeless situation I found myself in my whole life, including the AIDS ministry ten years later. No matter how bad things are, there's always this pilot light of hope. After that I began drawing wishbones, which became for me a symbol of hope, of hope against hope.

Would you say that Pine Ridge was a pivotal moment of release or liberation for you, like, "I'm not looking back anymore. I'm not going to try to 'cure myself' of this supposed affliction of being gay"?

You know how sad you can be when you're young? At some point many years later—it may have been during the COVID pandemic, when we were all isolated in quarantine—I realized that the person I wanted to be when I was at Pine Ridge is the person I finally am now. The tears that came over me that day in the chapel, I imagine it's the grace Ignatius felt so often at Mass, just tears of overflowing joy.

It was beyond being gay. It was, "This is a word for you, for your whole life—hope against hope." It was a realization that God will take care of you no matter what comes. All the times I felt myself on the outside, not invited, not part of the group, I've since realized that I set myself up for those experiences throughout my life. By choosing icons, many years later, *in being chosen by icons*, I was able to leave all of that need to fit in behind. When I go into the work, that's the moment of release and liberation.

I'm especially struck by your image of hope as a "pilot light." When it's flickering and about to go out, someone comes along and shelters the flame from the wind, helps us keep it going. "We're all born with a brilliant light inside of us," you said in an earlier conversation, but there are forces that are always seeking to put out the light.

And so, when a terrified, dying man asked you what was going to happen to him when he died, and you gave him the card with the picture of Jesus embracing a man at the gates of heaven, you were replacing his image of an unforgiving God with an image of God as all-embracing love; in those last moments, perhaps restoring his faith that what he understood to be impossible might actually be possible. When John Staudenmaier invited you to come on retreat at Pine Ridge, he was offering you a first step out of the desolation that you felt, and God followed with an image of consolation: "hope against hope."[1]

Exactly. I'm sure you can look back now and see people in your life who were there for you at critical moments. For me there were other Jesuits besides John Staudenmaier, like Dan, like John Padberg, whom I mentioned earlier when I came to Boston. I sometimes think of them as "male mothers," which Robert Bly talks about in his book *Iron John*. I believe every young person needs these kinds of mentors along the way. When I was at Georgetown University recently, I was told that teachers today are afraid to get too close to their students because they risk being accused of "grooming." It's a terrible ripple effect, especially when there seems to be so much

loneliness among young and older people alike today.

Arrows into the Heart of the Church

Speaking of hope as a kind of pilot light, I'd like to turn to the art that came out of the AIDS epidemic as you were experiencing it through the hospice ministry. We touched earlier on your role in bringing St. Aloysius Gonzaga to the forefront as a patron saint for people with AIDS and their caregivers. But there are other powerful drawings and paintings from this period, some of which, years later, would get you into trouble with the "icon police" and hard-right Catholics who found them objectionable.

Yes. We should probably start with *The Epiphany: Wise Men Bring Gifts to the Child*, which was the first painting I ever did related to AIDS. As far as I know, it was the first Catholic painting ever done about AIDS. It was printed by almost every Catholic magazine and newspaper, and caused quite a stir.

Having become familiar with the image of the arrow in Christian art—the idea that God or an angel would shoot the arrow of love into your soul or heart—it came to me that God was calling me to become an archer in my work. While doing a drawing or painting about AIDS, I would pretend that I was taking that image and shooting it into the heart of the church.

The Epiphany painting was carefully thought through, designed, and contemplated, bringing together a lot of images in one painting, in gouache and watercolor. It took me several months to complete. It was not done primarily for people with AIDS, because there is so much suffering in it. It was done for the church, to show the church what the attitude of the saints and the Mother of God and Santo Niño, the Child Jesus, was toward people with AIDs, who were outcast and suffering.

The saints that I felt helping me most in the hospice ministry were St. Francis and St. Aloysius. I had learned a lot about Francis when I became a

The Epiphany: Wise Men Bring Gifts to the Child

Third Order Franciscan. After he had been converted and began to attract others around him, he demanded that they work with lepers. You need to meet Christ, he said, and the lepers are Christ. You need them more than they need you. Above Francis in the painting is the crown of thorns, and falling from the crown are wishbones, my symbol of hope. Out of suffering, hope comes. For people considered the lepers of our time, I was trying to say, Francis sees you as Christ. Francis is holding a man named Robert, one of the first men I visited who was dying of AIDS.

I had seen a photograph of a statue in Rome of Aloysius holding a man who is dying of the plague. That image burned itself into my memory. I almost immediately got the feeling that Aloysius wanted to be patron of people with AIDS. At the time I thought, This isn't a good idea. Jesuits, as I mentioned before, thought

of Aloysius as a prig, with his "modesty of the eyes" and the fact that he is "patron of purity" and "patron of boys"—all of that was against Aloysius. But when I read the book on the Gonzaga dynasty, I understood why Aloysius was so painfully modest and strange around women. As I mentioned before, when Aloysius was at the court of King Phillip in Spain, they had these parties where women would make a sport of molesting the boys.

I thought his story was a lot like Maria Goretti, who was stalked by her murderer.[2] She was eleven; her stalker was nineteen. He would whisper things in her ear, and she never told her mother because she feared it would bring trouble between the two families. Who knows what Aloysius went through, but I felt strongly that he really wanted to be involved, to be a part of this contemporary plague. I read everything that

75

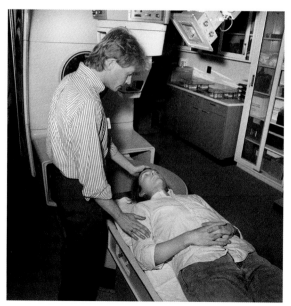

Fr. Bill with Jeff in hospital
© 1987 Rosalind Fox Solomon

You said that Epiphany *is the first of the AIDS images, and it's such a bold concept. The very idea that the gifts the Magi bring to the Child Jesus—the Magi being Francis and Aloysius—are men dying of AIDS, naked, and covered with Kaposi sarcoma lesions. It's not hard to imagine that the painting made a stir, as you said before. Where did the painting appear?*

When I finished the painting, I had it framed and they hung it in the hospice office. But it was reproduced in all kinds of Catholic magazines. The thing is, it wasn't controversial in the sense that people objected to the subject matter. It was shocking in the way it was meant to be—like an arrow shot into the heart. These are the plague victims of our time. What are you doing to care for them?

Rise Up and Follow Him Home

In Christopher Summa's beautiful 2016 film about you, The Boy Who Found Gold, *you are reflecting on your art from this period and you say something that I've never forgotten: "AIDS had to have a face that was compassionate. Christ had to be there. Mary had to be there—the deaths were so quick, and so fast, I kept trying to do drawings that would put Christ into it." There's archival footage of an interview you gave in which a TV reporter asks you whether the AIDS epidemic has something to teach the Catholic Church. Without hesitation, you responded, "God is giving the church an opportunity to love him with a different face. Will you love me if I look like this? How much will you love?"*

I could about him, and Jesuits began to print the pictures I did of him in Jesuit newspapers and magazines. They accepted the research that I did and maybe that helped to change attitudes toward him. For people dying with AIDS, it didn't matter, I already knew he was their angel.

The drawing of Aloysius at the bedside of a patient is a really tender image.

The person in the bed in that drawing is my friend Lenny. I asked Lenny if he would be okay with it, and he said yes. I had my camera, and I asked him to look up and to imagine that Aloysius was standing right over him. I made the drawing from that photograph. I put patches on Aloysius's garments because, being from the great Gonzaga family, he was so famous when he entered the Jesuit novitiate that lots of important people would come to try to meet him—cardinals and politicians and court people. He would try as hard as he could to get his cassock dirty, so he wouldn't look good. I put patches on his cassock—both in the *Epiphany* painting and in the drawing—as a sign of his humility.

I'm grateful for Christopher's film—it took him a long time to convince me to do it—partly because it captures a lot of things from that time that might otherwise have been lost or forgotten. Michael's book does the same thing—in different ways, both are like arrows into the heart of the church.

I mentioned earlier how I wore the button with St. Anthony holding the baby, because people would tell me they couldn't pray to Christ, or to the adult Jesus, because they felt he was judging them. I would tell them to take the baby, hold the baby and talk to him; he won't judge you. The *Epiphany* painting was another way of trying to say the same thing. He loves you, he wants to love you, let him come to you.

Eventually the painting came back to me, and the only thing that's faded over all this time is Mary's turquoise cloak. I wanted Mary to be Our Lady of Guadalupe, not a white Mary but a brown Mary. And her clothes don't symbolize whiteness, like Fatima or Lourdes. Guadalupe's clothes are a very rich turquoise with a salmon color underneath. I wanted the Santo Niño, the Holy Child, on her lap. He is practically jumping out of her lap, the way little kids do in a store when they see something they want. Mary is holding him back, but he's leaning toward Robert, wanting to be held by him.

Mary is sitting on the throne from the book of Revelation. I don't think the rainbow was yet a gay symbol; that would come later; but for me, it had to do with Caird's commentary on Revelation, where the throne is a rainbow. The waters of death are also in the painting. We say at the funeral, "Lord, carry them over the waters of death," so it became a powerful symbol for me.

I wanted there to be a pathway—like the glowing luminarias that people light at night in New Mexico—so I put red vigil candles in the water, as if to say, if it becomes dark and you can't find your way home, follow the vigil lights home. I got that from the song "Clara, Clara," in *Porgy*

St. Francis 'Neath the Bitter Tree

and Bess. It goes, "Clara, Clara, don't you be downhearted, Clara, don't you be sad and lonesome; Jesus is walking on the water, rise up and follow him home, follow him home."

"Rise up and follow him home." That is such a beautiful image, especially when I picture the luminarias that many people in Colorado and New Mexico light during the Advent and Christmas seasons.[3]

Fr. Bill, let's turn to another of your drawings, Francis 'Neath the Bitter Tree. I notice that Christ is reaching from the cross into St. Francis's embrace—much as the Child Jesus is reaching toward Robert in the Epiphany painting. But the focus here is on the crucified Christ as a person suffering with AIDS.

You Must Meet Christ in the Wounded

That drawing is after Bartolomé Esteban Murillo's famous painting of Francis beneath the cross, where Christ has loosed one of his arms to embrace Francis. As I mentioned before, in *The Little Lives of the Saints* by Daniel Lord there was a version of that painting, and that's why as a child I thought it was Francis beneath the cross. I didn't yet know about John. The Murillo painting is really, really beautiful.

I've given Christ the wounds of people with AIDS, the Kaposi sarcoma wounds. AIDS left you with no immune system, no defense, nothing to fight off infection. The image is saying the same thing that Francis said to his novices: *You must meet Christ in the wounded,* in the afflicted, in the lepers. Above Christ's head are the terrible things people called those with AIDS— "drug user," "AIDS leper," "homosexual"—just as Christ was mocked by the words above the cross.

The words that Christ said to Francis, "Francis rebuild my church," was another arrow I wanted to shoot into the heart of the church. How did Francis rebuild the church? When you look at his life, it was by embracing poverty, the way of humility. I love Francis as much as I love Aloysius. I love him because there's a wild side to him, like Hosea and Jeremiah.

AIDS Crucifixion, 1986

It's true that it's drawn a lot of attention. The Catholic right called it blasphemous, not when it first came out, but more recently. When it came out, everybody understood it; nothing negative was said about it. People knew what I was saying.

Really?

Yes, it was clear that the sign above Christ's head— "faggot," "pervert," "sodomite"—was mockery. I'm sure the Catholic right today knows that, too; they understand it completely. But they used the drawing as a way to attack Jim Martin, because we're friends, and he has always supported my work. They called it "the sodomite Christ."[4] This was during the time of Pope Benedict, and Jim, of course, was coming under a lot of attack for his outreach to the LGBTQ community, as he still is.

Of all the drawings that came out of the AIDS pandemic, the one that is best known—some would say "infamous"—is AIDS Crucifixion. *Michael O'Loughlin titles the final chapter of his book after this image. I've looked at the drawing many, many times, and still, each time I contemplate it, there are details that grab me in new ways, or elements that puzzle me, the New York skyline in the background, for example, but then a desert foreground with cactus. And the weeping moon and sun. The male figure embracing the woman beneath the cross looks like you. There is a lot going on this image, and the more I see it, the more sophisticated it appears to me.*

You may have heard this story about a priest from the United States who brought Jim's book *Building a Bridge* to Rome to give to Pope Francis. Before handing it to him, he said something like, this is Fr. Martin's new book and it's causing a lot of controversy. Francis said, "Oh, then it must be about the Gospel."

It sounds just like something Pope Francis would say. I know that Fr. Martin has been received very warmly in several private audiences with Francis, who has encouraged him in his ministry, and Jim has since been appointed as a consultor to the Vatican's Dicastery for Communications.

Where was AIDS Crucifixion *published?*

It first appeared in *Christopher Street* magazine. But this and many of the AIDS drawings I had printed up as cards, and sold them after the Healing Masses. People sent them all over the place.

I can only imagine how comforting it was for people with AIDS and their caregivers to have images of Christ and Mary and other figures from the Gospel placed right in the middle of the AIDS crisis. You said earlier about Epiphany *that it was the first Catholic painting you are aware of to have AIDs as its subject. It's probably hard to overstate the further impact of bringing the crucifixion, this central image of the Christian imagination for two thousand years, into the AIDS epidemic.*

For a long time, artists have been depicting Christ on the cross in different cultural images and races, which is very powerful. Grünewald's famous crucifixion was done for a hospital for people who were dying of skin diseases. That's why Grünewald did Christ in the way that he did. I got it from him, really. If you are dying of a skin disease and you look up and you see that Christ's skin is all mangled, then you can connect to him. You wouldn't connect as much to a very bloody Christ—the Spanish and Mexican artists did a lot more with blood and realism—or an idealized Italian painting or icon. The *AIDS Crucifixion* was done with the same kind of forethought that I gave the *Epiphany* painting.

I was also very aware of Fra Angelico's crucifixions. He would often put the Mother Pelican on top and on either side of the cross. The crucifixions of Luca della Robbia would have the sun and the moon in the sky both screaming, just screaming. I wanted the sun and the moon

reacting. I wanted Manhattan in the background. I wanted Mary Magdalene to be there. I put my friend Cissy, who helped me so much with people with AIDS, as Mary, and me as John, comforting Cissy.

Then there's this guy on the right who takes the part of those screaming at Christ, like the thief who mocked him, *Why not save us if you're God?* He's holding up the Bible, yelling, and he has a pro-life rose on his lapel. No wonder people are upset, but it's a "staged, feigned, melodramatic upset," because it is aimed at people like them, people mocking and yelling at a suffering Christ. They know, or should remember, the story of the extreme humiliation of the crucifixion. And, as I said, at the time everyone understood what that drawing meant. Jesus said "Woe to you when people speak well of you."

It's Not Easy to Turn That Negative Energy into Grace

It occurs to me that all of this is happening before the Internet—you wouldn't have a website to show your art until decades later. For people to see them, they'd have to be reading magazines or newsletters linked to the gay community or the Catholic Church, or getting them more directly through the prayer cards you gave out or sold through your ministry.

Yes, I mentioned *Christopher Street* magazine, which was named for the street in the West Village where Stonewall Inn is located, and the center of the gay rights movement in the 1970s. They published a full-page version of *AIDS Crucifixion*, as well as *Epiphany*. There was also the first public art exhibit about AIDS, at Louis Abrons Art Center on Grand Street in Manhattan, where I was invited to exhibit my work with the other artists. I wrote an essay for it, "Art: *Apocalypsis* and *Veronike*," which you've seen. I know there is intense anger in that essay. I was angry at the sub-human way people were being treated.

Yes, there is anger. I was determined to include the essay as a postscript to this book, and I'm glad you agreed. There is a prophetic edge in your writing that one doesn't always hear in conversations with you, or, I imagine, on a first impression, when people are meeting you for the first time.

Not everyone has seen that side of me. I'm not sure Michael O'Loughlin saw this side of me—in his book he emphasizes my gentleness. I was younger then. I was able to hold a lot more in.

But I also learned a lot from Caird's commentary on Revelation, the famous passage about "the iron rod" smashing the nations "like clay pots," where the iron rod is the cross. When you are attacked, or rejected, or injustice is done to you—when you are experiencing the cross—and if you let it spin around inside of you, and you don't give it back, with God's help you can transform it, almost like having convulsions. If you can hold on and not give it back to the attacker in a spasm of bitterness and violence, that's what the cross is.

People have often said to me, You're so peaceful. And I think, How did I pull that off? Well, I am peaceful under the right circumstances. But when life electrocutes you, it's not easy to transform that negative energy into grace . . . in a way that others can receive as a gift.

Were you getting reaction from the Jesuit community about the AIDS illustrations?

I don't think so. The reaction was to me in general, not to the drawings. As I said before, if you were a man at that time working with people with AIDS, you were gay. Simply the fact that I was doing this work meant that I was coming out. And when the article came out in the *New York Times* that I was doing a Mass for people with AIDS, that was effectively my coming out to the nation, to the Jesuits, and *as* a Jesuit, though I didn't say anything about being gay in the article. It made it hard for the Jesuits and hard for me. It was just the times that we were in.

The Land of Burning Children

Speaking of shooting arrows into the heart of the church, Fr. Bill, I'd like to go back to your first encounter with Fr. Daniel Berrigan near the beginning of the hospice ministry in New York. You said that you had read some of Dan's work during novitiate, thanks to Fr. O'Flaherty, and you greatly admired him, but never imagined you would actually meet him, much less become friends. In fact, you said that before you knew him, you were terrified of Dan, intimidated by him. I have the sense that he was a critical influence in your life during these years, as Robert Lentz would be some years later in your study of iconography. Dan was one of the older Jesuits in New York who really supported your AIDS ministry. Can you say more about meeting Fr. Berrigan and how your relationship with him evolved?

One day in Manhattan—it was sometime between the fall of 1983 and winter of 1984—I was taking the Uptown #1 train from Seventy-Second Street, the subway doors opened, and there he was sitting right in front of me. Hanging on the subway pole, I stammered out that I was a Jesuit and had read everything he'd ever written and was utterly grateful. He invited me to have a picnic on Staten Island, and so later we met, took the ferry over, and I told him everything. He then asked if I could introduce him to Sr. Patrice, and he joined the AIDS Hospice team. Thus began a friendship that was both rocky and sublime.

Fr. Bill in Ireland with Fr. John Dear and Daniel Berrigan, SJ

"This Child is set for the rise and fall of many... a sign that is spoken against a Child born to make trouble and die for it... we say killing is disorder life and gentleness and community and unselfishness is the only order we recognize... How many indeed must die before our voices are heard?"

Holy Prophet Daniel Berrigan, SJ

It's true, I was so in awe of Dan that I thought if I ever met him I'd be seared by his fire and utterly withered. Through him I met some of the greatest writers and peace workers of our time, including his brother Phil, Phil's wife, Liz McAlister, their kids and their extended family. I designed a poster for Dan, and three of his book covers. When I became an apprentice iconographer, he gave me a book of icons that had belonged to William Stringfellow. And he encouraged me, saying that his friend Thomas Merton had loved icons, adding that it took him ten years to get over Merton's death. I never wanted "to be Dan," but I needed to experience how he could take such continual blows and still keep going.

As Adrienne von Speyr says in her book *The Mission of the Prophets*, Dan was so much "here," so focused on human suffering, that he could not be comforted. The prophets are inconsolable. Honestly, I have to say that I had been prepared to read Dan by reading Jim Douglass's book *The Non-Violent Cross*, in 1969, which confirmed everything I intuitively knew in my heart. And then Dan's book *No Bars to Manhood* just shook me to my core. One of my cherished memories was accompanying Dan to an upstate New York retreat center where a group of Vietnam Veterans had asked him to give them a retreat. They felt he was the best priest to understand their suffering, a man who had shown the true meaning of compassion, "to suffer with." I'd say it's very similar to the Bodhisattva vow.

Dan was part male mother to me and part searing prophet. I used to say the prophets have a "blowtorch mouth." When they turn the explosive fire on a huge religious institution or corrupt government, it's necessary, fearless, and right, and we all applaud them. When they turn it on you personally, it can be devastating. From Dan I definitely got both the mothering and the blowtorch fire.

I remember once I went to see him to tell him my problems. I'd been asked to write a diary of my work with people with HIV-AIDS, and because it was all so intimate, personal, and confidential, I refused the offer. The publisher had even suggested he could get Dr. Mathilde Krim, a famous research scientist who was bringing HIV-AIDS to public attention, to write an introduction. I said to Dan, what do you think? and waited in silence for him to answer. Finally, he said, "Well, pretty classy problems." So, we had a drink and I went down to my apartment, humbled, tail between my legs.

There are so many other stories, but what stands out for me today with the war in Ukraine, with all the horrible school shootings here, with the child sexual-abuse crisis in the church, is his constant reference to the "war on children." Most people remember his famous statement about burning draft files in Catonsville, Maryland, May 17, 1968, "Our apologies, good friends, for the fracture of good order, the burning of paper instead of children." He mentions children so often in his writings that in my icon of him I had to place the Christ Child in his arms, with a prophet's fierce flame over his head.

New York City Remembers AIDS Vigil

I just looked up Dan's statement during the trial of the Catonsville Nine, a group that included his brother Phil, of course, a Josephite priest at the time. Dan goes on to say, "For we are sick at heart, our hearts give us no rest for thinking of the Land of Burning Children. And for thinking of that other Child, of whom the poet Luke speaks. The Infant was taken up in the arms of an old man, whose tongue grew resonant and vatic at the touch of that beauty. And the old man spoke; this Child is set for the rise and fall of many in Israel, a sign that is spoken against. . . ."

Further on, speaking directly to "our fellow Christians," he asks, "When, at what point, will you say no to this war? We have chosen to say, with the gift of our liberty, if necessary our lives: the violence stops here, the death stops here, the suppression of the truth stops here, this war stops here."

I can certainly see why you call him a "blowtorch

fire." Thank you for sharing these memories of Fr. Dan. I'm sure you carry many, many more in your heart.

The Light Is Pouring across the Water

I'd like to go back to AIDS Crucifixion *and ask about the New York skyline in the background, which is also reflected in the water below. Why set New York City behind the crucifixion scene?*

I loved New York so much, and of course, this was a major epicenter of the AIDS crisis, of Stonewall, the dawning of awareness of the suffering and persecution of LGBTQ persons everywhere. New York was like the proverbial stone—or maybe it was a boulder—thrown into a pond of suffering and contention.

For me, the drawing that I did for the Aids Candlelight Vigil captures all of this—not just my love of New York and the pain and the suffering but also the love and solidarity and hope that came to birth in those very difficult years. I knew all the people who were involved with the Vigil, ACT UP, the Gay Men's Health Crisis, the secular side of the movement. They trusted me and commissioned me to do the poster for the event. Everything in me was poured into that drawing. The candle, the symbol of hope, like the Easter Candle, is bigger than all the skyscrapers. The light from the candle is pouring across the water.

You were a Catholic priest and they trusted you. Given the times, that says quite a lot. It occurs to me, this is twelve years before 9/11—the illustration really shim-

Cover of *America* Magazine

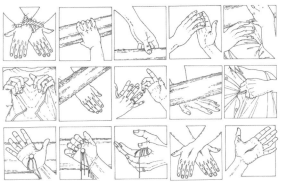

Stations of the Cross of a Person with AIDS

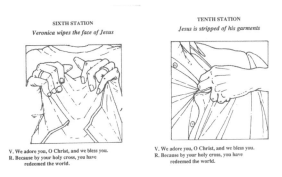

Veronica Wipes the
Face of Jesus

Jesus Is Stripped
of His Garments

mers with love for New York and with hopefulness. We haven't talked about the event itself—I see the date is June 17, 1989, in Central Park—but I can only imagine what it was like to be there.

It's hard to separate the drawing from the event and from the years that led up to its creation. As I've said before, there are certain drawings, icons, and paintings that I really love, but this is one of those drawings that I know didn't really come from me; it came from another place.

I want to say this. I feel the atmosphere right now is just as it was back then during the AIDS crisis. People were feeling hopeless and rejected, terrible fear of the world around them. Try to imagine, there was only one funeral home in the whole city that would take people who had died of AIDS, Redden's Funeral Home on Fourteenth Street. Imagine driving around New York City with the body of a loved one in the back seat, try-

ing to get a funeral home to take them, and none would. I wrote about that in the meditations that accompany my *Stations of the Cross of a Person with AIDS*.

It was a terrifying time for people. As Michael O'Laughlin's book reminded me, President Reagan didn't say the word "AIDS" until 1986, and Pope John Paul II didn't say it until 1987. People weren't even saying the word. I started my work in 1983, but the crisis really began in 1982. It's very similar to our time now. How does one live in this kind of a time?

I'm glad I was younger then! I was better at handling the sense of hopelessness. I'm still having trouble with it, but right now I'm doing Sr. Thea Bowman's icon. Being with her keeps me hopeful.

I think you've just put your finger on one reason we wanted to do this book. Every generation goes through trials and is tempted to think it's never been worse.

Yet there is light—beautiful, fierce, sometimes terrible light—to be found in the darkness, light "shining across the water." Of course, it's not easy to see or believe when you're getting battered under the storm clouds.

I know that the impact that certain works of art can have on us is not explainable in a strictly logical or rational sense, but I still find many of your pieces from this period to be profoundly consoling, even those that are visually unsettling. It's counterintuitive and kind of amazing. Sr. Thea is amazing. I've always felt her to be the patron saint we need most today in the U.S. Catholic Church.

Doing her icon is getting me through. It actually is.

CHAPTER 7

Midwives to the Second Birth

The juxtaposition of life and hope with the passage through death, or what Bill calls "the Second Birth," provides a through-line for our explorations of Fr. Bill's art in this chapter. I begin by asking him about two images that appear frequently as "totems" during the AIDS ministry: the wounded deer, or hart, and the zebra. Among other striking images, the wounded deer becomes a key symbol in a remarkable book of meditations that Bill did with his friend Jesuit Fr. Bill Dobbels, while Dobbels was ill with HIV/AIDS. When it came to providing resources that might provide comfort or consolation to people dying from AIDS and their loved ones, Fr. Bill says, "There was nothing from the church."

Two other drawings take primacy here, The Incarnation, *which Bill created at the bedside of his dying father, and* Down in Yon Forest, *inspired by an old English Christmas carol. Once again, the Child, the infant Jesus, and the joyful anticipation of Christmas stand as counterpoint to the anguish of accompanying people in the passage through death. Fr. Bill shares a pivotal lesson that Teresa of Avila learned from a vision of Jesus—"I must not give up anything that awakens love in me"—and his musings on why young people are leaving religion yet still are deeply drawn to images and narratives of hope.*

Chris: Fr. Bill, you mentioned that after your retreat experience at Pine Ridge, the wishbone became for you an important symbol of hope, of "hope against hope." But there are at least two other images that appear repeatedly in your early illustrations: first, the wounded deer, or "hart," an old English term for deer, which is also your middle name. And second, the zebra, or the stripes associated with a zebra, which show up repeatedly in your drawings. Can you explain why you refer to these images as your "totems"?

Fr. Bill: The first time I ever used my middle name "Hart" was on my high school gradua-tion announcement, where I used my full name, "William Hart McNichols." I thought, That sounds like an artist's name, like Thomas Hart Benton or something. Then I discovered that "hart" was an old English word for "deer," probably from reading the King James Bible, "As a hart longs for running streams," from Psalm 42. It really opened things up, because John of the Cross in his spiritual canticle speaks of the "wounded hart" or the "wounded deer," the deer wounded by its love for God.

When I did that drawing of the deer with the arrow in it, all of these images came together for

All My Eyes See

Wounded deer totem

me. Of course, the arrow is from God, like the famous Bernini statue of the angel holding the arrow, getting ready to pierce Teresa's heart as she leans back in ecstasy.

As I've probably said in many different ways, I've always had this emptiness inside—I think a lot of people do—and when I read *The Drama of the Gifted Child*, the famous book by Alice Miller, she helped to put it all together for me. Despite its title, the book is not really about being "special" or anything. It's about the experience of an emptiness, even from childhood, that nothing can really fill. Around the same time, in Caird's commentary on Luke, I came across something like, "The only requirement for entering the Kingdom of God is an emptiness that only God can fill." That was it. I said, Okay, I get it.

And I get why the emptiness doesn't go away, because you can never have enough of God. Anytime you think you've got God, or think that you know God, in my experience, that God will become an idol. Then you have to wait, realizing, Okay, I don't know God, because I made him into an image that I like, a God who works for me, a God that doesn't disturb or trouble me or make demands.

Right after I moved to Albuquerque, in 1990, my cat was poisoned. Twenty-four hours after

she died, I had just gotten out of the shower and was in the bathroom shaving. Suddenly I felt her come up and rub against my leg. Without question she was there. We had been taught that animals do not have souls, period. Once they're gone, they're gone. There is no way that could happen, and no way I could have expected it, because I believed animals didn't have souls. But it did happen, and reminded me how little I know. I thought, Oh boy, I know nothing, I really ought to give up right now.

Wounded by the Love of God

It reminds me of some of your childhood experiences of God, or the devil, or of angels catching you when you fell out of bed—and your realization that the unseen world is real. It was your grandmother, Mimi, the one who told your mother, "Don't get too close to this one, he belongs to God," who insisted that your middle name be Hart, is that right?

Manhasset, Long Island, 1985

Yes, the name was from her side of the family. And once I made these connections for myself—the deer from Psalm 42 and the wounded hart from John of the Cross—it became a natural "totem," as it were, for my spirituality and for the AIDS ministry.

Early in the hospice years, I made a pamphlet with the wounded hart on the front and the quote from John of the Cross. *"Return, little soul and alight, for on the hill above appears the wounded hart."* And from Jeremiah: *"For I will restore health to you, and your wounds I will heal, says the Lord, because they have called you an outcast . . . and you shall be my people, and I will be your God."* The deer also has a flame above its head. Behind the wounded hart I put a desert with cactus in the background, because of John of the Cross. When people would come to see me, they would ask what I charge, but I just couldn't charge them anything. On the back of the pamphlet, it said they could offer a donation if they wished. Sometimes I would get $5, sometimes $100, but I was able to get by and be taken care of. And the Jesuit province, too, was giving me money to support my living expenses.

From that time on, the deer began to mean a lot to me. One time I was taking a train to Albany to visit with a friend of mine. I was looking out the window, and the Hudson River was covered over with broken ice. Suddenly I saw a deer, just like the one I had drawn, on top of the ice floe on the river, and it frightened me, to see my totem on the broken ice like that. Later on, I wrote a poem about it. When I got to my friend's place, he told me that he had AIDS. It felt like a premonition.

The image of the deer is prominent throughout the book you did with Bill Dobbels, An Epistle of Comfort, *which is filled with your illustrations.[1]*

Bill Dobbels, as I've said, was my dearest friend. When he was diagnosed—I'm not sure I should go into more of that story—but when I was working in the AIDS hospice, I had nothing to give people to read that would give them comfort. There were popular books by people like Bernie Siegal—a kind of "power of positive thinking"

Cover of *An Epistle of Comfort,* 1990

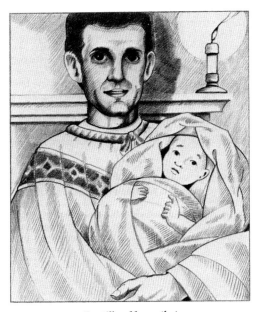

*Be still and know that
I am God.*
—Psalm 46:11

Illustration from *An Epistle of Comfort*

As a hart longs for the running waters,
so my soul longs for you, O God.
—Psalm 42

Cleanse me of sin with hyssop,
that I may be purified;
Wash me, and I shall be whiter
than snow.
—Psalm 51

Heal me, Lord, that I may be healed;
Save me, that I may be saved,
for it is you whom I praise.
—Jeremiah 17:14

Blessed are they who mourn,
for they will be comforted.
—Matthew 5:4

Father, into your hands
I commend my spirit.
—Luke 23:46

Behold, I make all things new.
—Revelation 21:5

Illustrations from An Epistle of Comfort

approach—but there was nothing at all from the church. I said to Bill, I desperately want to give something to people, but I can't write it, because I don't have AIDS. If I tried to write something about AIDS, people would say, "Oh, sure, you can say this, you don't know what it's like."

I made a list of chapter titles and themes that I thought needed to be talked about, and I asked Bill to write it. Because he loved *Meditations on the Tarot* so much, a book written "to my unknown friend," Bill decided to take that voice for his book, "My dear unknown friend." We had decided on the title, *An Epistle of Comfort*, taken from the title of Robert Southwell's book for English Catholics who were being persecuted during the Elizabethan period. I thought, why not make the deer, the wounded hart, the symbol for the book, so it became the cover and it was there in many of the drawings.

Thank you for sharing the backstory for An Epistle of Comfort. *I have to say that when I first paged through this little book—it was before I knew your history as an illustrator and I knew only the icons—I was so moved by the drawings. Unlike the other AIDS drawings we've talked about, these drawings are not explicitly scriptural, excepting the deer images. They depict ordinary people, helping and giving comfort to one another through loneliness or illness—very down to earth, recognizable scenes to anyone. There's a vulnerability and tenderness in them that could only come from direct experience.*

Was Bill already sick at the time he wrote the book? Was he able to complete it before he died, at the same time you were doing the drawings?

There's So Much about Ourselves That We Don't Understand

Yes, it was like Thérèse of Lisieux, who wrote her autobiography as she was dying. Bill had a real devotion to Thérèse, even though in some ways he was her opposite. Sometimes we choose people to love or to be friends with who have something that we don't. It makes perfect sense to love

someone who can help you with something that you don't have. That's how Bill was with Thérèse.

Did he get to see the book in print before he died?

Yes, he did. I asked Dan Berrigan and Sr. Patrice to write blurbs for the back, and Basil Pennington and Murray Bodo, a famous Franciscan writer, also wrote endorsements.

Next to the chapter on "Sin and Suffering," there is a drawing of a young man that is very striking, full of emotional depth. I thought it might be modelled after you, actually.

Yes, that is me, right next to the chapter on "sin and suffering"!

Well, I didn't mean to suggest a direct link . . .

Again, for me, these drawings stand apart in your work as especially "realistic" representations of adults who look like anybody you could recognize on the street. And the way the images are paired with the text is quite evocative. In the chapter on "Comfort and Strength," for example, a man carries a woman in his arms, with the sea in the background. But others are a bit shocking—like the deer being dragged along the ground by hunters after it has been shot. There's a poignancy and tragedy in that drawing that exposes, I think, how people with AIDS were being treated at the time. It's really a special book.

You know I haven't read it since it was published, because I couldn't bear to read it after Bill died. I miss him so much still. He died December 22, 1990.

Bill was very practical, but he did have a mystical side, which frightened him. He was also Jungian, studying with Robert Johnson when he got sick. He made fun of me all the time, because of the way I am and the way he was. He would say, "You take guided tours to the underworld every week. I like to go once a year." "What do you mean?" I'd object. He'd say, "Oh, you go down there all the time."

We don't really know ourselves. We think we do, but there's so much about ourselves that we don't know or understand. Like any good friend, Bill helped me see things about myself that I didn't see.

Let me just say, he was right. You spend a lot of your time taking tours to the underworld, and I spend a lot of my time trying to find you down there.

This might be a fitting bridge to your other totem, the zebra. Why the zebra?

The Infinite Imagination of God

When I was teaching high school, I would take the kids on drawing expeditions, to the Forney Car Museum in Denver, for instance, or the Denver Botanical Gardens. And then I took them to the zoo. I said to my students, Try to be shocked when you gaze on the animals. Because we should be; we should be totally shocked. For example, we think of snakes as bad, as evil and frightening. But they're not frightening to God at all. *Try to see them like you've never seen them before.*

When I gazed on the zebra, I thought, my God, what's going on here? You don't ride a zebra like a horse. *What are they for?* To me, the zebra is a symbol of being different, of *being made different*. On the outside, people don't know what you're for. What do they do? What are these stripes *for*?

I called up my friend JJ, the Jesuit poet Jim Janda, and said, You have to write a poem about zebras.[2] He said, Do you know that no two zebras have the same stripes? It blew my mind. It's very Ignatian. He called again and said, Did you know that Ignatius went into ecstasy when he saw an orange leaf? No, I said, I didn't know that. For me it represents the infinite imagination, if that's the right word, *of God*. The way that every leaf, every snowflake, every fingerprint, every zebra, is wholly unique and different. If you contemplate that for two seconds it's overwhelming.

It makes much more sense to me now why the wounded deer and the zebra keep showing up in your illustrations during the 1980s, when you were doing AIDS ministry, and coming into your own sense of identity, very publicly, as a gay priest. Your point that it's "very Ignatian" not just to acknowledge or tolerate difference but to positively celebrate the diversity of creation, the uniqueness of every creature, is really wonderful. It's the vision of the famous "Contempla-

The Zebra Appears on 16th Street, New York City

tion to Attain the Love of God" during the Fourth Week of the Exercises, where Ignatius has us ponder God's love and dynamism pouring out from every creature, every pore, of the universe. Love is shown in deeds, says Ignatius, more than in words. The Divine Lover desires nothing more than to share everything with the Beloved.

I'd like to turn to two more color drawings, The Incarnation *and* Down in Yon Forest. *Both bring us back to the image of the child, evoking the season of Advent and the Feast of Christmas, which I know is your favorite liturgical season of the year. You always tell me that you begin celebrating Advent as early as possible, I think beginning at Michaelmas, the end of September?*

The Incarnation sums up for me so much of your work, where hope comes to humanity in the mystery of a child. With this drawing we're jumping ahead about ten years, to the late 1990s, but theologically, it exemplifies a golden thread linking your illustrations with the icons. There's a candle being lit by the flame of a match, which is at once the figure of a child; a large hand is sweeping the flame and child down toward a candle from the sky, while a crescent moon looks on from above. It is quite striking.

Like the *AIDS Vigil* drawing, which also centers on a candle, this is another drawing that I love so much, and don't feel bad about saying so. I imagine it's very similar to the joy and wonder of having a child, where you don't really feel it's from you, or came from you, but the child *came through you,* and that's how I feel about the drawings. Somehow, they came through me, not from me.

When my dad was dying, I would fly from New York to Denver to visit him in the hospital. It was November 1997 and I had a commission from *America* magazine to illustrate a poem or something about the Incarnation. I had to do it in the hospital, with Dad lying next to me, because I had a deadline, and in those days, you had to mail it to them overnight.

I was sitting next to Dad, and I closed my eyes, and all of a sudden, I saw this hand of God the Father lighting this candle, and the candle was

the location where the child would be born. God strikes the light, the light comes into the world—as it says in John's Prologue—and BOOM, the flame hits the candle. Inside the flame is the baby, joyfully coming to Earth, and the Holy Spirit is the flame. I was pretty much in a trance when I did it.

There are some things that I do, and I'm so joyful when I'm doing them, not aware of anything, just so happy. And knowing what I'm bringing into the world, it doesn't really matter whether anyone gets it. But for me, *oh . . .* You know I would like to put that drawing all over the world, send it to everybody.

It's also the experience of being with my dad when I was doing it. While I had a lot of trouble with my dad when I was young, we loved each other so much when I got older. By the time of his death we were completely healed. So, there is a father and a child in that drawing. I think it just came out the way it did because of the peace I felt with Dad lying next to me, being with him before he died.

I've always felt that Advent is the season I come most alive. I actually begin Advent on August 15, and it goes all the way until January 6. I get that from St. Francis. At the end of his life, when he was overcome by depression and feeling like a failure, Francis said to Br. Leo, "We're going to make St. Michael's Lent together." So, Francis and Br. Leo went up to La Verna on August 15, the Feast of the Assumption, in order to fast for forty days. They came down September 29, the Feast of St. Michael. Later on, in English schools, it was called Michaelmas. While at La Verna, Francis said to Br. Leo, I have to be alone; do not let anyone come to me. And that's when he received the stigmata.

Francis totally opened up for me the season of Advent, technically not Advent, but August 15 to September 29, traditionally called "St. Michael's Lent." Francis received the wounds around September 14, and Padre Pio on September 20, 1918—so for me, that time before the Season of the Holy Souls in November and then Advent is the "Season of the Wounds."

The Incarnation, 1997

It never would have occurred to me that your painting of St. Francis receiving the stigmata would be linked with the season of Advent and Christmas.

You know there is something palpable that comes over the world during Advent. Much later, I learned that for Jews, the season of Hanukkah is when the Shekhinah begins to descend upon the Earth.[3] Christians call her the Christmas Spirit,

but there is something palpable that comes; and the reason it's palpable is because when its gone, you know it's gone. You feel its presence, so to speak, by its absence.

Midwives to the Second Birth

It strikes me that in The Incarnation *you were creating an image centered on the joy of birth, of new* life and hope coming to Earth, precisely at the moment your father was leaving the Earth. The two realities, life and death, love and loss, are held together in a single moment of inspiration.

I've heard you refer to your years in the AIDS hospice as being a time when you were a "midwife to the Second Birth." In other words, it was a ministry of accompanying people through the dark night of illness and death into the promise of resurrection and what awaits us in the afterlife—not incidentally, this is the drama of the Third and Fourth Weeks of the Spiritual Exercises. You were not just a witness to resurrection faith but an active participant, a "midwife" to it. Like so many of us who have sat at the bedside of a sick or dying loved one, it seems you were a kind of midwife for your father, too, as he passed over.

More darkly and hauntingly, Mirabai Starr has described your particular vocation as an artist and iconographer as "bringing Nativity into the Apocalypse."[4] I want to come back to this later, but this strikes me as a brilliant mystical insight, almost singular among commentaries on your art. Again, I think you would say that this is not unique to your vocation but, in distinct ways, the calling of every Christian.

Down in Yon Forest, 1987

Fr. Bill as St. Francis, following the enactment of the Transitus, Bronx, NY, October 1984

Staying with the theme of Nativity, let me ask you finally about Down in Yon Forest, *a vivid color drawing and one of the first of your illustrations that you sent to me. As a fan of Canadian musician Bruce Cockburn, I know that it was inspired partly by an old English Christmas carol, but I don't know much more, other than your deep affection for it. I've always gotten the sense that this image stirs something elemental in you.*

Many years ago, I heard the song "Down in Yon Forest" for the first time, listening to the 1966 Joan Baez Christmas album, *Noel*. I was immediately captured by the lyrics and the refrain, "I love my Lord Jesus above anything," repeated over and over again, like a mantra. Bruce Cockburn's version is much darker, really enigmatic,

which I love. In fact, he describes it as one of the spookiest Christmas carols you can imagine, with its verses describing a flood of blood and water running beneath the crib, and thorns growing up and around the cradle, and the moon shining over it all.

All of this came together for me when I saw this little crib, no bigger than what a doll could fit in, with little bells on top, at the Metropolitan Museum of Art in New York City. The Crib of the Infant Jesus, "Repos de Jesus," was from the South Netherlands, Brabant, and was carved and painted in the fifteenth century around the same time the carol was written. It was made so clearly out of love.

I made the drawing in 1985. Those years in the AIDS ministry, 1985 through 1988, were really terrible. It went from epidemic to pandemic to just an explosion of death. Anything that would touch my heart like that song—"Over that bed the moon shines bright / The bells of paradise I heard them ring / whichever blows blossoms since He was born / And I love my Lord Jesus above anything"—and anything that would help awaken in me childlike wonder and faith, like the crib at the Met—the drawing was my way of trying to hold onto that feeling. Teresa of Avila says we must not give up anything that awakens love in us.

There's a passage in Teresa's autobiography that JJ typed out for me, where she describes feeling guilty about having too many pictures in her

Bill with infant at baptism, 1980s

> ### *When Someone Becomes Christ to You*
>
> When someone becomes
> Christ to you
> then you must
> stop,
> be seated with Mary,
> and drink in
> every word, glance,
> and touch.
> It is time to
> listen
> for Love is letting
> that precious nard flow,
> and are there not
> too few
> who will catch it?
> No time to busy oneself
> with Martha's running about,
> nor time
> to hasten to harbors
> of distraction.
> No time
> to fill the loneliness
> with religion
> or busywork,
> or plunge into readings
> or meditations to find love
> deep inside or elsewhere . . .
> for Love
> sits before you
> longing to be heard
> and loneliness
> can wait

room, holy pictures, so one day she took them all down. Jesus appears to her and asks, "Why did you take all those pictures down?" She says, I thought it was a weakness, an imperfection to have nice pictures. Jesus asks her, which is better, poverty or charity? If charity or love is better, he says, you must not give up anything that awakens love in you. Jesus brings her, very gently, to a new realization. "I must not give up anything that awakens love in me."

That is beautiful, and terribly poignant. It goes a long way to refuting the Jansenist spirituality that you've mentioned, where everything is "no"; if you enjoy it, it must be a temptation or a distraction; you'll have to give it up. It's also a pretty good description of your work, if I may say so.

Thank you. I hope so. I certainly want my work to be brimming with love, you know?

I think it also may be why young people today are pulling away from formal religion and flocking to movies like *Avatar*, and *Lord of the Rings*, films that give a visual language of hope against hope, a kind of mythology that feeds the imagination in times of great crisis. *Avatar*, with its great Tree of Souls at the center, and Eywa, the Great Mother, and the seeds of the Tree floating on the wind like dandelion seeds. . . .

I'm thinking of characters like Treebeard in Lord of the Rings, *and the Ents marching against Saruman, who has burned the forest down to build an army and forge the machinery of war. The "Last March of the Ents," from "The Two Towers," is one of the more memorable scenes I can recall in any film in the last twenty years. Both films seem to suggest that the wounded, suffering Earth is fighting back.*

Yes, and it's also why I think Hildegard of Bingen—her notion of "Viriditas," the greening power of the Divine within creation—is so hugely important now, and why she's such an important doctor of the church. I feel the same way about Nicholas Black Elk. For me, the two go hand in hand.

It goes back to William Lynch on hope and imagination, or Jung, who spoke of the collective unconscious.[5] All of these illustrations inspired by the symbols of Advent and Christmas—the Epiphany, the Magi, the Child, the crib, the Incarnation, the candle—for me, these symbols have always been inside of me, inside of all of us. They point to the dawn of a life that would dramatically change human history and all of creation, and they point to the night of the end of life on Earth and into the life of eternity—Incarnation and Resurrection, Alpha and Omega.

This is how it is with all of us. It's how it was with my dad as he lay dying, and for me, sitting at his bedside. We have this brief life here on Earth, but we will live forever. I have felt both my father's and my mother's hands still lighting my life, with the beautiful examples of their lives and their steadfast love.

CHAPTER 8

The Flowering Wounds

Fr. Bill's color drawing of Martin Luther King Jr., Always a Drum Major for Justice, *among other African American figures in his work—and our visit to the Black Crucifix on the campus of Regis University—set the table for an exploration of art as a means of grasping another person's or community's experience "from the inside," heightened by the Ignatian spiritual practice of sensory and imaginative prayer. From a viewer's perspective, works such as* Stations of the Cross of a Person with AIDS, The Sower's Nightmare, *and* St. Francis' Flowering Wound, *can be both unsettling and beautiful at the same time, just as the Black Crucifix bears a "terrible beauty" in light of injustices experienced today by African Americans. "I wanted to create images that were strong," says Fr. Bill, "that would honor the actual thing that happened and not try to hide it."*

There are other Ignatian notes, here, too: What does it mean to speak of "evil spirits," to be "attacked by the devil," or "the enemy of human nature," in the language of St. Ignatius? It's not easy to ignore or dismiss such imagery, suggests Fr. Bill, when it is used by people who have direct experience with "the devil," as Malcolm X once described white people—or Ignatius, wrestling mightily with the sins of his past. As we conclude our conversation, Fr. Bill once again invokes images of hope from the Gospel: the sacred Child who dwells in all people, especially those for whom "there is no room at the inn, not even in the church." Where previously he has alluded to the dragon in Revelation 12, poised to devour the Mother's Child, here he invokes the massacre of the infants and the flight into Egypt from Matthew's Gospel. "You're trying to protect the baby. That's what my life feels like with my art."

Chris: Fr. Bill, you mentioned that you've been working on the icon of Sr. Thea Bowman, which was commissioned for a chapel at Georgetown University, and how being with Sr. Thea is keeping you grounded in hope. Among the drawings during your AIDS ministry there is the beautiful Black Madonna and Child. *Like the drawing of* Ignatius the Convalescent, *it's printed in blue ink, which sets it apart somewhat from the black-and-white drawings. There is also a drawing of Martin Luther King Jr.,* Always a Drum Major for Justice, *also done in color, with a flaming Black crucifixion in the background.*

In the decades to follow, there would be many more African American, African, and non-white subjects in your sacred images and icons, like Sr. Thea, Elijah McClain, the Black Madonna of Montserrat, Mother

Martin Luther King Jr., 1983

who would regularly attend, and whose picture I took along with many others. Just beautiful pictures. From that photograph of her I made the drawing and turned it into a prayer card. It was the first *Black Madonna and Child* I did, though Mary in the *Epiphany* painting we talked about earlier was a non-white Mary, Our Lady of Guadalupe.

The King drawing was done in 1983, not long after I began the AIDS ministry. I really wanted to do a Black crucifixion in the background, and because the Klan would burn crosses, there are flames surrounding the cross. It's a very strong drawing of King. I wish I had made it into an icon. I remember as I looked at the drawing, it was incomplete. I decided to leave it unfinished, and I'm glad I did. Because his work—the full acceptance of Black people—is still unfinished. This is way before Black Lives Matter. King's face, his eyes, his look of strength; it says, I am never going to stop being a drum major for justice.

Anybody who is murdered for being who they are—being gay, being Asian, being Black—becomes a Christ figure. The question is, Do we have eyes to see? The degree of hatred in our society today is much worse now than it was then. So many are being crucified in the background. The drawing speaks more to me now than it did even then. I'm very happy that it was given to me to do.

and Child of Kibeho, St. Bakhita Universal Sister, to name just a few. Is there a link or common thread that joins these drawings and icons with your life experiences?

Fr. Bill: Every month during those early years of the AIDS pandemic in New York City, I celebrated some of the Masses for the Dignity community on Saturday evenings. We would gather in the church basement after Mass for refreshments. There was a young Black mother with her baby

When you were in Denver recently, I brought you to see the Black Crucifix at Regis University that stands on a hillside in a meditation garden just outside the Saint John Francis Regis Chapel. The bronze corpus of Christ was done by sculptor Jan Van Ek, using a

life-cast of a Denver native, and the steel cross by Ray Fedde, who had also cast our chapel's bronze doors and Stations of the Cross. I don't think it's an exaggeration to say you were deeply moved by it, stunned, "electrocuted," as you sometimes say.

The day you took me to see the sculpture of the Black Christ Crucified, I was almost instantly aware that I was seeing a true work of art. I have

Black Madonna and Child, 1987

loved many crucifixes in the history of art, and I could probably fill a page with the most moving ones for me, whether paintings or sculptures: the Gero cross, the Eisenheim cross, the Cimabue and Giotto crosses, and Van der Weyden. I would now add the Black Christ of St. John Francis Regis University to that list. It's just a masterpiece and, I think it should be a place of pilgrimage. Each

Jan Van Ek / Ray Fedde Crucifix
at Regis University

of these crosses has a deeply embedded spiritual power that brings you directly into that Ignatian meditation during the First Week of the Exercises, where he asks you to carry on a "colloquy," or conversation, with Jesus as he is being crucified.

Yes, and to ask oneself Ignatius's three questions: What have I done for Christ? What am I doing for Christ? What ought I to do for Christ? I should say that the Black Crucifix at Regis has become a kind of pilgrimage site, a place of prayer and contemplation, for many of us who work there.

When I think of Ignatius's questions, I think of the Emmanuel Nine shot dead in a church basement in Charleston; ten shot dead in a grocery store in Buffalo; the far-right rally in Charlottesville that left Heather Heyer dead; Trayvon Martin, Eric Garner, Sandra Bland, Tamir Rice, Breonna Taylor, Elijah McLain—the litany of the crucified goes on and on. Jesuit theologian Jon Sobrino adds a fourth question: What am I doing to take the crucified peoples down from the cross?

99

Do you remember why you chose to do the King image at that time, in 1983? As you said, this is right at the beginning of the AIDS hospice ministry.

All of the Devils Came Out from Hiding

Why did I do that picture? I'm not exactly sure. For one thing, every race was affected by AIDS during the epidemic. Just like today, with the COVID-19 virus, it crosses all boundaries but especially ravages communities of color. And I always had this thing about the Ku Klux Klan because of the story my dad told me about them burning a cross on his lawn when he was a child. That story burned into me for sure.

You've also spoken to me about your love for Malcolm X. Did that come later?

Yes, when I was in Boston, I visited Roxbury, right where he grew up, and that's when I first read *The Autobiography of Malcolm X.* There's just something about him—like Sr. Thea—the strength of Sr. Thea, the strength of Malcolm X. He went through a long period of being totally against white people, thinking the "white man is

"For love is strong as death" (Song of Songs 8:6), from *Through the Loneliness*

the Devil." I completely understood that, in terms of what people thought about gay people, and the injustice of how gay people were targeted.

I did the King drawing at the same time I was doing the gay drawings, *The Akedah, Illustration of a Faggot,* and all of that, exploring injustices against gay people who were standing forward in the midst of burning crosses. And gay people were really targeted, especially gay Black people who had AIDS. The first baby I met that had AIDS was a little Black baby named Stevie. The nurses took me to one of the wards where there was nothing but babies with AIDS. It was so heartbreaking; I just wanted to pick them all up. They were so sick, but they weren't really crying.

When you read The Autobiography of Malcolm X, *you understood the anger he felt toward white people, in part, because of the injustices you were witnessing against gay people and people with AIDS. Do I have that right?*

Yes, I'm just remembering a quote by Susan Sontag, who said, "White people are the cancer of the earth," and then she added, "I really apologize to cancer patients for putting it this way." She was Jewish, so she understood. When you, when your whole community, has lived for centuries under the boot of white power—but all of this stuff is a hundred times worse now than it was then. All of the devils were locked up back then, at least most of them were locked up.

Every now and then in New York City, they lift up all the manhole covers and release all the fumes and toxic gasses that have built up. This is what happened when Donald Trump became president: they opened up every one of the manholes, and all the devils were released. It's like the Stephen Sondheim song in *Sweeney Todd,* "City on Fire." Trump gave power to all these groups that were in hiding. He exalted them, and they came out of hiding. We live in a much more difficult time than it was then.

It's a terrifying image. I wish it didn't feel so accurate.

» Il Monte della Verna «

Il Monte della Verna, 1984

There's something like this in the show *Cabaret*. At the beginning of the show, all sorts of people, every race, every sexual orientation, are out enjoying the cabaret together. It's accepted. But some people, notably Hitler, thought that German society had gotten way too open, way too decadent. As it's portrayed in the movie, you're at the cabaret and Liza Minelli is performing, and you look out and there are two SS officers in the back of the room, watching. You think, Oh, something is happening here. The next night, there are four. The next night, there are six. Now the situation is very dangerous, the mood very tense. That's what is happening now in our culture. People thought, Oh, these things could never go backward, gay rights, women's rights, will never go backward. But all of these issues are now up for grabs. I'm not saying they will go backward. I'm saying that it's happened before.

As you were talking, I couldn't help think of the Pulse Nightclub massacre. And we could name a hundred

other recent examples: *the mass shooting at the Tree of Life Jewish synagogue, Club Q in Colorado Springs, and again, Mother Emmanuel AME in Charleston, the Tops supermarket massacre in Buffalo.*

And an unarmed Black kid with sixty bullets in his back. It's just unbelievable, yet it's not really "news," in the sense of unexpected or unprecedented. This is America. Black people have been living under the shadow of threat always, as have Jewish people, Native American people, Asian and Hispanic people.

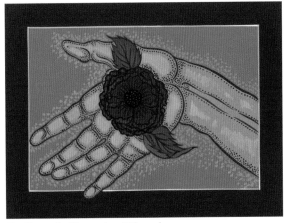

St. Francis Flowering Wound

To Feel and Understand from the Inside

I'm still stuck on your image of the manhole covers, and how to account for what feels like the release of powerful dark forces that had once been more or less underground, kept at bay. Ignatius seems to have lived under a strong sense of the devil, the bad spirit or evil personified, whom he calls "the enemy of human nature," frequently present in his writings. There was a time in my younger days when I would poo-poo that sort of language, dismiss it as mythological, a kind of naïve childhood image of the supernatural to be put to rest when you're older. But it occurs to me, with some embarrassment, that my attitude was partly a function of racial and economic privilege—never once having found myself targeted or under attack by malevolent forces, by "the Devil," to recall Malcolm X, because of who I am, the way I look, my political leanings, my economic or cultural background, my sexual orientation.

I certainly remember having nightmares as a child, even more recently, that frightened me terribly, that felt "demonic," that is to say, where I felt a sense of darkness or evil palpably present in the room after waking from the dream. But never have I been part of a community that is literally under attack in the full light of day. It begins to make sense why Malcolm X would refer to white people as "the Devil."

And Susan Sontag. The reality is, historically, we all came from one place, one root, in Africa. I remember reading that for the first time in an issue of *National Geographic*. And, as it turns out, all races are capable of both great good and horrific evil, as we saw in the Rwandan genocide, and now in all the present wars.

Yes, this was Malcolm X's great revelation during the hajj, the pilgrimage to Mecca, when he found himself surrounded by tens of thousands of pilgrims of every color from all around the world, and overwhelmed by a spirit of unity and kinship that his experiences in the United States had convinced him was impossible between the races—that all are human beings, children of One God, irrespective of differences in color. "What I have seen, and experienced," he wrote, "has forced me to rearrange much of my thought-patterns, to toss aside some of my previous conclusions." Behold, white people cannot be lumped en masse into pure good or evil any more than Black folks. As James Cone has written about so powerfully, Malcolm's experience of the Oneness of God, the Oneness of Humanity, brought him closer to the vision of Martin Luther King Jr., in the last year of his life, just as King was becoming more radicalized in the late 1960s.[1]

Fr. Bill, in light of all this, I'm able to understand this kind of imagery of Satan, the evil one, or the Devil, much better now than I did when I was younger, at least intellectually, if not fully emotionally or psychologically. How do you make sense, then, of this part of St. Ignatius's autobiography, where he seems to experience the demonic as such a palpable force in his life and in the world?

Boston College, 1996, writing the icon *Mother of the Incarnate Word*

In one of the illustrated versions of Ignatius's autobiography there's a picture of him in bed with two or three muscular devils literally beating him up. But you know Ignatius himself was never one to exaggerate. When he describes the temptations of the devil or being attacked by "the enemy of human nature," it's powerful precisely because you know he has experienced it directly. It's not easy to ignore these accounts, as you say, because he's been through it. Think of his terrible scruples and temptation to commit suicide in the cave at Manresa.

I was also thinking of Manresa. It was one of his most important spiritual breakthroughs, when he finally came to understand that his scruples—these ter-

Behold! I Make All Things New

rible regrets about his past that were leading him to despair and relentless self-doubt—were not from God but from the evil spirit. It's as if Satan, the "father of lies," the "enemy of human nature," was mocking him, convincing him that he would never be worthy of mercy, never be good enough. What honest person of faith hasn't felt this way?

God allowed him to learn alone in the cave at Manresa so that later he could truly help people because he had been through the experience himself. As I said before, I couldn't write a book about AIDS. Bill Dobbels had to do it, because he was going through it directly. If Ignatius was counseling someone about the devil, he had to have experienced it himself. He couldn't be abstract about it.

I hope this isn't too big a leap, Fr. Bill, but I would say that your series of drawings, Stations of the Cross for a Person with AIDS, *is similar to this, very*

Ignatian, because you are inviting the viewer to feel and understand from the inside something of what it's like to be crucified by AIDS—and not just by the disease, but by society, by the stigma imposed by society and often by the church on those suffering.

"Crucify him," that was our society's response to AIDS. It's what we Catholics say during the Passion narrative. "What should I do with this one?" asks Pilate, pointing to Jesus. The whole congregation shouts, Crucify him! That's our collective response, and that's what was happening at that time.

Jesus' Flowering Wound (cover image from Stations of the Cross of a Person with AIDS)

Whether it's AIDS or unarmed Black men with bullets in their back, you've suggested that the climate in American society today, some sixty years after King's assassination, is worse. We're back to Hawthorne's The Scarlett Letter, *this idea that we've got to purge society of all the impure people.*

Exactly. This is why it took President Reagan so long even to say the word "AIDS." People were actually saying: Good, get rid of the drug users, get rid of the Blacks, get rid of gay people. We don't have to do it ourselves, we have a disease now that will do it for us. People were very slow to act, because they thought it was going to clean up the miscreants.

A lot of evangelical Christian pastors, very public figures, said the same thing about Hurricane Katrina, that God was punishing the city of New Orleans for its debauchery.[2]

It's very interesting to me that Louisiana and New Mexico, maybe California, too, are the only Catholic states. What I mean is, they're not overwhelmingly Puritan or influenced by the American form of Puritanism in the culture. Louisiana is definitely not Puritan, as you can see every year at Mardi Gras; they're way over the edge. And the culture of New Mexico is clearly not based on the American Puritan ethic. It's definitely Hispanic and Native American. When I used to say Mass at Taos Pueblo, the people would say, "We keep our Indian ways, but we integrate them with our Catholic ways." They haven't thrown out who they are, though there were many people who came in and tried to do that.

It's like Ireland. They've been trying to make it Roman ever since St. Patrick, but they've kept their Celtic ways and culture. And now today, because there was so much child sexual abuse in Ireland, they've become more or less secular Catholics. It was so bad, much like the Native schools in Canada, that you just don't even bring it up. And all the Irish who came over here to Boston, New York, Chicago, including the Irish priests, they were all heavily influenced by this history of abuse.

To Acknowledge and Transcend the Violence

I wonder if we haven't stumbled accidentally on the reason why you did the drawing of Dr. King in 1983. The confluence of all these wounds, of people carrying the wounds of Christ in their bodies, in their collective memory, their "pain body," as you put it in an earlier conversation.

Yes, I think that's it.

I was extremely moved when I learned that in Russia they built a church on top of the place where they unearthed the charred bodies of the Romanoff family, and they called it "Church on the Blood." I thought, we would never do that here in America. Our whole impulse is to deny, to look away, to forget. Can you imagine if they tore down the grade school in Uvalde, Texas, where all those children were massacred, and built a church on the site called "The Church of the Massacre of the Holy Innocents." We would never do that here; but if we did, you would never forget it, because you're connecting the massacre with Jesus, with the murder of innocents everywhere, all the way back.

I wanted to create images like that, that were strong, that would honor the actual thing that happened and not try to hide it, like the Black Crucifix at Regis. You can never heal unless you honor it and face it in a way that is profound. I can't think of anything more healing, to build a church on the site in Uvalde with the pictures of the kids and their teachers. It would help us to acknowledge and transcend the violence. It's like when Jackie Kennedy refused to change her dress, splattered with the blood of her husband. No, she said, I want people to see what they did to him.

Mamie Till, Emmet Till's mother, did the same thing, insisting on an open casket after they pulled the boy's mangled body out of the river. "I want the world to see what they did to my boy."

I think this is what Robert Ellsberg was getting at when he used the phrase "terrible beauty" to describe your work. Look at who you're painting, the stories

The Sower's Nightmare, 1981

you're lifting up for us to see and remember: Elijah McClain, Sr. Dianna Ortiz, St. Henry Walpole, the English Jesuit who was "splashed by the blood" as a young man when he witnessed the martyrdom of Edmund Campion.

It's the difference between cheap grace—let's all smile and be hopeful, shall we?—and costly grace, as Jesus asks, Can you drink the cup that I am to drink? But you're also saying we mustn't overlook the beauty, the light in people, our capacity for tremendous love.

Yes. I hope people see the beauty, the light, the love coming from within the images.

I'm thinking now of your drawings like The Sower's Nightmare, The Mother Pelican, *and* St. Francis' Flowering Wound, *images that fascinated me and, to be honest, repelled me a bit, when I first saw them. Somehow, they're both terrible, or unsettling, and beautiful at the same time.*

I'm very fond of Jesus's parable of the sower for many reasons, especially the seed that falls into thorns, as we talked about in my 1977 drawing, *Self-Portrait with Symbols.* I did *The Sower's Nightmare* after a friend of mine had come to my apartment in Brooklyn to talk, after a rela-

Mother Pellican

105

tionship with a man she loved had ended. She just wept and wept, hardly able to speak. I used an avocado seed sprouting, with a halo of light guarding it, to show that even though this relationship did not work out, she could still have hope. The seeds were still in her like the presence of the Holy Spirit. In every relationship the seeds are so varied, the hopes, the shared conversations, the intimacy on many spoken and unspoken levels. They stay with us, and we can choose what seeds we nourish, that we'll grow and expand into.

The mythic legend of the Mother Pelican is one of the few symbols we have of the Divine Feminine. She would feed her own chicks from the blood of her breast—a symbol of Christ. Fra Angelico placed her at the top of some of his crucifixion paintings, and in old churches you'll see her near the altar or on tabernacle doors. I remember walking into St. Peter's Church in Brooklyn and being knocked breathless when I saw this great mosaic of the Mother Pelican covering the floor. I love it when these ancient symbols come alive again. The right wing wants to bring them back, but in a way that's dead, exclusionary, cultic. My whole being wants to include everything—Padre Pio, the Berrigans, the Hindus, the Buddhists.

I often don't know how my work comes across to people. So, when Robert Ellsberg described my work in that way, as "terrible beauty," it was a jolt to me, but it was also a gift. It's why, I suppose, whenever I've done a cross, all hell breaks loose. That last giant cross I did, *The Cross of Life*—it's seven feet by thirteen feet—is still waiting for a home. It nearly killed me to finish it.

I think Robert was trying to jolt me into the realization of how people see my work, the intensity, the seriousness of it. I know a lot of things I've done are pretty intense. My work is not used that often in the world of Catholic media, like it was in the first years of my apprenticeship. I think my "continual coming out" may have something to do with that. I say continual, because now everyone has Google, and thus, like it or not, you become a sign of contradiction. People have to

> ### Isaiah 60
>
> Something is happening.
> It's the flash and
> glare of light
> in Jacob Boehme's
> pewter dish.
> It's the sudden
> petal shower
> from Normandy's precious Rose.
> It's the awesome
> awakening of the Child
> in the arms of the
> Skeleton at Greccio.
> It's Damien
> transfigured and returned
> to the Emerald Forest.
> It's the reproach of
> seven years lifted.
> It's the end of the
> blood soaked sheets.
> It's the rider espoused
> and the pale horse fed.
> Its the Light in the
> darkness.
> It's the nations streaming
> to the outcasts.
> It's the empty tomb

keep making that decision to accept or reject you. Or maybe it's just not that good in some people's eyes, or maybe it's too serious for some people? Even the children's books, the Santo Niño book, for example, has the Christ Child going into prison![3] That's the legend, by the way; I didn't make that up. I also know that being out was very restrictive. From then on, I would be known as "the gay priest" who happens to be an artist, an iconographer; and some people would not use my work for that reason. I knew that would happen, but not the extent to which it would happen.

And still, "The world is charged with the grandeur of God"; it really is. Like Joni Mitchell says, If you're open to the miraculous, it's a very rich world. Of course, I grieve a lot, too. I grieve over what's happening in Israel and Palestine, the war in Ukraine. These things weigh on me, as they do on all of us. I tend not to look away from them.

When you introduced me to the work of Melissa Raphael, how she lifts up the experiences of women in Auschwitz, it was unlike anything I had read.[4] My God, I thought, this is *really looking at it*, eyes open, and still finding the experience of the Shekhinah of God in the middle of the horror, which nobody would ever dare to say. Ignatius, too, is saying just this, and it scandalizes: *find God in all things*, not just in the beauty, but also in the tragedy. If you don't live that way, it's hard to guide people into hope.

A Reality that Lives in All of Us

Abraham Joshua Heschel calls it the "will to wonder," and insists that wonder, for the person of faith, is not merely a state of aesthetic enjoyment. It includes the hard stuff.[5] It's also Johann Baptist Metz, who describes the spirituality of Jesus and the Hebrew tradition from which Jesus imbibed his sense of God, as a "mysticism of open eyes."[6] It also brings us back to Hopkins, and his beautiful prayer, your prayer, that "all my eyes" might see.

I have to say that when we first began to sort through all of your drawings and illustrations, I was stunned and a bit overwhelmed. I could see the clear connections to the Gospel in the drawings, the lives of the saints, Ignatius and other Jesuit saints—all of this was clear to me, and compelling. But there were other drawings—some beautiful, others unsettling, strange, haunting—that I didn't immediately "get."

What I'm trying to say is that the power of the drawings has emerged much more vividly for me in light of the life story that produced them: your childhood and teenage years, your Jesuit formation and AIDS ministry. If the eyes of our hearts are open, we become much more than passive readers or viewers. We become participants in the inner movements of a human life and its lessons learned through time.

On the one hand, it is difficult to separate the work from the life of the artist that produced it. On the other hand, the work itself, as you've said many times, takes on a life of its own that touches people in ways well beyond your control. People see things in your art that you have not seen, so that something unexpected, spontaneous, and free is birthed from the heart of another. Heart speaks to heart—cor ad cor loquitur—and does so potentially across cultural, temporal, religious boundaries.

Very early I fell in love with the symbols of Catholic art, the blood of the Lamb and the wounds especially, as you've noticed. I have a love of tradition that is very deep. I don't see the Catholic tradition as something that is static or negative. The love for those symbols was planted in me before I was born. Because I was gay, I related strongly to the child martyrs, all the young people who were murdered, or bullied, or humiliated, or raped. All the people, even today, for whom there is no room at the inn, not even in the church.

The desire to get the work out is not about me, it's not about defending myself or the work. It's the flight into Egypt. You're trying to protect the baby—these ancient symbols that speak to a reality that lives in all of us.

When people attack, I don't want to waste precious time fighting back. I've got to get this baby into Egypt—so hauntingly timely, as the Palestinians are desperately trying now to get into Egypt. I've felt very protective of my art, and it's difficult for me to explain why. Perhaps if I had real children and grandchildren like my siblings I wouldn't be as concerned.

It all comes from my belief that this art was given to me. Even when rejected, I feel obligated and compelled to share what was given. You're trying to protect the baby—that's what my life feels like with my art.

I'm reminded of your theology professor, some forty-five years ago, cautioning you and your classmates that priesthood can be a chaotic and lonely path, that you will plant the seeds for a church that you will never see.

Recently I read a beautiful portrait of Fr. Henri Perrin by Robert Ellsberg. And it was a huge revelation to me about the model of the worker priests that I seem to have adopted very early on, largely unconsciously. I feel I have lived at the tail end of this movement, which arose during World War II and goes back to an ancient apostolic way of living the priesthood, which naturally filtered into the inspirational documents of Vatican II. I believe the worker priests possibly inspired Pope Francis in his comments about some contemporary seminarians, voicing serious concerns about clericalism at the closing of the 2023 Synod.

This Spirit-led worker priest movement lasted only for a period of time, like the Beguines of thirteenth-century Europe. Both were ahead of their times, and, as a result, both were suspended, but I believe they foreshadowed contemporary lay movements like the Catholic Worker, the Focolare Movement, the San Egidio Community in Rome, and other recent lay institutes that include priests and women religious. I know these worker priests inspired me specifically about how to live during this era—this brief one hundred years or so, in the long, long life of the church, about which our teacher prophesied rightly, that if you choose to be ordained, "you will plant the seeds of the new church, but you will not live to see it."

"I John, was in the Spirit on the Lord's day"
(*Revelation 1:10*), color pencil, 1980

PART III

Iconographer: Friend of Prophets, Pilgrims, and Saints

To be created in the image of a (divine) other entails that creation is necessarily relational—a face-to-face event—God making us present to one another.

It follows, then, that the retrieval or even momentary restoration of a face is the restoration of presence.

~ Melissa Raphael, *The Female Face of God in Auschwitz*

The profound beauty of an icon is gentle. It does not force its way; it does not intrude. It asks for patience with the uneasiness of early acquaintance. More important, it asks the one praying to allow himself to be gazed upon by it. One must yield space within himself to the icon and its persistent beauty. . . .

It manifests to us the God who breaks through all signs and symbols with truth.

—Sister Helen Weir

Ah, but in such an ugly time the true protest is beauty.

—Phil Ochs

CHAPTER 9

Images that Return Our Love

As we begin Part III of our conversations, Fr. Bill and I explore his transition from the AIDS hospice ministry in New York to apprenticing with master iconographer Br. Robert Lentz in Albuquerque. What led him to make such a radical change, and what was it like to study with Robert Lentz? Solitude emerges as a critical aspect of Bill's life in New Mexico, and the rigorous discipline of painting six to eight hours a day. "This is work," Robert tells him, "you do it whether you feel like it or not." Fr. Bill begins to receive commissions, most notably for the icon Our Lady of the New Advent: The Gate of Heaven, *the official icon of the Archdiocese of Denver, and he is asked to present a second icon of* Our Lady of the New Advent *to Pope John Paul II during his 1993 World Youth Day visit to Denver. Following the example of his teacher, while developing his own distinctive style, Bill is led to ask, What is the treasury of the church? The answer that came: the wounded, the poor, the outcast. "We need to gaze on truly conversational, truly loving images," he says, "images that will return our love."*

After completing his study with Br. Lentz, returning to Boston and then New York, Fr. Bill is given permission to return to Taos where he will reside for fourteen years, alternately serving as a priest for the Hispanic church of Ranchos de Taos and for the Indian community at San Geronimo Church in Taos Pueblo. Celebrating the Mother and Child imagery so prevalent in Bill's iconography, spiritual writer Mirabai Starr describes his work as "bringing Nativity into the Apocalypse." To create such art is "a struggle" and a "gift of great humility," says Bill, but also "a gift of great joy, because every so often one can send a colorful love letter into the unspeakable suffering of a world haunted and destined for God." In the high desert landscape, with Taos Mountain looming above it all, Fr. Bill finds "the space I needed to listen, to take instruction."

Chris: Fr. Bill, I'd like to ask about the discernment process that led to your decision to study iconography with Br. Robert Lentz. You said that the inspiration came during your long retreat in tertianship, the last stage of Jesuit formation, a kind of second novitiate, when you make the Spiritual Exercises again.

Fr. Bill: During those years of the AIDS ministry, Bill Dobbels and I would go to Santa Fe for vacation every year in December. One year, I went into the cathedral in Santa Fe and saw the first icon that Robert was doing for the reredos there, and each year, there were more of them. A reredos is an altar screen, in this case, a huge screen holding fourteen "Saints of the Americas," each icon seven-feet tall. It took him two years to complete all fourteen icons. I'd look at them and I was just overwhelmed. These are magnificent, the height of detail, the height of perfection.

I first began to see Robert's work in New York. I would take my cards down to the Catholic store, and his cards were all there too. I would look at them and think, wow, this guy is really doing it. Robert is truly a giant. He single-handedly changed the practice of iconography across the world. He was the first to do Martin Luther King Jr., many Black Madonnas, a Navajo Madonna, an Asian Madonna.[1] I didn't yet think of studying with him, but I thought, someday I would love to do what the Renaissance painters did. All of them were apprentices, learning the technique of the particular art you were doing.

I wondered *who* in the world I would want to learn from, because everybody, it seemed, was doing modern art. I knew that I wanted to be a painter, but couldn't figure out where my niche was. I was very comfortable with watercolors and gouache. It's a language that you can either do or you can't. It's difficult, and you can't correct it once you lay it down. But yes, it wasn't until my long retreat in tertianship that I began to think of studying with Robert.

Can I ask why you did your tertianship in Austin, Texas? A lot of Jesuits choose to go overseas, to a retreat center in the Philippines, for example, or Japan, Australia, South Africa.

I chose to do tertianship in Texas because Bill had gotten very sick and I didn't want to be too far away if he died. Joe Tetlow was the tertianship director in Austin, steeped in Ignatian spirituality, and really beloved and famous among Jesuits as a retreat director. For the long retreat we went from Austin to Grand Couteau, Louisiana, the Jesuit retreat house in the very heart of Cajun country. Being in that Cajun culture, and with Jesuits from all over the world, was so rich, just amazing.

From day one, every time I prayed, it was totally dry. Nothing. When I would meditate on the Scriptures, for example, the Infancy Narratives, which I love, there was nothing. No move-

ment in my heart. As the long retreat came to an end, I'd go to Joe, and he'd ask, Anything? No. Nothing. Zero.

But then, during the very last few days of the retreat, I went in and said, Joe, I keep thinking of the name Robert Lentz. He asked, What does that mean to you? I don't know, I said, maybe he's sick and I should be praying for him. What else? he asked. Well, he's an iconographer, I said. He's a master. I've always wanted to do an apprenticeship with a master, like they used to do during Leonardo da Vinci's time. They all studied with a master. Right away, Joe said, *I think you should do that. When we finish the retreat, I want you to call the provincial and tell him this is what you want to do.*

I called my provincial, who, at the time, was Ed Kinerk. He listened, and said that I should call Robert. Unbeknown to me, my superiors were trying to find a way to get me out of New York. They were afraid I was getting eaten alive with the AIDS ministry. And I was. I was pretty well burnt out.

I called Robert Lentz and said, I don't know if you ever take on students but I would really like to learn from you. He said, "I sent you a letter, and I never got a response." He's very direct; he doesn't fool around or joke on the phone like I do. He told me that he had seen my painting *Epiphany*, and thought it looked like I was trying to do iconography, and wrote to me about it. I said to him, *I never got that letter.* He said, "Well, if you're willing to move to Albuquerque, I'm willing to teach you." A few days later, he called and said that he had found a house in Albuquerque where I could stay.

Everything started to line up. I called Ed Kinerk, told him that Robert had said yes, and Ed said, I think you ought to do this. I went back to my room, lay down on the floor and wept. I had thought that I would never leave New York, my work, all my friends there. My spiritual director even said to me, *You cannot do this. You are an AIDS priest; it's who you are. You can't go off and study painting. What are you thinking?* But it stayed with me. I really wanted to work with a master.

Everyone Had a Place at the Table

Besides your desire to study with Robert, you alluded earlier to elements of the desert Southwest, its Hispanic and Native American cultures, which were already familiar and attractive to you. When you did Epiphany, *for example, you said you wanted Mary to be Our Lady of Guadalupe, "not a white Mary but a brown Mary," and you placed "the Santo Niño" on her lap. You described the atmosphere of New Mexico as far removed from the "Puritan culture" that dominates much of the United States. Even in the* AIDS Crucifix *drawing, with New York City in the background, you placed desert cactus and rocks in the foreground, having visited New Mexico and feeling "at home" there.*

I wonder if there isn't a thread joining your sense of comfort both in the Northeast and in the desert Southwest with your attraction to Robert's work—to me, it suggests a kind of radical openness to the divine in all things, holiness manifest across all kinds of cultural, religious, and racial boundaries.

Just after the retreat in 1971 at the Pine Ridge Lakota Reservation, which was so important to me, I read *Black Elk Speaks*, a book of sheer spiritual, mystical, visionary poetry.[2] I can see now how the retreat and the book planted things in me that would flower many years later. It's like the guy in New York who told me, when he looked at my drawings, that I was destined to do some other kind of art.

One of the criticisms of *Black Elk Speaks* as told to John Neihardt is that Neihardt did not include the many years that Black Elk served as a wise elder and Catholic catechist. Nicholas Black Elk managed to do what my friends at Taos Pueblo do, which is to naturally blend their Catholic and Native spiritual traditions. My fourteen years in Taos working as an iconographer—I moved there in June 1999, after finishing with Robert and returning to the Northeast for several years—had a deep effect on me. I felt completely at home, though I would never pretend, and never tried, to fully understand the Taos Indian culture.

Black Elk: Wicasa Wikan

I'll never forget the first time I did Mass at Taos Pueblo. I had long hair and a blonde horseshoe mustache. I walked into the sanctuary, looked up

113

at the people, and said, Oh my God, I'm so sorry. I must look just like Custer! It just hit me at that moment when I walked in. I turned absolutely white—or whiter!—and then I turned completely red, and they just laughed and laughed. It really broke the ice, and from then on, I was fine.

Bill in Taos

Oh my gosh, that is very funny. I've seen pictures from this time and you do look like Custer.

After saying Mass in Spanish for a long time at Ranchos de Taos, a Hispanic parish, I asked the people, How am I doing? They said, pretty good for a white boy. I was there for fourteen years. I was extremely lucky to have that experience of many cultures. So yes, you can see why I jumped at the chance to work with Robert, whose work crossed all of these boundaries.

I can only say that this was a place for me, with its Native values and traditions, that made it possible *to be all of myself.* I often say that the Native Americans were right about just about everything. But for me and for the LGBTQ community, Native culture was uniquely, spiritually enlightened. Within these cultures there was an innate respect for LGBTQ people. Everyone had a place at the table.

Still, the initial transition from New York to Albuquerque—and from the AIDS ministry to iconography—must have been rather jarring.

Your Art Is a Lot about Pregnancy

Just before I was supposed to leave for Albuquerque, I said to my dear friend Louis, who was dying of AIDS, "I can't go. I can't do this, Louis. What if you die while I'm gone?" He said to me, *"Listen, it's time for you to go. It's time for me to go, too,"* he said. And he did. A few days later they called and told me that Louis was gone. I rushed over, and they already had him in a body bag, zipped up to his neck. I asked, "Can you please open it." His face looked just like Christ to me. He had a little beard, and his face was marble white. I did his funeral on September 3, 1990, and flew to Albuquerque on September 7.

There was an old adobe house that Robert had arranged for me to live in. I settled in and slept for nearly a month. I was exhausted, physically and emotionally, so much had happened. Finally, one day, Robert came and said, "When are we going to start lessons?" We began on October 4th, St. Francis Day. I thought, maybe I'll do this for a year. I had no idea. I didn't know the spirituality

Fr. Bill celebrating a baptism, San Geronimo Church, Taos Pueblo

of icons. I didn't know anything about them. He had done Martin Luther King, Stephen Biko—I just knew his work was so powerful.

Isn't that strange? I can still remember a time when I knew nothing about icons. Or knew nothing about gay history. Or knew nothing about Black history. When it all comes back to me, it's very strong. I think to myself, Oh my gosh, God really was leading me. . . .

Just after I got to Albuquerque in 1990, I got a letter from Archbishop Stafford's office in Denver, saying he wanted me to do an icon of Our Lady of the New Advent. Even though I was just starting with Robert, I wanted to tell him, you just happened to pick the perfect person, because I come alive in Advent.

A woman who knows my work very well once said to me, "Your art is a lot about pregnancy." In the book of Revelation, the dragon is attacking the pregnant woman, waiting to devour her child. What does it mean to give birth to something that will threaten the world with its goodness, its joy, its beauty? Mirabai Starr, as you mentioned, described my icons as "bringing Nativity into the Apocalypse."[3] And Dan Berrigan saying that so much of our world is constructed almost literally as a war on children.

I remember reading Mirabai's comment in her Foreword to your book with John Dadosky, Image to Insight. *That phrase just stopped me, and I thought, what could she mean by this?*

When you described your experience at age five of being abused, Fr. Bill, you said you could feel this figure in the doorway filled with rage at the light in you—it occurs to me now, it was like the Beast in Revelation, poised to devour the Child. In your drawing of The Akedah—*you were 31 when you did that picture, almost a decade after the shock therapy—you said that you had finally come to realize that you were doing this to yourself, trying to violently put out your own light, as it were. What's remarkable to me is how your experience of carrying these wounds—some inflicted by others, some self-inflicted—gives birth to the promise of rebirth in your art, and gifts this promise to a wounded world.*

In your essay "Art: Apocalypsis *and* Veronike,"[4] *you say that art born in the midst of war or persecution is given "to warn, encourage, and to reach out to hold the hands of those in the struggle against the Beast." To create such art, you write, is "a struggle" and a "gift of humility because it is so difficult"; on the other hand, it is "a gift of great joy because every so often one can send a colorful love letter into the unspeakable suffering of a world haunted and destined for God."*

Yes, love letters, or flaming arrows. And Robert Lentz was the best teacher I could have ever had. He was very stern, extremely intellectual, very unromantic about it. *This is work*, he taught me; *you do it whether you feel like it or not.* He explained to me about the traditional practice of fasting when you're writing an icon. I thought, well how can you fast when you're doing iconography every day, as your livelihood? Traditionally iconographers would do a few icons every year, and during that time they would fast. But I was doing almost one each month, working every night, so I decided to eat very little, and that has worked for me.

Kidnapped into Icons

After studying with Robert for a while I came to feel very strongly that God was calling me to be an iconographer, that it was my vocation. I very badly wanted to do it as a Jesuit, and I wanted the Jesuits to be excited about it and support it. My superiors struggled to understand why I couldn't do icons while living in a community. When I'm doing an icon, I'm deeply in relationship with that person. I need to work in solitude, but I'm not alone. When I live by myself, I have a lot more energy to give to the icon.

It reminds me of Merton's battles with his abbot for many years over his desire to live as a hermit. Solitude, for Merton, wasn't an escape from community but a way of life within the bounds of monastic discipline to see and experience with greater clarity, to see through the fog. It seems your vocation to iconography is at once a vocation to solitude, without many paral-

lels in contemporary Jesuit life, which has caused you some difficulties along the way. By the way, not only did Abbot Fox eventually give Merton permission to become a hermit, he became one himself in the last years of his life.

I was drawn to the Jesuits partly because the door was wide open for what kind of a Jesuit I wanted to be. You can be like Dan Berrigan or you can be like Teilhard de Chardin. But being a Jesuit *and* an artist was not always easy. Sometimes, I still want to say to the Jesuits, these icons belong to you. God gave me this gift, this vocation, for you. Once the desire came up during long retreat, all the doors opened. Once I began to do the work, I knew that icons were my way of giving to the church. Others can do talks, lead retreats, teach and write, or other Ignatian things. But who else was called to write icons? I was very aware that God had given this gift to me as a Jesuit.

The way God works, you often don't notice what's going on until much later. Essentially, I was kidnapped into icons, because before that I really had almost no relationship with them. I had no idea how demanding it would be, in terms of stepping away from other things. I was fighting it, with all kinds of distractions, and Robert had to really lay down the law with me.

What You Gaze Upon You Become

You began studying with Robert in 1990, at age 41, and finished in 1996. You've told me that the essay Robert wrote for a Jesuit magazine at the completion of your apprenticeship—we've included it in the last part of the book—says everything you could ever say about icons but much better.

Yes, he gets right into the heart of the spirituality of icons with very few words. But of all the books on icons, Paul Evdokimov's *The Art of the Icon*: A *Theology of Beauty*, is probably my favorite.[5]

Many Catholics in the West, I think, have come to icons through the little book by Henri Nouwen, Behold the Beauty of the Lord, *a book I've taught in my classes.*

Nouwen says that icons are not easy to "see" because they "speak more to our inner than to our outer senses. They speak to the heart that searches for God."[6] Jim Forest, a Catholic Worker, longtime friend of Merton and peace activist who later converted to Orthodoxy, also published a wonderful book with Orbis called Praying with Icons.[7]

My own favorite description of icons is still yours. "What you gaze upon, you become." "You gaze on the icon, but it gazes on you too," you once said. "We need to gaze on truly conversational, truly loving images, images that will return our love."[8] That statement -- "What you gaze upon you become"—has become very personal for me. It's why I'm especially drawn to your icons of St. Joseph, asking for the grace to become a better, more patient father. In your icon St. Joseph on the Rio Grande, *for example, the way Joseph is present to Jesus, his cloak surrounding the boy, protecting him—if I thought I could be present to my kids in that way, even after I'm gone, I would die a happy man. And to show Joseph and the boy Jesus as exiles,*

Bill with Pope St. John Paul II, presenting *Our Lady of the New Advent: The Burning Bush*

St. Joseph on the Rio Grande

like migrants today, crossing the Rio Grande—as you said before, it's the flight to Egypt. "You're trying to protect the Child, get him to Egypt safely, and back home again."

I was so happy when Pope Francis declared 2021 the "Year of St. Joseph." I did *St. Joseph Flower of Jesse* that year, one of those images that just seems to have been channeled through me. I wanted to evoke Joseph's journey as a young man, before he met Mary, before the birth of Jesus, praying and trusting that God would reveal his life to him—a period we all go through, I think, when we're young.

I love it when these ancient symbols come alive again—the flowering cross, the blood of Christ, feminine images of God, Mary, the martyrs and theologians, flowers blooming in the desert—but they have to be living symbols, not dead, not nostalgic, not cultic.

Sometimes you do things in a way that people call "being in the zone," or almost completely directed by the unconscious imagination. I like to believe the Holy Spirit, who sees all things, guides your heart and hand to produce an image that mysteriously ministers to you, and also goes out into the world as something that is a contemplation for others to feel inside their souls too.

You say that you got the commission from Archbishop Stafford very soon after beginning with Robert?

Yes. The first icons I did while studying with Robert were three icons of the face of Christ. I was in the middle of writing the second one—it was February of 1991—when I got a letter from

117

Our Lady of the New Advent: The Gate of Heaven

the office of Francis Stafford, then the Archbishop of Denver. I couldn't believe it. He was going to ask Pope John Paul II to declare a new feast day for Our Lady of the New Advent, and wanted me to do an icon for the archdiocese. They wanted the icon to include the Colorado mountains and the state flower, the columbine, and Mary's cloak to be purple, for the season of Advent.

When people saw the icon everything kind of exploded. They brought a print of it to Rome when a delegation from Denver was meeting with the pope about World Youth Day. They asked Pope John Paul II to give the archdiocese a new feast day for Our Lady of the New Advent and to come to Colorado for World Youth Day. He said yes to both. The feast day of that icon is December 16. Robert said to me, *You better surrender. God is telling you that this is your vocation.*

When John Paul came to Denver in 1993 and I met him—I was allowed to present a second *Our Lady of the New Advent* icon to him—I had a lot of my own prejudices about him: first, many of us Jesuits were angry about his treatment of Fr. Arrupe; but second, there was the gay thing. Neither of my groups liked him. But the minute I stepped on the stage and looked at him, I loved him. We saw each other; he saw me, and it was staggering. I was overwhelmed by a sense of his love and holiness.

His mission was the New Evangelization, and I thought my vocation as an artist could fit right into that vision. I was doing Rutilio Grande, all these new saints, and all these old saints—I always felt that images were a powerful way to evangelize, to reach and inspire people.

You Open Yourself Up in Prayer and Things Come to You

Can you explain the distinction in your work between icons and images?

There are very strict rules about icons, and Robert, of course, was deeply aware of all of that. He would get hurt by criticism that he was "breaking the rules," being the first to do a Navajo Madonna,

doing Mary of all different races, Christ of all different races. I see a lot of artists doing icons in this way now, but they never acknowledge Robert. He led the way, saying that this is something that needs to be done for the whole world, and not just for one race. Of course, I strongly agree.

Fr. Bill writing an icon

When doing a commission, often I would model it after the original, or what they call the prototype. Other times, if doing a subject who didn't yet have an icon, I would have to imagine how to represent that person. The image of Matthew Shepard with the red body, the blue sky, the moon—technically it's not an icon but what I call an image, which allows for greater freedom in creating it.[9]

The process of doing an icon or image is a beautiful process—I imagine it's like when you are writing a book—where you open yourself up in prayer and things come to you. It's what Joni Mitchell says about songwriting: being open to the miraculous, opening yourself to the mysterious.

Living alone, you're protected from a lot of distractions. I could create the space I needed to listen, to take instruction. Almost every day I would take a nap so that I could paint that night. As I lay down, I would be getting instruction, in my spirit. When I did *St. Joseph Flower of Jesse,*

119

a young Joseph with the hollyhock rising from the ground, that image just came to me, as I said before. It's wonderful to be in the zone like that. I'd be flying, I'd be so happy. The first ten years I was painting all the time.

I imagine it's quite intense spiritually, not just intellectually. You want to "get it right," as it were, and when you're writing an icon, the medium allows you to make changes, if something isn't feeling quite right. And things rise into your consciousness unbidden, unexpected. Is that correct?

Things that have been inside me for a long time, like the lamb, or the Mother Pelican, would come out of me. The Holy Spirit as a dove is in a lot of my icons. So is the Mother Pelican. I wanted to unearth those symbols and give them back to the church. The Mother Pelican, as we've talked about, is significant as a eucharistic symbol and as a female symbol of God—the idea of giving our blood for the people we love, being fed by the Eucharist and then giving it out again.

I know that every parent feels like they're giving their blood for their children. Mothers literally do, but so do fathers. With all that you and Lauri have been through with your family, I know that you do.

It brings us back to our earlier conversations about how the wounds we bear can link us to others, or images being like arrows shot into the heart of the church. Sometimes these arrows are painful, disturbing, unsettling—thus Robert Ellsberg describing the "terrible beauty" of your work. I would call it the prophetic voice, rendered visually, sometimes shocking the viewer out of complacency. But there is also the tenderness, sometimes heart-rending tenderness, of the mother or father cradling the child.

A Theology in Lines and Colors

Looking back at this period, what did iconography allow you to express that went beyond the earlier paintings and drawings?

Robert Lentz took a form, the icon form, and transformed it into a very powerful set of images

for today, *about* people today. Dorothy Day, Martin Luther King, Stephen Biko, and on and on. And he took a lot of criticism for it. The Orthodox and the right-wing Catholics went wild after him.

But you've suggested that he could take the heat.

Oh yes. When he would answer his critics, it was very lawyerly: point one, two, three, four, five, responding with facts. I remember thinking, *I hope I never get this kind of blowback.* In my mind, I still thought of myself as an AIDS chaplain. I knew what it was to take criticism, but I thought, to receive it as an artist, as an iconographer, I hope that doesn't happen to me.

And how did that work out for you?

It's funny, isn't it? I knew that when I went to study with Robert I would be on the hit-list for a whole group of people. But he was so good. He wasn't just mimicking others and pouring forth stillborns. A lot of people follow all the techniques—a certain kind of wood, a certain paint—and what comes out, there's no life in it. Robert made the art alive again. Of course, they don't like to call it "art," because it's writing theology.

"A theology in lines and colors," says Evdokimov.

Yes, a theology in lines and colors. But it has to be alive. I remember Robert asking me, do you think if Andrei Rublev was alive today he would be using egg tempura? No, he said, he'd be using oil or acrylic. He wouldn't be following the strict rule just for the sake of following it. And that made a lot of sense to me. Now, apparently when icon teachers teach people, they point to Robert and me as examples of *what you should not do.* It's like when Dylan went electric.

Of course! I couldn't have come up with a better analogy.

People really attacked him. And the same thing happened to Robert. But you know he studied at

Our Lady of the Apocalypse

St. Padre Pio Mother Pelican

Holy New Martyr Jean Donovan

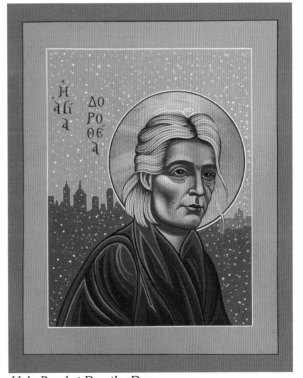

Holy Prophet Dorothy Day

the Orthodox monastery in Brookline, Massachusetts. He learned everything you can learn about how and why the Orthodox do icons the way that they do. He's a very strong intellectual thinker, very detailed in everything that he does. Even though he's a Franciscan friar, he is nourished deeply by Orthodox history and spirituality.

We spoke earlier about a thread that joins your 1983 color drawing of Dr. King and later icons of people who have borne the wounds, whole communities still being crucified, like the flaming cross behind King in that drawing. That Robert Lentz would lift up people like Stephen Biko and bring them into the icon tradition is something that you've carried on in your work and have also been attacked for. I'm thinking of your icon of Ben Salmon, the American conscientious objector, whom I knew nothing about.

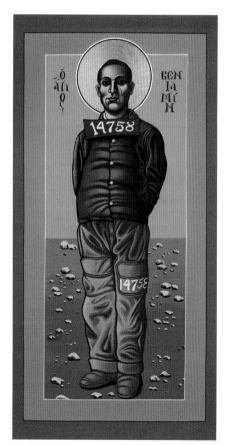

Holy Prophet Benjamin Salmon

Ben Salmon was like Franz Jägerstätter but much earlier, in the United States, during World War I. He was a pariah for so many years until finally people began to recognize the courage and holiness of what he did. I had read about him in Robert Ellsberg's book on the saints, and the fact that he was from Denver really drew me to him. I knew how he grew up. I knew what Denver was like before it became the contemporary Denver. I knew the attitude of people toward Catholics and anybody else that's not accepted. A conscientious objector in World War I? It was unthinkable.

The Denver paper had an article about Ben Salmon with the headline, "Denver's Man with a Big Yellow Stripe on His Back," and his kids grew up with that. He was sent to Leavenworth, tortured there, and wrote a book, saying, "There is no such thing as a just war." And he did it all with an eighth-grade education. The prison chaplain refused to give him communion. My God, can you imagine?

Yes, I can. The marriage of church and state. Civil religion. God and country.

Dorothy and the Catholic Worker Movement began to try to dissolve that, and then, of course, the Berrigans as well.

Take Us to the Treasury of the Church

I should say that long before studying with Robert, my predecessors in the art world go back to a 1972 exhibit at Boston University around the theme of the artist as social critic. I walked into that exhibit and saw Goya, Daumier, Picasso's "Guernica," Heinrich Kley, Käthe Kollwitz, all these people *who had put the suffering of real people into their art*. It was so powerful to see what you could do with art.

Because of my dad, and then Dan Berrigan, I had a lot of people in my life who spoke up for the outcast, for the underdog. And I thought art could really be powerful in that way. I had just done the Viet Nam chapel. Robert Lentz was infusing that kind of social justice art into

Nuestra Señora de las Sandias

Nuestro Salvador de las Sandias

icons—Stephen Biko, Dorothy Day, King, and other Americans—examples of a different kind of spirituality, an American spirituality, which was unusual.

Through icons he was highlighting a particular witness that was coming out of the American experience, people whose lives were resonant with the Gospel and the Hebrew prophetic tradition.

Yes. I knew my work would never be as perfect as his. It's like Salvador Dali said, "Don't worry about perfection, you'll never reach it." But Robert did. Working with him three times a week, two-hour lessons, for six years, I dove in so deeply, and tried to read everything I could about the Orthodox tradition. Paul Evdokimov's book on icons, as I mentioned before, was number one.

Looking in depth at the history of the church has always been part of my life, and wondering how my art might add to the treasury of the church. You know the story of St. Lawrence,

when his captors said to him, Take us to the treasury of the church, he took them to a house for the poor, opened the door and said, here are the treasures of the church. They were so enraged they martyred him immediately. That story is from the third century.

All those stories taught me to ask, Okay, what is really the heart of the church? *The treasures of the church are the wounded, the poor, the outcast.* That's from the earliest days, and it hit me really hard.

When I read your work, Chris, I feel you're tapping into that heart of the church, both ancient and contemporary, living and new. Even where you're critical of the church you're not trying to tear it down but preserve what is best out of love, in a way, like Dan Berrigan, who could be extremely critical, or Dorothy Day, or Merton. I can be critical of the church, but I'm fully aware that my sins are also part of the church. I think of Jesus in Matthew 5, when he warned the disciples, and I'm paraphrasing, Yes, you can be critical so long as you guard against hypocrisy.

123

St. Francis Church, Taos

Fr. Bill beneath icon for St. Francis Church, Taos

In other words, the way you live your lives matters as much as any words you speak; it's what will give your words their authority and integrity. Of course, it's easier said than done. We all fall short every day.

Indeed, we do! Thank you, Fr. Bill. I do hope my work seeks to "preserve what is best out of love."

After completing your studies with Robert, you returned to Boston College for a year as artist-in-residence, and then were back in New York from 1997 to 1998. What finally brought you back to New Mexico, and Taos, in 1999?

In 1998, I was invited to go on pilgrimage to Akita, Japan, and when I got back to New York, I got a call from a priest friend in Ranchos de Taos, New Mexico, asking if I would do a painting for the iconic church there of St. Francis receiving the stigmata. With permission from my superior, I returned to Taos thinking I would only be there for a little while, but it became my home, and I would eventually set up my studio there.

I loved living in Taos so much because, in the midst of the mountains, I felt properly small. And looking at them, I also felt I was part of the natural world. Nothing could ever define me that

was too small of a category or box, because Taos Mountain kept pointing to infinity.

John's Gospel has a similar effect in that right from the beginning you are led out of this world to a kind of aerial or cosmic view of all things in relation to God's loving movement in creating the world. St. Ignatius does the same in the Spiritual Exercises, where he "takes you to heaven" to overhear a conversation of the Blessed Trinity about lovingly sending the Word down to Earth to save humankind.

"In the midst of the mountains I felt properly small." I love that insight, and I certainly felt it palpably when I visited you in Taos many years later. None of our categories or boxes can contain the mystery of God, nor the mystery of our own humanity. Taos Mountain keeps pointing us back to infinity.

CHAPTER 10

Splashed by the Blood

The atmosphere of mystery endemic to Native American culture—not only reverence for nature, but also for those whose gender and sexuality doesn't conform to a neat binary—opens our conversation. "It was the first time I ever felt honored by a culture. Not only am I not sick, or perverted, or an aberration, but no, this is a gift." While being given a distinct and sacred vocation in the community is beautiful, "it can also be quite frightening." This leads us into a conversation about Bill's departure from the Jesuits in 2002, after 35 years in the Society. The circumstances surrounding the break still clearly trouble him, yet, "I realize a lot of things couldn't have happened, probably many of the icons, if I were still a Jesuit."

Fr. Bill's love for the Jesuit poet Gerard Manley Hopkins exposes a vulnerability he shares with Hopkins since his heart collapse in 2012—"I'm way too open." Two recent paintings of the child Mary and a young Joseph invite us to contemplate their "hidden years," before they met, and as both were "coming to a gradual awareness of some extraordinary vocation." From there we discuss what one Jesuit mentor calls his masterpiece, Mary Most Holy Mother of All Nations, *a work surrounded with mystery for Bill, and several recent icons of Joseph, which push against the "militant" Joseph of the Catholic right.*

As both a priest and iconographer, Fr. Bill comes to realize that "some contemplative concepts can only be represented through visual art." A film like Oppenheimer *may awaken many people to the nuclear threat in ways that political discourse has failed. While presiding at Mass, he describes seeing in the eyes of adults how "the light" has gone out or is being extinguished by others. It is not only children whose personhood is threatened by forces of darkness. We conclude with three images very close to my heart:* St. Henry Walpole, SJ, The Passion of Matthew Shepard, *and* Elijah McClain. *To be "splashed by the blood" is to be marked, body and soul, by trauma. "It may not be comfortable, but it sears you."*

Chris: I'd like to begin with the period between your return to New Mexico in 1999 and your departure from the Jesuits in 2002. I remember one of the first times we talked about New Mexico, Fr. Bill; you described a sense of mystery in the landscape that draws people in, but there's a harshness as well. A lot of people, many famous people, come to visit, enchanted by the landscape, but find that they can't stay.

Fr. Bill: Everyone, I think, has a landscape in their soul, and when they find it in the outer world, that's where they want to live. I know many people on the East Coast will say they could never live in the mountains; they need to be near the ocean. I love the ocean, but I have to be near the mountains, and that's because I grew up with them every day. I was aware of the Native American presence as a child, but I didn't know any Native people until I eventually moved to Taos.

Growing up as a child, because Dad was governor, he was invited to Native dances and ceremonies, and often he was given gifts. I remember him coming home from a ceremony one evening and showing me a medicine bag that they had given him. Much later in my life, when I left the parish in Taos, a lot of people from the Pueblo came to the reception, and afterward they gave me a medicine bag. I asked my Native friend Jeralyn, an artist, what was in the bag, but she wouldn't say. There are things about their ways that they aren't quick to disclose, even to a friend. I still have that medicine bag.

I remember as a kid going into downtown Denver to pick up Dad from work, and seeing Native American men lying on the sidewalk, drunk, or leaning against a building. It was scary for me as a child, seeing their suffering. It also taught me how the Native culture in Colorado has been ravaged—there it was the Plains Indians, not the Pueblo Indians as here in New Mexico, which is a very different culture.

The thing I realized is that they are very strict about rules, in a way, like the Jesuits are. To stand out is not a good thing. You're not meant to stand out from the community. You're not applauded for succeeding. Robert Mirabal, the famous Native American flute player from Taos, says "I'm known everywhere, except Taos Pueblo." But this is an outsider's view; just my impressions.

When I hear Native people speaking about relationships, about God, or the Earth, everything is totally spiritual. We so desperately need that reverence for nature that they have and speak of. It just shocks you how secular our culture is, by contrast, when you hear them speak.

But whether it's the Hispanic or the Native or the Black culture, I don't ever pretend to really understand. There's a mystery that remains, and it's important to honor that mystery.

Honoring the Mystery

Your painting Approaching the Mystery of Crazy Horse *is a beautiful blend of multiple images, visually unusual because it's not square or rectangular but made in the form of a circle. The frame created for it by your friend Roberto Lavadie is equally gorgeous. They go together hand in glove.*

When Roberto and I work together I feel we can do anything. He is such a spiritual craftsman.

The story of Crazy Horse is very, very mysterious, and very somber—a little like reading Melissa Raphael, women's narratives from the Holocaust—because you're hearing the beginnings of genocide, as the Wasichu, the white people, are coming in. He's describing visions that the Native people had of these people coming in and taking everything and putting the Native people in these tiny square houses, instead of tepees, in the worst part of the land. Of course, they were foreseeing life on the reservations.

As a little boy, Crazy Horse was called "Jiji Kin," because he had light brown curly hair, and he was made fun of because of it. When he was around twelve he had his "vocation dream," which tells you what you will do with your life. His story stirs up so much in me, partly from that sense of solitariness that comes when you have a vocation that requires you to be solitary—to be "claimed by the inner life," as Robert Johnson puts it, at such a young age. Though you didn't ask for it or expect it, you recognize that it's real and you give in to it.

You've talked with me about the idea and practice of "Two Spirit" people in Native culture, and how learning about this had a great impact on you.

The Lester Brown book *Two Spirit People* was decisive for me.[1] I had never heard of any pre-Freudian designation or concept about gay people that didn't say that gay people were sick, mentally ill, an aberration. I hadn't known that some Native communities believed that these persons had been touched by God, and are different for a reason. They serve a different role in the community. If you were born Two Spirit, it means that you were born for a mission—a teacher, a nurse or doctor, a priest—to serve the community in a spe-

Approaching the Mystery of Crazy Horse

cial way, not going off to war. It was the first time I ever felt honored by a culture. Not only am I not sick, or perverted, or an aberration, but no, this is a gift.

That's quite powerful.

Then the Christians came in. They thought that all of these things—the medicine men, the sacred tree, the Two Spirit people—it was all demonic, and began to teach the Natives that this was wrong. "You can't dress like a woman." It's the same thing we're dealing with now.

To make it into a sacred vocation is so beautiful, but can also be quite frightening. To be called out to have a special role in the community—like Crazy Horse or Black Elk or Robert Johnson—it implies a surrendering that can be painful. It cuts you off from other avenues that you might rather pursue.

Thank you for sharing this. I remember also learning from you about "third and fourth genders" in

Native culture.[2] For LGBTQ people, I can only imagine how liberating it might be to know that there is another cultural possibility than what we're currently experiencing in the United States—to know that there are cultures, much more ancient than ours, that practice an embodied wisdom and spirituality that is so affirming.

Yes, they recognize that this boy does not want to be a boy, and they aren't afraid of it. Because the Two Spirit people were "in between," so to speak, they had an intuitive knowledge across genders, so they could mediate conflicts in the family, between husbands and wives, and so forth. Learning about all this really affected me and, in a way, invited me to try to bring some of this into our culture, even if just a little bit.

As we've talked about before, it's hard to separate all of this for me from the dark history of the Klan in Colorado. Trump and his followers have brought all of this cruelty back to the surface. He's made it cool to be cruel, which is sad and ugly, but also terribly frightening for anyone in the crosshairs.

Mentors and Companions in the Lord

Fr. Bill, the story of your departure from the Jesuits has been told elsewhere, and I know it's a sensitive topic, layered with histories and various personalities. I understand that part of it had to do with an interview you did for Time *magazine in May 2002, defending gay people and gay priests who were being scapegoated during the church's sex abuse crisis in Boston.[3] Michael O'Laughlin writes that when you saw the story in the magazine, you were "mortified," and that it "felt staged." In black and red block letters, next to a full-page photo of you with your hands folded together in prayer, the headline proclaimed: "Inside the church's closet." As Michael writes, "Rather than joining a chorus of voices fighting against injustice, Father Bill was somewhat alone in pleading for compassion."[4]*

When I was called by *Time* magazine, I said I wouldn't speak unless they called me back and read me word for word what I said. The woman who called said, "Oh, we never do that." I said, Okay, then I'm not going to talk to you. The next day she called and said she'd gotten permission, so I spoke to her.

I knew it had to be as perfect as I could make it because no one would talk; but I had a chance to talk about Jesus in *Time* magazine. Every priest had turned her down. If you read it now, you'd probably say, "What is the problem? There really is nothing offensive here at all." But since gay priests were being scapegoated, I knew I had to do it. The article is still very good, but the awful title of the article is just one of those things they do to grab your attention. A friend laughingly told me, You know Billy, if it wasn't for "Spider Man," you'd have been on the cover of *Time*![5] Imagine the horror of that.

At that time, the whole thing was utterly taboo, so speaking at all was taking a huge risk. But I knew what I said was true and helpful. I received letters from Jesuits around the world thanking me. I kept them for a long time after; then during my last move, from Taos to Albuquerque, I finally threw them away.

I can't go into the trouble it brought me from my own Missouri Province of Jesuits. This is what I was told, and I believe it is true, that it was actually only a couple of people who wanted me out. It was made out to be an issue of obedience, but I don't think that's a fair rendering of what happened. I've chosen not to tell my side of the story,

because I know those who were involved are not permitted to comment on anyone who leaves. I could go into the depths of the whole situation, but they cannot respond. And I won't do that.

Many Jesuits who leave really try to play the victim, and it goes nowhere. This is a holy religious order of innumerable saints that has been around for five hundred years. Who am I to criticize them, when it was actually only a couple of people who wanted me gone within a huge brotherhood of about three thousand? I never really knew how much I was loved, until I left. I had been focused on a couple of extremely negative voices and missed the supportive, loving, positive ones. I suppose what hurt and confounded me the most was being asked to prove my fidelity or commitment to the Society, to a Jesuit way of being.

After I left, I had a commission from Creighton University to paint a triptych of St. Ignatius, St. Francis Xavier, and St. Peter Favre, a favorite of Pope Francis. Fr. Dave Fleming, my former provincial, commissioned me to do *St. Ignatius and the Passion of the World in the 21st Century*. He said to me, "Billy, everything you do, you do in a Jesuit Way. You are completely Jesuit." So, I was still doing Jesuit work. And I thought I was okay.

But my body reacted in shock. I had an operation for diverticulitis that spring where they accidentally nicked my vocal chords, and I couldn't speak for six months. Then I fell and had a massive retina tear in my left eye and had to be operated on again. My whole being was in shock and out of control because I'd been a Jesuit for thirty-five years, since age nineteen.

I was actually in Maryland at the time I finally left, keeping vigil for Phil Berrigan, who was dying. He died December 6, 2002. That night they asked me to do the burial. It was—I don't know what word to use—a magical, mythical burial, almost like King Arthur was being buried. It was winter, and everyone came out with torches in the night. I had spent days painting the coffin. We stood in the dark with these burning torches, remembering Phil. I came back to Taos around December 8 or 9, and left the Jesuits on December 16, the Feast of Our Lady of the New Advent. I

Triptych of Jesuit Saints: St. Ignatius, St. Francis Xavier, and St. Peter Favre

had planned to leave on that day so that I would associate the day with something joyful, and not just the extreme sorrow of the day I left.

Sometime in August 2003, St. Ignatius appeared to me in a dream. I know that sounds outrageous, but I know it wasn't just a dream. I can still see him as he was that night. He didn't say anything to me but looked at me with great love, strong love, and his gaze communicated, "I am not going anywhere, I'm still with you, and you're not going anywhere." At that time, I assumed he wanted me to return, and years later, I tried and failed.

Yet my relationship with his Society is really wonderful, and I've had the support of Jesuits like Jim Martin, Mike Tueth, Frank Clooney, Kevin Burke, Jim O'Brien, Mark Bosco, Steve Kelly, Myles Sheehan, Ron Anton, Bill Cain, and others. And laymen who work in Jesuit apostolates or universities, like Alan Mitchell, John Dadosky, Michael O'Loughlin, and you, Chris. Alan Mitchell brought me a medal of St. Ignatius from Loyola, Spain, which I treasure and haven't taken off since the moment he gave it to me.

This was all predicted or communicated, unbeknown to me, that August of 2003, in a dream, without a word from Holy Father Ignatius.

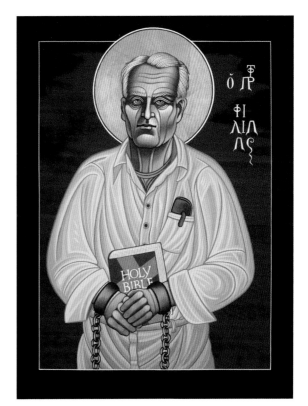

Holy Prophet Philip Berrigan

Thank you for sharing this part of your story. It's quite clear to me when you speak of Ignatius, not to mention the sheer number of drawings and icons you've done of Ignatius and other Jesuits, why you still consider him to be your spiritual father. Your icon St. John Francis Regis and Brother Bideau, *I can tell you, is beloved at Regis University.*

I'm incredibly grateful for my years in the Jesuits. I still consider so much of my work as being done for the Society, that it really belongs to them. But it's also my life story, always wanting to belong and not quite fitting the mold. As soon as I think of Joseph, or Francis, or Padre Pio, compared to the crosses that they had to carry, I'm doing okay.

Just today, while saying Mass, I was in between the consecration of the bread and wine when the names of particular people came across to me. That's happened to me a lot since I was ordained 44 years ago. I realize I must have gotten that from Ignatius, because he was always having illuminations during Mass. Why did this person's name come to me? It's important for me to tell the person when that happens—the consecration is such a sacred part of the Mass, and for someone to come into my awareness at that part is really beautiful and significant.

I want to say, Chris, that some of the people in the Jesuits that were hardest on me were also massively important to me as mentors. When Fr. O'Flaherty had us read Hans Urs von Balthasar's book on prayer during novitiate, there was one line that has nourished me for fifty years. Something like, "God might ask you to do something today that he didn't ask you to do yesterday." Nobody else says that. It opened me up completely. If you're locked into a single way forward, then you can't listen, you can't hear. For me, Fr. O'Flaherty was like Robert Lentz, a teacher who was tough but from whom I learned everything. Fr. O'Flaherty loved Dan Berrigan and he loved von Balthasar, and he gave them both to me.

Just like many of us experience in the church, or in our families, as I look back I realize there were equal parts conflict and equal parts mentorship. I want people to see me for my good parts,

St. John Francis Regis and Brother Bideau

and I also want to give that to them. I think of our faults as a way of acknowledging the wounds, the wounds of prejudice, non-acceptance, rejection, ego-striving, all of those. We all have them. I certainly have them. As I remember and speak about all of this, I realize a lot of things couldn't have happened, probably many of the icons, if I were still a Jesuit. God pulled me back so strangely. But that's a story for another time.

O Look at All the Firefolk!

Of the many Jesuits who have impacted you deeply, you speak often of Gerard Manley Hopkins, and how studying his poetry with a very gifted teacher in high school really impacted your artistic imagination. You've done two icons of Hopkins: Gerard Manley Hopkins: The Poet's Poet, *and one of my favorites in all your work,* Gerard Manley Hopkins amidst the Firefolk.

Gerard Manley Hopkins: The Poet's Poet

Hopkins was a glass torch. I always tell people you have to read Hopkins's poems out loud. So rich and absolutely unique. Words so lush, filled with longing love, wanting to express love, and misunderstood in his own time. He was considered by many as way too eccentric.

Forgive me, I know you didn't intend it, but this description sounds pretty close to your own life, your art, your personality—and how some in the church have responded to you.

He was a sad person in a lot of ways. When he died—it was June 8 in Dublin—his last words were, "I'm so happy." He was in his 40s. There are the dark sonnets, and all the things he went through. I think some of it had to do with being gay. I've read that he was a lot of fun to be with, and that the people he lived with didn't see his melancholy side. He certainly felt out of place at times in Ireland. The Irish "pain body," as we've talked about, is heavy. You feel it when you visit, and, of course, all of these revelations of abuse in Ireland are partly behind this.

Not many people know that he was an excellent artist. He did beautiful drawings, very much in the style of the Victorian era, the pre-Raphaelite era, very astute studies of nature. He really grieved over the loss of the wild. In this sense he is an ecological saint, responding to changes of the Industrial Revolution. In *The Poet's Poet*, you see the kingfisher, symbolic of the Holy Spirit, appearing to him as an apparition. There's a factory in the background, with smokestacks belching smoke. The other one, *Gerard Manley Hopkins amidst the Firefolk*, is taken from one of my favorite poems. "Look at the stars! look, look up at the skies! / O look at all the fire-folk sitting in the air!"[6]

I definitely have a side that is sensitive to tragedy all the time. It's gotten worse since my heart collapse. I'm way too open. It's like what my brother's first wife said to me after I came out of the coma, describing how she felt after her mastectomy. She said, "Billy, I would see a child and wonder where its mother was, and start crying." You become very vulnerable to the pain of the world.

Being involved with the church can also make you extremely vulnerable—reading, for example, about some of the terrible things that right-wing Catholics are saying about Jim Martin, attacking him all the time. Luckily, he has tremendous support from the Jesuits and a number of bishops. That's just our world right now. The Catholic world is just as divided as the political world. Never apologize, never admit you're wrong or that you have something to learn. Just keep pushing. Keep attacking.

Yet still, for all the divisiveness and violence,

there is so much beauty. "Look at the stars! look, look up at the skies! / O look at all the fire-folk sitting in the air!"

I think the image of a "glass torch" is from Paul Evdo-kimov, who uses it to describe the spiritual power a true icon can have on the believer. You've also described Daniel Berrigan as a "blowtorch."

Yes, a blowtorch of honesty. His vocabulary was as rich as Hopkins's. A total poetic genius called to be a prophet.

And a revolutionary against the war on children.

Yes.

Get Ready, Something Is Coming

We talked earlier about St. Joseph on the Rio Grande, *an icon that is especially dear to me as a father, and you mentioned* St. Joseph Flower of Jesse, *the young Joseph at night with his hand over the hollyhock as it rises from the earth. You said you wanted "to evoke Joseph's journey as a young man, before he met Mary, before the birth of Jesus, praying and trusting that God would reveal his life to him."*

In New Mexico, the hollyhock is called the "staff of Joseph." I wanted it to be a kind of apparition of the hollyhock growing from the ground. He's wondering what his life will be, and he goes out-side and sees this red flower bloom. It touches some part of his soul. "Get ready, something is coming. Something you could never imagine." These portrayals are not directly derived from the Gospel, of course, and imaginative render-ings of the lives of saints and the Holy Family can sometimes feel inauthentic or forced. But for some reason I have been really inspired by a few.

When I look at St. Joseph Flower of Jesse, *I can't help but associate it with* The Child Mary Soon to Become the Ark of the Covenant, *which you did not long after. I've never seen any images of Mary like it, nor had I heard of Mary being associated with*

Bill holding *St. Joseph Flower of Jesse*

The Child Mary Soon to Become the Ark of the Covenant

the Ark. Like the Joseph image, it invites us to contemplate Mary in the years before we meet her in the Gospel.

When I began my apprenticeship with Robert, I had already read many of the mystical lives of Mary, which go back to the *Protevangelium of St. James*, the ancient story where we learn the names of Anna and Joachim, Mary's parents. During the Year of St. Joseph, declared by Pope Francis in 2021, I found a mystical life of St. Joseph by Mother Maria Cecilia Baij, OSB, which led me to ponder the young Joseph and his gradual realization of his vocation. I put this contemplation into *St. Joseph Flower of Jesse*.

For years I had planned in my imagination to portray Mary, the Shekhinah, and the Ark, all in one image. I chose to make Mary about eight or nine years old, as if she too, like Joseph, was coming to a gradual awareness of some extraordinary vocation she would embody. This, of course, was all revealed to her by the Archangel Gabriel at the Annunciation. Most scholars agree that Mary was around fourteen or fifteen.

I will never forget when I first saw Thomas

Christ Unveils the Meaning of the Old Testament. Drawing by Thomas Merton. Used with permission of the Merton Legacy Trust and the Thomas Merton Center at Bellarmine University

Merton's mystical drawing *Christ Unveils the Meaning of the Old Testament* on the cover of your book *At Play in Creation*.[7] Once again, I realized that some contemplative concepts can only be represented through visual art. In 2022, at the beginning of Rosh Hashanah, I finally felt it was the right time to bring this symbolic, inner vision of a youthful Mary to life.

Merton's drawing is truly remarkable: a young Jewish girl sits in the foreground with vibrant eyes and long, dark hair, her face being "unveiled" by an older Christ-figure, who stands behind her. Merton rarely titled his drawings. In this case the title, Christ Unveils the Meaning of the Old Testament, *begs the question: Is she a figure of the sacred feminine, Proverb, Wisdom, Sophia, who "plays" before God at the dawn of creation? Is she the image and likeness of God who shines in each of us? To connect it to your image, Merton might say that we all bear, as it were, the "Ark of the Covenant" within us—the capacity for deep intimacy with God. Yet each of us must cooperate with God in our own discovery.*

I want to ask you about several other icons of Mary and Joseph, quite different from these. Let's begin with Mary Most Holy Mother of All Nations. *According to John Dadosky, one of your Jesuit mentors called this icon your "masterpiece." I have to agree. And John adds this: "I like to think of it as [Mary] preserving our planet from the negative consequences of climate change."*[8]

I think that work is prophetic. I still don't fully understand it. I tried to do different things, but I kept getting instruction about the way it should be. We've seen Mary on the globe, we've seen her stepping on the dragon. I didn't know what I could add to the iconography of Mary. I had to think about it.

And then all of a sudden, I saw her holding the Earth and the Holy Spirit engulfing the world in twelve flames, hovering above the atmosphere. Yes, I thought, that has not been done, I guess she wants me to do it. I can't say a lot more about that icon. How it came about is still a mystery to me, but I do know that it speaks to people.

Mary Most Holy Mother of All Nations

The Triumph of the Immaculate Heart of Mary

Yes, it does—for me, it is a breathtaking visual theology in lines and colors. It reminds me, as you have said, that sometimes more can be expressed in a single image than in many books about the signs of the times, whether it be climate change, racial justice, immigration, and LGBTQ issues, or the nuclear threat.

I feel that way about the film *Oppenheimer*.[9] It is really very different from any film I've ever seen. A most unusual visualization of scientific con-

cepts and realities that we inhabit right now—another way of saying, "Get ready, something is coming"—but that we deny or don't want to face. Artistically it breaks completely new ground and, I can't help but hope that our book touches people in ways that are also artistically unique.

Regarding the nuclear threat, your icon The Triumph of the Immaculate Heart of Mary *pictures Mary clothed in purple and blue, an anguished expression on her face, with an atomic mushroom cloud rising up behind her, rendered in shocking reds and blacks. Quite a different portrayal than* The Child Mary Soon to Become the Ark of the Covenant.

At the time I painted it, Our Lady of Fatima was so much in the consciousness of the church. Many were saying that it was her intercession that saved Pope John Paul II when he was shot. It struck me that Mary had appeared to the children at Fatima in 1917, during the First World War, and she had warned that there would be another world war, much worse, if people didn't turn away from war and violence.

Of course, the atomic bomb is the worst kind of war that anyone can imagine, and with the Russian attack on Ukraine, so many are anxious about the possibility of a nuclear strike. At the time I did the icon I was very close to Phil and Liz Berrigan—Phil had served in the Second World War—and I sent it to them. It was at Jonah House for some time, though I don't know where it is today.[10]

Recently the Ukrainian bishops wrote to Pope Francis asking him to consecrate the "immeasurable pain" of the Ukrainian people "to the Immaculate Heart of Mary of Ukraine and Russia, as requested by the Blessed Virgin of Fatima." In her vision, Mary says, "In the end, my Immaculate Heart will triumph."

Let me ask about St. Joseph Mirror of Patience, *in which Joseph leans against the wall, one hand to his heart, with an anxious expression on his face. You've said that so many fathers have told you that this icon of Joseph captures precisely what being a father so often feels like.*

The mystical life is harrowing. Joseph is being attacked nearly every day by someone, usually neighbors, who are riled up against him, because he's so good. So, I painted *Mirror of Patience* for all fathers who feel like that too. So far, every father who sees it sighs and says, I know exactly how he feels.

During the Year of St. Joseph, I reread my two favorite books on him, *The Mystical Life of St. Joseph*, which I mentioned earlier, and *Joseph Shadow of the Father*, by Fr. André Doze. I'd pick titles from the Litany of St. Joseph that called out to me, and so far, I've painted three images from the Litany.

Including your most recent icon of Joseph, St. Joseph Terror of Demons.

Yes, that icon was a response to what the right wing was doing with him. I came across an article on "Joseph Terror of Demons" about "reclaiming masculinity," where Joseph is holding the child Jesus, looking very militant, and Jesus is holding a spear and pointing it at a dragon. I thought, this is not how Christ used his power at all; it's not the way he handled conflict. If you want to reclaim masculinity, then let's look at how Christ and Joseph used their masculinity, how they used their power during their lives. *They don't need a sword, they don't need a gun.* A word alone from Christ would drive out demons.

It's very important for me to make this point. It's partly from being a gay man, never being looked at as a symbol of masculinity, and so having to discover the meaning of masculinity. Is it all posturing? Yet even today, with all the division in the church, all the news about the destruction of the planet, we still see beauty. It hasn't been destroyed yet. "Look at the stars!

In the studio, Arroyo Seco

St. Joseph Mirror of Patience

St. Joseph Terror of Demons

look, look up at the skies!" Who knows what may happen.

The Radiant Child (in All the People)

We don't often think about the spirituality of Joseph, or the spirituality of Jesus, for that matter. Talk about "Get ready, something is coming"! One wonders how Jesus prayed through all of these things he would experience, from childhood to adolescence — the hidden years of Jesus — and preparing for the start of his public life. It brings me back to the icon of St. Joseph on the Rio Grande, where Jesus is a boy, and how Joseph's cloak is partly wrapped around the child, covering his halo.

Joseph had to protect Jesus and his wife from shining too brightly before God was ready to bring them out. In that icon, it's autumn, a sign that Jesus is growing older, and they're walking along the Rio Grande. Joseph is aware his son is shining, and that he has to protect him. The moon

in the sky over the Sandias is Mary, so the whole Holy Family is there.

Once again, your work is about protecting the Child, guarding the light. It's about the flight into Egypt.

Yes. And you can snuff out the light of adults, too, by denigrating them, by censoring them, by mocking them. Sometimes when I'm presiding at Mass, I look out into the eyes of people, and I see adults whose light has been snuffed out. You can see it in their faces. When they were young, or maybe it's happening with their partner right now, there's someone who continues to oppress them, put them down, not want them to shine, to become who they are. And I've seen priests humiliate people too.

When I was working with people with AIDS, I came across a book called *The Radiant Child*, filled with stories of adults who were recalling the moment in their life that their light was shut out, when they were censored or shut down as a child. It was very powerful because I was working with gay men who, their whole life, had to hide, could not be who they are.

I'm reminded of Merton's meditation on Holy Wisdom: "She is the Child who is prisoner in all the people, and who says nothing. She smiles for though they have bound her, she cannot be a prisoner."[11]

That says it all, doesn't it? "Unless you become like a child...." We need to be nurtured by others, male mothers, and female friends, to really grasp and believe this in ourselves.

Don't we ever! Bill, I'm quite moved by your description of looking out at the congregation while presiding at Mass and seeing in people's eyes their present suffering, their inability to know or trust their own light. In another famous passage, at the corner of Fourth and Walnut in Louisville, Merton said, "There is no way of telling people that they are walking around shining like the sun."[12] It's a peculiar grace, he says, to be able to see others as God sees us, much less to see oneself in that way. For some people, as you say, the slow or sudden "extinguishing of the light" is happening right now in their relationships, their job, their families.

It happens in marriages all the time, between spouses, or parents with children. Some saints are called to stay and live through the suffering. Some are called to say, No, I can't stay and allow you to do this. To know the difference, which direction the Spirit is calling me, is one of the most painful matters of discernment. In any case, that was my experience with the Jesuits.

It's the flowering wound, as expressed in your art, something we all have to deal with when there's a breakdown. Can there be healing, new life coming to birth, from this trauma?

Most people in families understand this, some kind of break due to addiction, divorce, trauma, abuse, and we want to keep going; it's too hard to separate. I had an experience of this with someone in New York, and my confessor said to me,

"If you allow this person to keep abusing you, you are enabling them in their sin." That changed everything for me.

There are some people that we can't let back into our lives because they're abusive. You can't keep going back for more and more. Narcissists are like that. They rarely change. They might change through a flood of grace, but we can't provide that. Other situations we're called to stay and live through it.

Sharing in the Passion of Christ

As you know, Fr. Bill, your icon St. Henry Walpole, SJ, one of the English Jesuit martyrs, is very dear to my family, to my son Henry's story in particular. We light a candle in front of that icon every night before sitting down at the table to eat.

Yes, I did the icon with your Henry in my heart. He carries so much in his "pain body," you know? The pain body of Haiti, of being separated from his birth mother, of neglect in an orphanage, all of it, and he's trying to come to terms with these things now as a teenager.[13]

Henry Walpole was literally, and figuratively, splashed by the blood. He was a young man, just 23, right up in front of the crowd, when the Jesuit Edmund Campion was drawn and quartered, when they pulled his heart out—just horrible, unthinkable. He was so moved by Campion's witness that he wrote a little book of poems to honor him, at considerable risk to himself during the persecutions in England. He later became a Jesuit, and was himself martyred.

What does it do to a person to witness martyrdom? It's similar to what a living prophet or saint does to you when you meet them. It may not be comfortable, but it sears you. It marks you.

I had heard you use the phrase "splashed by the blood" many times, but I never understood it until you told me the story of Henry Walpole. In your icon, it's a bit unsettling to see that he has a crimson smudge across his chest. To be "splashed by the blood," you explained, is to be marked, body and soul, by trauma. It is also

Elijah McClain

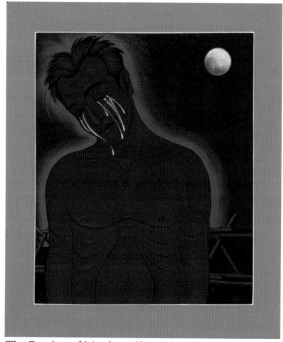

The Passion of Matthew Shepard

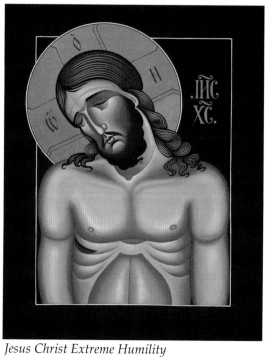

Jesus Christ Extreme Humility

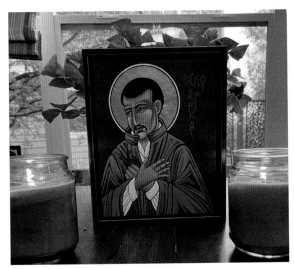

St. Henry Walpole

what a living prophet or saint does to you when you meet them, like Campion's impact on Henry, or Daniel Berrigan's impact on you, or Merton's impact on me. It may not be comfortable, but it sears you.

Your icon Jesus Christ: Seraphic Guardian of the Blood—*as strange as this icon was for me when I first saw it, I'm drawn back to it now in ways I can hardly understand. It seems to get to the heart of something you're trying to say in these images, and say urgently, about our world right now, and where God is to be found, where healing can be found, if at all. I mean the daily mass shootings, Ukraine, Gaza, Haiti, all the tragic murders, wars, all the violence. Can you speak about this icon?*

Any innocent person whose blood is spilt needlessly, their blood is Jesus's blood. It's that line in my poem about the Sisters: "They taught him a Secret of the Kingdom; To see the blood of Christ everywhere." Not just in the sunset or the Sangre de Cristo Mountains, though I do see it there, and especially in those struck by the stigmata: Francis, Padre Pio, Adrienne, etc.

In September 1224, while on Mount La Verna, Francis was visited by a vision of Jesus crucified, wrapped in the wings of a Seraph. Having tried to follow literally everything about Jesus in the Gospels, he had asked two graces of the Lord before he died: "Now, I'd like to share in your pain on the cross; and also, to know, How did you forgive those who put you there?" – my paraphrasing of the beautiful medieval text, "The Five Considerations on the Stigmata." His answer from Jesus was to receive the five wounds, and also the love of a Seraph. No one else has ever seen this vision of the Seraph with the exception of St. Padre Pio, who likewise received the wounds, in September of 1918.

In the case of Francis and Padre Pio the blood-soaked cloth bandages were used to heal people, and that's a great and awesome mystery of the cross and resurrection; of sharing in the passion of Christ; of miraculous healing coming out of suffering. And also—and this is hugely important to me—the mystery that no one can silence them, even after they die. Jim Douglass has said, "We kill our prophets twice. First, we kill their body and then we try to kill their reputations." But goodness will not be silenced. St. Thomas Becket is another powerful example.

Jesus Christ: Seraphic Guardian of the Spilt Blood

139

The bulk of my work is not about tragedy, but sometimes an individual's untimely death is "calling to me" to be memorialized. A person's death creates a huge amount of attention, and then, sometimes, change begins to occur. Daniel Berrigan once said to me, The first murder in the Bible is a brother killing a brother, and it's been the same ever since. In Genesis 4:10, God says to Cain, "What have you done? The voice of your brother's blood is crying to me from the ground." The truth, whether beautiful or terrifying, will find its way into the light.

We all have ways of reacting to tragedy, and my way is through art. In 1992, during the second year of my apprenticeship as an iconographer, I read about the terrible murder of a gay, 22-year old Navy seaman named Allen Schindler—this was six years before the murder of Matthew Shepard. *Jesus Christ Seraphic Guardian* is taken from a fresco by Giotto, and I dedicated it to Allen Schindler. It is almost impossible today, as you said, not to be overwhelmed by the violence of our world. My friend Nadia Bolz-Weber of Denver has wisely counseled, Pick one thing to concentrate on—it is simply impossible to give attention to everything. So, I listen to the people I feel are calling to me.

Fr. Arrupe, in his letter to me as a young Jesuit, affirmed the incredible power of art and his blessing of my work. Many years later, Sister Wendy Beckett did the same. Both have been a great impetus for me to keep on working. I learned in the AIDS pandemic that the art given to me was also saving my own life.

Thank you, Fr. Bill, you've helped me to better "see" this icon, which has long eluded me. There are two other images that I associate with the mystery of the blood and the wounds, as you've so powerfully described it here: The Passion of Matthew Shepard, which was the first painting of yours that I ever saw, and Elijah McClain. Over twenty years separates the violent death of these two young men—Matthew Shepard in 1998 and Elijah McClain in 2019. In your book with John Dadosky, John points out the striking resemblances between your Matthew Shepard image

and your 1993 icon Jesus Christ: Extreme Humility, *emphasizing "the parallels between Matthew's death and the passion and death of Jesus." "An aura of pain, perhaps from the shivering cold, surrounds [Matthew]. He is covered with blood save the tear streaks." You dedicated the image "To the Memory of the 1,470 Gay and Lesbian Youth Who Commit Suicide in the US Each Year and to the Countless Others Who Are Injured or Murdered."[14]*

I can hardly talk about him. It's the nightmare of every gay boy come true.

I heard his mother, Judy Shepard, say in an interview that she hoped that Matthew didn't die alone—she was heartbroken to think that he died alone, fell into a coma out in that field, alone. I put the moon in the sky above him to reassure his mother that he wasn't alone.

In Catholic symbolism, as you've explained to me, the moon often symbolizes Mary, who, as Catholics pray, is with us, "now and at the hour of our death." Matthew Shepard was beaten, tortured, and left to die in an open field outside Laramie, Wyoming, his body suspended from a fencepost. Elijah McClain died six days after an encounter with police and paramedics in Aurora, Colorado, during which he was injected with a powerful dose of ketamine to sedate him. His last words included him saying to the officers, while clearly struggling to breathe, "You all are phenomenal. You are beautiful and I love you. Try to forgive me. I'm a mood Gemini. I'm sorry. I'm so sorry."[15] What moved you to do an image of Elijah McClain?

He was a very gentle person, a lot like Matthew Shepard. He reminds me of Nat King Cole's song "Nature Boy": "there was a boy, a very strange, enchanted boy." The song ends by saying the boy is there to teach us that the greatest thing you could ever learn *is to love and be loved in return.*

Elijah is that nature boy—you remember him playing the violin for animals in the shelter—giving a love that goes around the world. He is a child of the light, still. And the light is always hunted by the darkness. It's Revelation 12: "I will go after her and all her children."

In an interview after his death, one of Elijah's regular massage therapy clients said that he "was not conditioned to the norms of this world." That description has haunted me. I've given prayer cards of your image of Elijah to colleagues at Regis, and one of them hangs in the hallway of our classroom building.

Splashed by the blood. The nightmare of every lesbian, gay, or trans boy or girl and every parent of an LGBTQ child. It's the nightmare of every Black child, every mother and father of a Black child.

It's why we keep lighting the candle.

CHAPTER 11

What You Gaze Upon You Become

The spiritual practice of gazing and the call "to share what you have contemplated" center our conversation as we explore more of Fr. Bill's icons and the vital, living presence of those whose witness he celebrates in his work. Servant of God Sr. Thea Bowman, Ukrainian martyr Fr. Nestor Savchuk, St. Lazarus of Bethany, scientist Rachel Carson, Sr. Dorothy Stang, St. Hildegard of Bingen, and even the Holy Spirit's action in "greening the world," at that moment when "life as we know it began to swirl from the void"—in each of these cases, says Fr. Bill, "An icon takes time to sit with, to converse with, to get to know, the same time it may take to get to know and love a friend."

As with the work of his teacher Robert Lentz, Fr. Bill's work celebrates figures both within and beyond the Christian tradition: a Jungian psychotherapist and spiritual writer; a young Irish woman who learns Zen practice in a Japanese monastery and is honored by her teachers as a "Soshin"; a ninth-century Sufi mystic and poet whose descriptions of oneness with God greatly impacted Thomas Merton. As an iconographer for some 35 years, Fr. Bill has gazed on innumerable lives of holiness and has shared what he has contemplated. In the words of Sr. Wendy Beckett, his icons "are not 'works of art' in the worldly sense but functional, living theology, uniting us to Our Lord as we look at them." We are always "growing into God," says Fr. Bill, citing Sr. Wendy. "It's the direction that matters." Finally, we reflect on the story of a young Catholic woman from Colorado who captured both of our hearts as this book was being brought to publication.

Chris: Across the years, Fr. Bill, your icons have covered an astonishing range of subjects; just so, the range of spiritualities expressed in your work, schools of spirituality, if you will, is remarkable. We've talked about Damien of Moloka'i, Joseph and Mary, Ignatius and a host of Jesuit saints who have shaped your spirituality, and there are musical artists like Joni Mitchell and k. d. lang, Bach and Pergolesi. But there are others whose names come up with almost equal frequency as sources of inspiration. I'm thinking of St. Francis of Assisi and St. Padre Pio, for example, and Adrienne von Speyr.

Fr. Bill: Ever since I can remember there has been Francis. I remember during theology studies, our teacher, Fr. Emerich Meir, OFM, said in his homily at the Mass on the Feast of Francis, "Francis had an I–Thou relationship to all of creation." Of course, Pope Francis builds his encyclical *Laudato Si'* on this relationship, citing St. Francis's hymn to Mother Earth, and the "groaning" of all creation that St. Paul writes about. But it was my bus trip in 1984 from Assisi to Mount La Verna, where Francis received the wounds, that has been burned into me ever since. With both

Francis and Padre Pio, as I mentionerd before, the blood-soaked bandages were used by their contemporaries to heal, and so the blood became a miraculous salve. I think that's part of what Henri Nouwen was trying to say in his famous book *The Wounded Healer*.

Adrienne von Speyer has meant a lot to me because she says things that will nourish me for 35 years, an insight that I couldn't figure out for myself but that helps me see what is going on. What she says about Clare of Assisi, for example: she says that Clare "is a born Martha," but the fact that "she also receives a share of Mary is something she owes to Francis." By disposition, Clare "would have preferred to leave contemplation to others," but she learns from Francis that "contemplation is the mother of action." And from this, "she allows herself to be fashioned into what God wants to make of her."[1]

When I read Adrienne's insight—that Clare let herself be molded by God—I realized I experienced this when I began to do icons. It's a heartbreaking insight in a certain way; it speaks to what it costs you to do something that God is asking you to do. When I understood it as "a busy AIDS priest arrives in Albuquerque," then I knew that God was speaking to me through her words. *Contemplation is the mother of action.* You're a painter now. You're not supposed to be traveling or going out and speaking in public. You've got to be alone and in relationship with these people, the subjects of your icons, otherwise they'll come out wrong. They'll come out like stillborns, which some icons do.

Contemplation Is the Mother of Action

You've recently completed your icon of Sr. Thea Bowman, who was a Franciscan Sister of Perpetual Adoration, and I know that you spent a better part of a year with her, researching her life and praying with her, while you wrote the icon. From our many conversations and from my own writings you know that she has long been one of my heroes in the church. What is it about her story that draws you in?

It's true, this icon came from almost a year's prayer, a lot of preliminary work, including a study—meaning a small version of the icon to work out some of the detail—and many spiritual meetings with those African Americans whom I have especially admired during my lifetime: Dr. King and Coretta Scott King, Malcom X, James Baldwin, Elijah McClain, and, of course, Sr. Thea. When I was commissioned to write the icon for Georgetown University, my next worried thought was why did Thea pick me? And how can I place a very vibrant, warm, extremely intelligent, literally glowing, often wonderfully "rowdy" woman—her own word about herself—into an iconic form? This question gets to the very purpose and meaning for having an icon, as opposed to having a photograph or painted portrait of someone. How to make Thea into an iconic presence?

I say "presence" because an icon is supposed to give you the opportunity to pray with Thea as she is now, in heaven. In other words, a true icon is more real than a photograph or painting. I know this is a very strong claim to make, but this is my own experience and that of many others down through the tradition. Also, it is more challenging when a prototype or original of an icon does not yet exist; when you are called upon to create the prototype. An icon takes time to sit with, to converse with, to get to know, the same time it may take to get to know and love a friend.

One vivid example comes to mind. In 1995, I painted or wrote the icon of the Ukrainian Holy New Martyr Nestor Savchuk. In 1996 an Orthodox Church in Atlanta asked to purchase Nestor because he had been martyred in 1993, and the youth in that church had a great devotion to him. It was very hard to give him up, but I had his photograph and I thought I'd frame it and he'd still be with me. After taking the icon to be shipped to Atlanta, I came back to my room at Boston College and his "presence" was gone, even though I had his photo. This is how I learned the very real presence and need for an icon.

I Want to Share My Treasures with You

Can you describe a bit of the process of painting/writing Sr. Thea?

I started by asking Louise Davis, an African American Catholic from our parish here in Albuquerque, to pose for me. Louise not only posed for me, she gave me many symbols to work with, including the acacia tree, with the word Umoja, or Unity, written beneath the tree, near the bottom of Thea's dress. This word means, "to define ourselves, name ourselves, cre-

Holy New Martyr St. Nestor Savchuk

ate for ourselves and speak for ourselves." She told me that this tree is the symbol of the African American Catholic community. I chose the Nsoromma star, meaning "child of the heavens," for her headdress: the Nsoromma ne Osrane, star and moon, a symbol of faithfulness. And finally, the ladder, Owuo Atwedie, "all people shall climb the ladder of death." Around her neck are leaves and berries signifying Thea's abundant life-affirming power while she was here on earth and now as one of our intercessors.

She also wears the Franciscan Tau Cross. I painted the cross red to honor the Franciscan charism of the five wounds, the stigmata. Above Thea is the dove, the Holy Spirit, painted in brown, signifying God is "all races." This brown Spirit I first saw and copied in a nineteenth-century icon of Mary called *Mother of God Your Lap Has Become the Holy Table,* in which Mary, the Child, and the

Holy Spirit, are all deep brown. Rays of the Spirit surround Thea as she opens her arms in "Marian fashion" to receive all of us.

In writing about Sr. Thea for your blog, you included one of my favorite quotes, which captures for me her spirit of childlike wonder and possibility, her ability to "work a room" and bring diverse people together. She says, "I think that children carry a message just by the way they are, and it's a message that needs to be heard. . . . My approach is: teach me. I will learn. I want to learn. I want to keep learning until I die. But I also want to teach. I want to accept your gifts. Please share your treasures with me, but I also want to share my treasures with you."[2]

She represents a whole group of people who don't feel part of this culture. In the icon, I made the Franciscan Tau Cross red to symbolize the suffering and the blood of the Black community. Of course, she really knew pain, sickness, and suffering in the last months and days of her life. But also, the experience of being the only Black woman in her religious order. Her father said to her, *Do you realize you'll be on the outside your whole life?* She said, *Dad, I'm going to make them love me.*

The truth is I've been exhausted since I finished Thea. When I finished it, I realized that I had been worrying that people who knew her would not find it resonant with their image of her. She speaks for the Black Catholic Church so eloquently. Yet, like Dorothy Day, she belongs to the whole church now. We never have needed her so much as we need her right now.

I agree. Her witness as "Servant of God," prophetic truth-teller and preacher of love in the U.S. Catholic Church, is being recognized and celebrated more and more.

What was coming through for me in doing the icon and researching her life was some of her pain, which she was not known for in public. She's known for her joyful singing and dancing, her singing with children in the classroom. I was focusing on being able to see her, and *to be seen by her.* Which might be difficult if she is singing and laughing and so on. I'm focusing on her inner life, the inner Thea.

You wanted to highlight her solitude, her receptivity.

When you do an icon, you want people to relate to the subjects as they are now, the heavenly Thea, something whom I hope people will sit in front of and feel they can talk with, especially Black peo-

Our Sister Thea Bowman

ple, who are being killed every day. As I said, the Tau Cross is for her Franciscan charism, painted red for the blood and suffering of her ancestors, which she was very aware of, and for her final years with cancer.

Vulnerable to the Pain of the World

I'm grateful you trusted those instincts. As you know the icon has meant a lot to me and Lauri and our daughter, Sophia, during her treatments for breast cancer. During her recovery from surgery we had the prototype of the icon hanging on the wall by her bed. For me, it was a comfort just knowing she was there. Again, these things are difficult to explain, so generally, I don't try to. But between Henry Walpole *and* Elijah McLain, St. Joseph on the Rio Grande, *and* Thea Bowman, *your work has become quite personal to me and my family in ways I could never have predicted ten or twelve years ago.*

Let me ask you about a number of images and icons that take us, as it were, to the brink of death, the fluid boundary line between the living and the dead. What's the story behind Lazarus' Tomb?

That was from my experience in Israel. I had this beautiful photograph that I took from inside

Lazarus' Tomb

St. Lazarus of Bethany

Lazarus's tomb, looking out at people on the out-side. I did the image from that perspective, from Lazarus's viewpoint, and the people calling him forth at the opening of the tomb are Jesus and Martha and Mary.

Your icon St. Lazarus of Bethany *takes the more traditional approach of icons, inviting us to look directly into the eyes of Lazarus, to try and see, as it were, what he has seen. And, as you suggest, to be seen by him, as he is now, from the other side. For me, it's one of the most striking icons in all your work.*

Lazarus is a very shadowy figure to me. He was overshadowed by death—just imagine, they wanted to kill him after he was given life again by Jesus! When I did him, I thought of my own heart collapse, and what it was like to die and come back. As I told you, you never get over it, that trip, you're changed by it. In his eyes, I wanted to convey the sense of some-

body that is here, but has also got a foot in the other world.

I did that icon for Jim Martin when he was doing his book on Lazarus.[3]

How do you imagine the passage through death, or what you have called our "Second Birth"?

When I woke up from my heart collapse, people asked me, What happened? What did you see? They all expected I had seen Jesus, my parents, or friends who have died, *something*. I was so dis-appointed when I had to say, nothing happened. Of course, they had given me a lot of medications so that I wouldn't be able to think, or dream, or anything.

I don't know who I'll meet when I go. My mom or dad, maybe Nestor, or some other saint, will come out and say, "Hey, I've been watching you for a long time. . . . You really caused me a lot of trouble!"

The Souls of the Just Are in the Hands of God *is inspired by the famous passage in the book of Wisdom, chapter 3. Like* Approaching the Mystery of Crazy Horse, *this one is also circular. I don't quite have words, but it says to me, though you feel the loss of your loved ones, perhaps desperately, you need not be afraid, they are being cared for.*

Yes, it points to the delicate, palpable presence of the dead, especially during the season of the souls, in October and November.

The Greening of the Earth

If we can widen the lens, Fr. Bill, to ponder the "wounds" of the earth itself, you've done two images celebrating women who dedicated their lives to the protection of the natural world: Environmental Prophet Rachel Carson *and* Holy Passion Bearer Sister Dorothy Stang; *and a third,* Viriditas: Finding God in All Things. *The latter is a very large piece commissioned by Loyola University Chicago, comprised of many panels, one of which features St. Hildegard of Bingen standing alongside St. Ignatius, and another panel with St. Francis receiving the stigmata. Of course, the title* Viriditas *refers to the "greening" of all things that Hildegard writes and sings about in her mystical visions.*

hopefully unfolds into insights that lead all of us, the whole human community, into action. The saints are grounded in the blood of Christ, which feeds the world as our mother's own blood feeds us in the womb. The Holy Spirit is seen just at that moment when God speaks the Word from Genesis: "Let there be light," and life as we know it began to swirl from the void. We are part of

The Souls of the Just Are in the Hands of God

Yes, the blood of Christ nourishing all of life and the cosmos.

When Jesuit Fr. Mark Bosco commissioned me to paint his dream of three saints holding up the world, St. Francis, St. Ignatius, and St. Hildegard, my question to myself was, How do they hold up the world?

Viriditas: Finding God in All Things was what came to me, a kind of sacred map that tells you where to go, but you have to actually make the journey. The map is a prayer, and the journey

that creation of life from the void, called to participate with the Holy Spirit's action in greening the world.

The piece is 5' x 10', one of the largest you've ever done, and was brought to Loyola in 2015. The frame is truly marvelous, itself worthy of contemplation. I can only imagine the sheer physical challenges of getting such a large work assembled, transported across the country and installed.

Environmental Prophet Rachel Carson
(after Hiroshige)

Holy Passion Bearer Dorothy Stang

Holy Spirit detail of *Viriditas*

Viriditas: Finding God in All Things

Yes, isn't it? I have a little book of prayers written by Hildegard with Robert Lentz's masterful icon of her on the cover, published by Franciscan Media. Looking through them, you could choose just about any prayer and it would speak to us today. Such is the power of Hildegard's connection to God.

Hildegard, Rachel Carson, Dorothy Stang—all of these women foresaw the crisis that we're presently living in. Rachel Carson was a very brilliant, very gentle woman with insatiable curiosity and deep reverence for the ocean, for mountains, for plant life. Her book *Silent Spring* was the red alert for all of us, a whole generation.[4] She was very stoic, hiding the fact that she had cancer. There's something deeply spiritual about her love for the waters of creation. She was mocked for it as a "nature goddess" in a lot of political cartoons and such. Of course, she was right.

Sr. Dorothy Stang was a lot like Nestor of Savchuk. She was given a task to do, in her case to prevent the rape of the rainforest of Brazil and the indigenous tribes who lived there. She knew

Yes, the frame was done, like all my frames, by my dear friend Roberto Lavadie, master woodworker of Taos. It sings the "Holy, Holy, Holy," just as in Hildegard's inspired chants, immersed in God, she heard "the Living Light, Heaven and Earth are full of God's glory." Christ the Deer, or Hart, is at the bottom standing in precious water, which nourishes all life.

The frame "sings," you said—that's a curious and wonderful thing to ponder.

Bill painting Holy Spirit of *Viriditas*

149

she had to stay, even though her life was so clearly in danger.[5]

Like Nestor, who was killed in 1993, at age 33—apparently by icon-thieving bandits who repeatedly targeted his church—and also like the monks of Tibhirine, in Algeria, who decided to stay and continue to pray and serve the people in the midst of civil war, and who were martyred.

Exactly like that. Again, you have to discern when you can't leave, that this is your vocation. This is where God wants you, even if staying is full of risk. Or, when you have to leave, that it's time to leave.

Claimed by the Inner Life

I want to stay with Viriditas *and the panel of St. Francis receiving the stigmata at La Verna—as you explained before, the five wounds he received during a vision in which he felt himself united with Christ on the cross. It takes us back to your painting of St. Francis receiving the stigmata for the Regis High School Chapel, and two other images:* St. Francis' Flowering Wound, *and the striking color drawing,* I Make All Things New.

A most mysterious part of the resurrection is that Jesus kept the wounds. In the post-resurrection accounts we watch him speaking and acting oddly, mystically, differently, and healing with his wounds. We all have wounds, but it takes courage not to hide them. Shortly after my trip to La Verna I joined the Secular Franciscans because I wanted to participate in their charism, which includes the stigmata, which Sr. Thea Bowman also participates in as a Franciscan. And that's partly why I have her holding her hands with her palms outward toward the viewer. Though you don't see the wounds, they were there.

I'm very moved by that insight about Sr. Thea, holding forth her hands in the icon with the hidden wounds. It's a connection I wouldn't have made on my own.

You've told me that Dorothy Day also had a deep devotion to St. Francis.

Yes, and to New York! I always think of Dorothy in New York. In my icon of her, I put her in brown to symbolize her Franciscan poverty, with the snow and Manhattan in the background. I wish I had met her. I got to New York in June of 1980, and she died in November. She really did like St. Francis, who was told, "Rebuild My Church," and Dorothy did that in America. She changed the American church.[6]

There are many other figures you've chosen to paint as sacred "images," Fr. Bill, that stand outside the official canon of Catholic saints, many who would identify as Christian, some as non-Christian, Hindu, Buddhist, secular, and so on. One of these is Robert Johnson, the Jungian psychotherapist and spiritual writer whose image of the "slender threads" has been so important to you.

The words that have always stayed with me are from his autobiography, words, I think, that his teacher Carl Jung said to him: "You have been claimed by the inner life."[7]

Almost all the people who come to me for counsel as a priest or friend are people claimed by the inner life, but often they don't know it. Whether they're seeking something in their job or their marriage, restless for some deeper meaning or whatever, once you tell them this, everything fits into place. They have a longing they can't explain, and they feel embarrassed by it. Robert Johnson gave me the words to tell them what that longing is, and I'm ever grateful for it. It's why I so much wanted to do him.

I had never heard of Maura "Soshin" O'Halloran before seeing your image of her. Her story is truly remarkable, and tragic, dying in a car accident in Thailand at age 27. But not before studying Zen at an iconic monastery in Japan—a first for a Western woman—being honored with the Dharma name of "Soshin," or "Genuine Heart/Mind," and writing what has become a classic treatise on Zen, her book

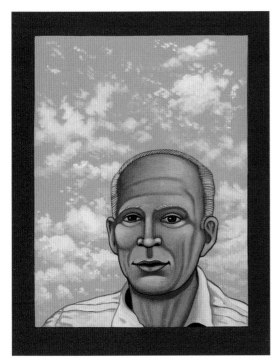

Robert Johnson in the Golden World

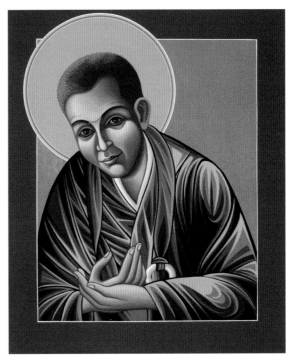

Maura Soshin O'Halloran

Pure Heart, Enlightened Mind. *Photographs of her are . . . simply radiant.*[8]

Her life really is astounding, almost shocking. To think that, by all accounts of those who knew her, she had reached enlightenment at the age of 27. I don't recall reading about any contemporary Buddhists who have reached enlightenment, whether Pema Chodron, or the Dalai Lama, or Joan Halifax. In fact, Pema will say, I wish I had attained it, but I never have. So, what is that grace that was given to Maura?

She was an otherwise "ordinary" person, born in Boston in 1955 to Irish parents, raised in Ireland from age four, completing a degree at Trinity College in Dublin in, of all things, mathematical economics. Who could have predicted what would unfold next for her? As Robert Johnson might say, she was claimed by the inner life and followed the "slender threads," allowing herself to be led.

Another "ordinary" saint you painted is "Holy Martyr Al-Hallaj," the ninth-century Persian Sufi mystic and poet. He was a lay teacher of Sufism,

Holy Martyr Al-Hallaj

151

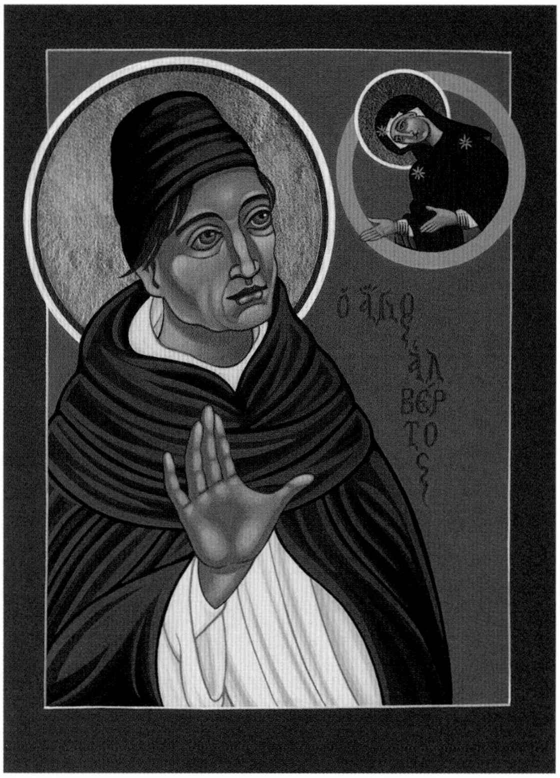

St. Albert the Great

unusual for the time, and a devoted husband and father, which seems to have aroused animosity in traditionalists, especially as his following grew.

I see him in jail, waiting to go out and be crucified. His son watched it happen. His connection to God, to Allah, was so profound that literally he said, "I am Allah," "I am God."

Of course, this opened him to the charge of heresy, of being an "incarnationalist," too close for comfort like Christ or the teachings of Christianity.

Yes. The four volumes on Hallaj by Louis Massignon are just amazing.[9] That a married man would be so taken up by God—so many of my married friends don't feel like they're equal to the saints and martyrs—but it's not true at all.

It was Massignon's work on Sufism, and through him, al-Hallaj, that so captivated Thomas Merton, especially al-Hallaj's description of "le point vierge," *literally, the virgin point—"a point or spark" in all of us, says Merton, "which belongs entirely to God," like "a pure diamond, blazing with the invisible light of heaven." It is "the center of our nothingness where, in apparent despair, one meets God—and is found completely in His mercy." In some of his most iconic passages, Merton translates this communion with the divine to the natural world: "The first chirps of the waking birds—*le point vierge *of the dawn, a moment of awe and inexpressible innocence, when the Father in silence opens their eyes and they speak to Him, wondering if it is time to 'be.'"*[10] *For Merton as for al-Hallaj, the inner landscape is inextricably tied to the natural landscape, the Earth, like a Child nourished within the Mother's womb.*

Yes—literally "God in all things"—like Hopkins's love for the wild, and his utter grief for the loss of the wilderness amid the factories of nineteenth-century England. . .

We touched on Rachel Carson, who, like the French Jesuit Teilhard de Chardin, was a scientist and also a kind of nature mystic. You also did St. Albert the Great, calling him "the Great Patron of Scientists."

I've always loved Albert and the Dominicans—my confirmation name is Dominic. He was very centered, dispassionate, like a lawyer, defending the faith against heresy, whereas Francis said, I won't preach against anybody, I'll preach Christ alone. And that appeals to me more, but I do have that other side. There are so many different gifts in the church, different spiritualities. I don't tend to fight with words, but I have fought with images, so to speak, sometimes disturbing images, like those of Käthe Kollwitz, and other artists, whose work really woke people up.

I love that Albert was interested in everything, like Hildegard. Of course, he was Thomas Aquinas's teacher, and the first to notice the genius in Thomas, whom they had called a "dumb ox" in grade school. Albert also had a great devotion to Mary, which I love.

To Love and Feel Loved in Return

There are two more icons that I find fascinating, Fr. Bill, almost "cosmic," in their portrayal of the Gospel vision: The Second Coming of Christ the King *and* St. John the Forerunner. *Both strike me as highly "Orthodox" in style, which is to say, very far from the European, American, or otherwise Aryan depictions of Jesus and John the Baptist that one finds everywhere in American Christianity and often in Roman Catholicism. You and I have talked about Susanna Heschel's landmark book* The Aryan Jesus, *which exposes how depictions of Christ in art, liturgy, and theology — all the public languages of the church — were used to reinforce racist tropes about Jews and every aspect of Nazi ideology.[11]*

When Susannah Heschel's book was published in 2010, I sent it to everybody. This was long before the recent rise in anti-Semitism, and now it's more important than ever.

I've taught select chapters from The Aryan Jesus, *and for students raised as Christian or Catholic who have never been exposed to these realities, much less thought about the Jewishness of Jesus, I can tell you, the book is a real shock to the system. But so critical for understanding the roots of anti-Semitism in a complex cultural stew too often infused with Christian imagery, language, doctrine.*

Fr. Bill, I know that Jim Douglass has used several of your icons, including The Second Coming of Christ the King, *as covers for his books.*

Jim has been a mentor and friend, and you can't imagine the honor I felt when he chose my art for his books. You remember I read *The Non-Violent Cross* just after entering the Jesuits, long before I actually met him, and it changed my life forever. Later he wrote *Lightning East to West: Jesus, Gandhi and the Nuclear Age*, based on Matthew 24, where Jesus is speaking about the return of the Son of Man, and says, "for just as the lightning comes from the east, and flashes even to the west" — and he used the icon on his cover.[12]

Some people interpret the Second Coming to

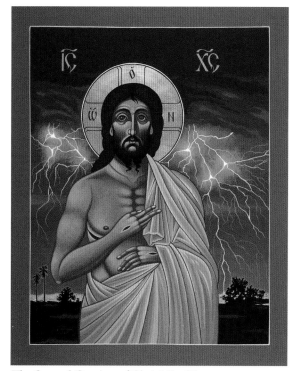

The Second Coming of Christ the King

mean that when Christ returns we will all realize Christ-consciousness, aware of the Christ within us. I believe in a literal Second Coming, but I didn't want Christ to appear frightening, like, "Okay, times up, run for the hills," like the bumper sticker, "Jesus is coming back again, and boy is he pissed." I didn't want that. I wanted to portray someone coming that you would love, and feel loved in return. I interpret the lightning imagery to say, "Don't worry, you won't miss it. You'll know when it's happening."

The icon resonates beautifully, I think, with Jim's portrait of a nonviolent Jesus, a far cry from the sword-wielding Christ of certain forms of evangelical Christianity who bears the saved up to heaven in the so-called "Rapture," while the streets run with the blood of the unsaved. I'm still shocked by how pervasive this narrative seems to be in the minds of many American Christians.

Tell me about your icon St. John the Forerunner. *I mean, wow, what a wild image.*

St. John the Forerunner

Sister Wendy Beckett

It is almost a direct copy of the sixteenth-century master Greek iconographer Michael Damaskinos. In Eastern iconography, John is called "the angelic man," and that's why he has wings, because he survived alone in the desert, led by the Holy Spirit. In Orthodoxy he's always right next to Christ, with Mary on the other side. I love John the Baptist. He and Jesus were almost the same age, maybe six months apart. John had the connection with God that Mary and Jesus had, not as intense, but maybe a little stronger than Joseph.

Fr. Bill, if I may, I can't help but associate this icon with Sr. Wendy Beckett, the beloved British nun and hermit who hosted a BBC TV program on religious art for many years, and whose portrait you painted for Robert Ellsberg. In her correspondence with Robert, recorded in their book together, Dearest Sister Wendy, *she offers a meditation on* St. John the Forerunner *that I find remarkable, unexpected, provocative in the best sense—which is to say, it opens me up in prayer.*

She says that St. John in your icon "has worn himself out with longing for the Kingdom, and he stretches himself out painfully to the Holy Spirit. The Spirit is there, but enclosed in his own heaven world, our world, the baptism world, which is not John's. It is an orb which the Spirit completely fills. And of his own power, John cannot reach it." For each of us, she concludes, "God will give us what for us is best. For John, it was the longing and the inability. Perhaps we who have the ability through grace do not have the longing."[13] Looking with fresh eyes at the icon, I can see the painful longing in John, the "reaching" but not attaining, that Sr. Wendy sees.

Henri Nouwen says that icons are not easy to "see" because they "speak more to our inner than to our outer senses."[14] The point is, I don't think I could have seen what Sr. Wendy saw in your icon of St. John without her help. But with her help, "all my eyes" come alive. I not only "see" but I feel John's own longing to know God, to draw near to Christ, a desire which, for me, remains elusive.

As you know, Sr. Wendy also considered the possibility of doing a book-length commentary on some of

*your icons, but finally decided against it. Her expla-
nation moved me deeply. "The thing is, dear Robert,
these icons are profoundly full of the presence of God
for me. To talk about them, I have to take some steps
back, and I can't do this without pain. . . . When I look
at [them], I fall into prayer, and that's it. . . . They're
not 'works of art' in the worldly sense but functional,
living theology, uniting us to Our Lord as we look at
them. The kind of distancing that is necessary for a
book seems to be beyond me. So will you please admit
my failure to our dear Father Bill? And I apologize to
you as well."[15]*

Sr. Wendy really helped me appreciate my own
work. It was very comforting to me, and very
humbling. She was very opinionated, but Robert
was able to stay with her, and open her up in a
way that I think very few others have been able. I
did that painting of her for Robert.

We're Always Growing into God

*There's a Dominican slogan you taught me that comes
to mind here, Fr. Bill, that you've said is very important to you. It's a Latin phrase that I don't remember
precisely . . .*

Comtemplata aliis tradere—to share what you have
contemplated, to share what you have seen. I've
always loved that saying, and maybe it's a good
description of our book.

What I would like for this book to be is what's
authentically been given for me to see, not trying to mimic other people's voices. I don't think I
have an agenda. I hope I don't, and I trust you so
much because I don't believe you have an agenda.

Images in Christian art are like the wounds
of St. Francis, the poverty of St. Francis. If Francis could find the places you were wounded,
the way you were poor, that was the doorway
through which he could relate to that person.
While doing Sr. Thea's icon, I watched a documentary in which she spoke of the two wounds
in her chest, the incision sites where she had
chemotherapy. It showed me a side of her that

isn't the usual happy, singing, glowing image of
Thea. It showed me her suffering, her solitude.

When I first read William Lynch's book, *Images
of Hope*, it struck me that part of his brilliance was
having come through real darkness himself, the
humiliation of being a priest and not being able
to access God.[16] They say the same about Mother
Teresa, who experienced long periods of profound darkness. It's one of the reasons why ordinary people, especially intellectuals, really love
Merton. With Merton I get the feeling that what
people love about him is that he's equally a regular person as well as a genius. He comes across
as not completely belonging to the monastic
world. "I still belong to your world." He stands
for something, like all saints stand for something.

Padre Pio stands for this capacity to cross
between the natural and supernatural without
distinction. Edith Stein stands for something
totally different from Padre Pio, worlds away,
but no less an image of hope. And all these people we've been talking about are images of hope:
Damien of Moloka'i, Dorothy Day, Dianna Ortiz,
Nicolas Black Elk, Sr. Thea.

Bill kisses his mother at his twenty-fifth
anniversary of ordination

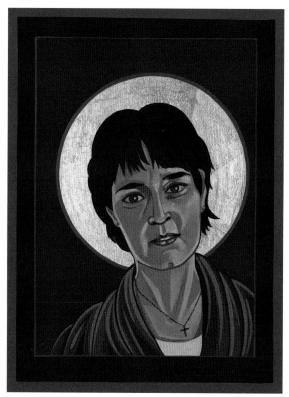

Holy Living Martyr Dianna Ortiz

we find hope, when the source of pain and darkness is the church itself? I'm thinking of your image of Alana Faith Chen (with Our Lady of Sorrows).

We both learned about Alana through a remarkable podcast created by a young man named Simon Kent Fung, who collaborated with Alana's mother, Joyce Calvo-Chen, to tell her story.[17] Much like Alana, who as a young woman had desired to become a nun but was deeply conflicted about her attraction to women, Simon grew up as a very devout Catholic who dreamed of becoming a priest, though he, too, was gay. When Simon heard about Alana's experience—while being counseled by a young priest and several nuns she had befriended in an intensively conservative Catholic community at the University of Colorado in Boulder, and after allegedly being encouraged to go through a kind of conversion therapy, she committed suicide— he reached out to Joyce to try to understand more fully what had happened. In fact, he moved from San Francisco to Alana's hometown near Boulder, Colorado, and for two years committed himself to telling her story through the podcast. Can you talk about this

We're always growing into God. I think this is the way to look at piety, as Sr. Wendy says, rather than you've lost everything and it's your fault when you don't feel the ecstatic rush you did in the beginning. "It's the direction that matters," she says. When I get into one of those places of dryness or even despair, I've learned to accept it, not to panic. What can I learn from this situation?

Artists or writers who articulate feelings that evoke this mystery, things I already had inside of me but didn't know how to articulate—like Adrienne, or like Jim Douglass in *The Nonviolent Cross*, a book that almost made my whole childhood make sense—these are some of the artists and writers who feed me.

Fr. Bill, so many of the subjects of your art, the people whose lives you have contemplated and shared with the world, exemplify a capacity to transcend terribly dark situations, suffering at the hands of others, through the light of faith. But what do we do, where do

Alana Faith Chen (with Our Lady of Sorrows)

image, why you chose to do it, and why learning about Alana so much affected you?

You remember when I was a high school art teacher, Chris, I always took my students to the Denver Zoo, because I wanted them to see the infinite imagination of God's creativity. At the time I was fascinated especially by zebras, because, unlike a horse, they seem to have no practical use. They are just beautiful, and no two zebras have the exact same pattern of stripes. It's no different than the way God fashions human beings with infinite creativity. But if you lack imagination, it's almost hopeless to really grasp this, and then it takes a tragedy like Elijah McClain, Matthew Shepard, or Alana, to open all your eyes.

I shared with you about how I went through "aversion therapy" as a nineteen-year-old Jesuit novice—which began with "nausea therapy" and then proceeded to shock treatments—and when I finally told an older priest mentor what was going on, he exploded with anger. "Billy, why in the world are you letting someone abuse you?! God made you this way and you're never going back to that doctor again!" Later on, that same mentor helped me understand that a person's sexuality is connected to everything, your art, your creativity, your *élan vitale*, your life force. The point is, it took a great deal of struggle and prayer for my own eyes to see what it means to be set apart, to be a "sign of contradiction" to the culture – that the hatred and suspicion and ever-looming threat of violence are not from God.

Another turning point came when I learned of the Native American concept of Two Spirit People, that LGBTQ people were specifically made, set apart by the Great Spirit, to serve the whole tribe as spiritual leaders, healers, artists, the go-between in family disputes, and so on. I was incredibly relieved to find a culture that highly valued and venerated the infinite variety of the Great Spirit's creation. In fact, at this very moment the Catholic Church is on her way to canonize Nicholas Black Elk. This would have been unthinkable in my childhood, and now we have Kateri Tekakwitha, too. When I served at

Taos Pueblo they told me, "We have our Indian ways and our Catholic faith. We have woven them together."

After over 50 years in religious life and 44 years as a Catholic priest, I can count on one hand the number of "authentically straight" people who, in my experience, truly care about LGBTQ issues. I'd like to warn young people that if you come across a person who is obsessed with your or any of your friends' sexuality, turn and immediately run away. There's a good chance they are hiding something and projecting onto you their own self-hatred. I have met so many people who, because they are afraid to be themselves, have had to come up with an alter ego, and you can feel it a million miles away.

We're always growing into God, you said. It's the direction that matters. It's when we fail to listen and learn and humbly grow as our understanding evolves, clinging to "old wineskins" for fear of personal or institutional metanoia, or loss of authority, or showing any kind of vulnerability to human contingency and difference, then people like Alana pay a terrible price. Our impoverished theological imagination, as you've suggested, makes a mockery of God the Creator. After all, what are zebras for?! By allowing no room for doctrinal development, effectively we've created an idol, a single, fixed image of "right thinking" about human sexuality. And idols always demand victims. It pains me to think of how many people are caught in this web of self-denial and loneliness and shame.

When I read about Alana, I knew I had to paint her, but initially I felt so much anger I couldn't even begin the drawing. And by the way, as you know, it's not just happening in Boulder, it's happening all over the country in parishes, campus ministries, and so on. It's the exact opposite of Ignatian spirituality. It's fear of the world, and teaching fear of the world, and Ignatius teaches finding God in all things, the almost infinite variety in creation. But eventually the anger passed and then came the grief. I cried for her, cried for her family, and I cried remembering my nineteen-year-old self. When I imagined, who is she with now? I thought of St. Thérèse, one of her favorites, but then I thought of Our Lady of Sorrows. Who better to reach down to catch Alana and bring her home?

The colors came naturally, her salmon colored blouse, the vivid blue background similar to the deep Colorado sky, the purple border and the Hildegardian/*Viriditas* green letters. As I painted

I listened to St. Hildegard's haunting chant, "O Rubor Sanguinis," and then I turned to Pergolesi's masterpiece, "Stabat Mater." Through the process of creating this image I think I have met at least some of Alana, and spoke with her during the weeks I was painting. How I wish I had met her.

CHAPTER 12

Then We Shall See Face to Face

"*To be created in the image of a (divine) other,*" *writes Jewish theologian Melissa Raphael, "entails that creation is necessarily relational—a face-to-face event—God making us present to one another. It follows, then, that the retrieval or even momentary restoration of a face is the restoration of presence.*"[1]

Our final conversation delves deeper into the mystery of prayer before icons, as bringing us into a relational, face-to-face event, a living presence that is "more real" than a photograph. From Our Sister Thea Bowman *to* Jesus of Galilee *and* The Risen Christ, *an icon that gazes out from behind Fr. Bill in a photograph taken as he raises the chalice during Mass, in Bill's art we are invited to behold the light of God shining from within all things, and gazing back upon us, through eyes of love.*

The experience of communion between the living and the dead is captured in the eyes of St. Lazarus of Bethany, *and for Bill, in Stephen Sondheim's musical* Into the Woods—*a sense of living each day and writing icons with "one foot on the other side." In the figure of Thomas Merton, Bill sees a prophet and priest who, in the midst of a century shattered by war, is "inviting us to bring Christ into our world, a world so desperately in need of beauty and love." Merton's awakening to God as Wisdom-Sophia recapitulates St. John of the Cross, who says that each of us bears a capacity and freedom to welcome God into the world. Like Mary, Mother of Jesus, "Each of us is the midwife of God, each of us."*

The image of feminine strength amid great conflict emerges in Bill's icons Holy Quaker Martyr Mary Dyer *and* St. Kateri Tekakwitha, *among many others. In* The Bride: The Church, *Bill seeks to convey the mystical heart of the church, the church "outside the building," an eternal aspect of the people of God "that can never be hurt, destroyed, or "disappeared." A remarkable interview for Catholic radio exemplifies the gifts of spiritual conversation, those relational moments of "God making us present to one another." Then we can say, with Sr. Thea Bowman, "Please share your treasures with me, but I also want to share my treasures with you." Hearkening back to the AIDS ministry, Fr. Bill reflects, finally, on the trajectory of his life as an artist and priest. "Don't worry, you are heading toward the shore."*

Chris: *When we were talking about your icon of Sr. Thea, Fr. Bill, you noted that an icon is "more real" than a photograph, in the sense that it seeks to bring us into the presence of a living person, as they are now, in heaven. I'm sure I didn't understand this in my youth,* growing up as a Catholic in the United States, where icons weren't at all part of my parish experience, much less my prayer. Statues, yes, and plenty of them, but icons never.

I think I understand it now—which is to say, I expe-

rience it in prayer with certain of your icons, like Sr. Thea, St. Henry Walpole, St. Joseph on the Rio Grande, The Passion of Matthew Shepard, *and* Mary Most Holy Mother of All Nations, *to name a few. Over time, these images, these presences as it were, have stayed with me, even when I'm not physically in their presence. Your icon of Sr. Thea, I feel her very much opening herself to the person at prayer before her. It's a living image, not static. You said, "I know it's a strong claim, but that has been my experience."*

Fr. Bill: By far the bulk of my icons—I think I've done at least 80 of Mary and the Child—are not heavy or sorrowful, not focused on the wounds or death, but joyful. Some I sincerely love and realize I would not be able to do them if I tried today. *Virgin of Tenderness of Yaroslavl* is one of my favorites. My teacher Robert was with me, as he was with a lot of my early icons. He would be in the room while I was painting, pacing back and forth, and he would insist that I go back in and make the lines perfect.

When I ended my study with Robert, I thought, I'll never be able to do icons on my own. I needed him to be there. But then I did *Mary Most Holy Mother of All Nations* without him, and many more. When I left him, he said, "You'll be fine, you know a lot more than you think." I said, No, I need three more years. But the Jesuits couldn't get me any more time. So, I had to go out on my own.

Virgin of Tenderness of Yaroslavl

relli film Jesus of Nazareth, *but for me, your image is much less ethereal, more grounded than Jesus in the film portrayal. You've told me that your favorite depiction of Jesus in film is* The Gospel of St. Matthew, *made in 1964 by the Italian director Pier Paulo Pasolini. Merton also had a deep appreciation for that film, and the Italian peasants who played all the parts.*

Then I Shall Know Fully, As I Am Fully Known

I want to ask you about Jesus of Galilee. *It's a close-up of Jesus's face, his light brown eyes gazing directly out toward the viewer. There's what looks like desert vegetation in the background and then, I presume, the Sea of Galilee and a light blue sky at the horizon. Unlike so many of your Mother and Child icons, done in the traditional Orthodox style—the number of them that you've done over the past 30 years is truly astonishing, and many are indeed quite joyful—Jesus in this image is embodied, earthy, human. He reminds me of the actor who plays Jesus in the Franco Zeffi-*

Jesus of Galilee

Here's my question: How does one go about depicting Jesus? What do you remember about creating this painting? The eyes, the lips, the full beard—it really does draw me in.

That's a wonderful question. Thank you. I've never talked about this painting before.

Jesus of Galilee was initially a drawing, which I made into a painting for Jim Martin. Almost every year Jim goes to the Holy Land with groups of pilgrims. I imagined Jesus just before going into the synagogue in Galilee and giving his "inaugural" speech, reading from the prophet Isaiah, "The blind will see, the lame will walk," and saying that this Scripture is being fulfilled now. I was conscious of him coming out, so to speak, as who he was, and then the reaction. Everyone was shocked when he rolled up the scroll. What is he saying? Who does he think he is?

I was trying to picture that moment of awareness in Jesus that he was now a public figure, that he had gone from the hidden life to the realization that the time had come to "do my Father's

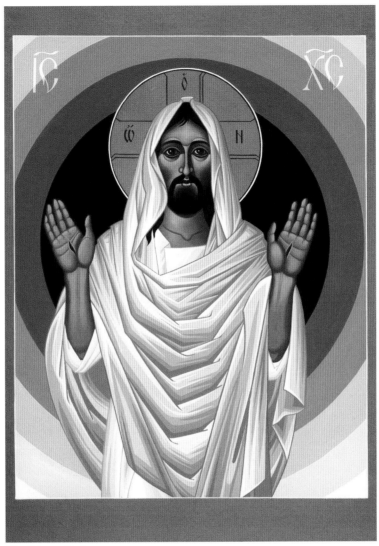

The Risen Christ

work," and he knew the hostility that would come to him as a result. Maybe a sense of conviction and a little bit of terror. He wouldn't have sweat blood in the Garden if he didn't know human terror.

I'm seeing it differently now in light of Luke's dramatic account of the beginning of Jesus's ministry in Galilee—deeply human, Jewish, prophetic—the whole story is touched with pathos. To stay with Jesus for a moment, there's a remarkable photograph that was taken of you while presiding at Mass with your icon The Risen Christ *in the background. You are raising the chalice during the Eucharistic prayers, as Christ seems to be looking directly toward you and toward the viewer. Of course, it's the image we chose for the cover of this book.*

A huge part of my vocation, and a part of my being gay, is that I'm a priest. Outside of New Mexico not many people see me in that role. The focus on the eyes of Christ in that photograph is really powerful. In the picture, it seems to me that the eyes of Christ that I painted have come alive.

161

Fr. Bill presiding at Mass

It's kind of a magical image, like Hopkins's "All my eyes see." The original icon is small, 18" x 24," and it was done for the Church of the Risen Christ in Denver. The church in Albuquerque had the reproduction enlarged, so it's easy for viewers to feel the eyes of Christ looking straight into their eyes.

For me, the photograph beautifully evokes the heart of your vocation, your love for the church, your love for the Mass. There you have your priestly vocation and your artistic vocation in a single photograph.

I think you're right, Chris. It was taken by a parishioner, Deborah Johnson, without me knowing it, and I'm very grateful.

I've just finished a new icon of Merton, and there are a handful of photographs of him saying Mass. It's not a side of Merton that people often

remember. But it was clear that he very much loved the Mass, and he loved saying the Mass.

Yes, Gregory Hillis writes about this in his wonderful book Man of Dialogue.[2] *I want to come back to your new Merton icon in a moment, but let's stay with your image of Christ a bit longer. I'm thinking of your drawing of the Incarnation, the one you did at your father's bedside when he was dying. The drawing is so unexpected and evocative, centered not on the adult Jesus or the Risen Christ but the infant Jesus and the Nativity.*

All of these diverse images of Jesus in your work move me to ask about your understanding of the Incarnation. The prayer cards you passed out during your AIDS ministry often included the quote from Colossians 3:11, "There is only Christ: He is everything, and He is in everything." How does this sense of Christ, Christ as "in all and for all," touch your faith life today?

From a prayer card during the AIDS ministry

God Is My Gift, Himself He Freely Gave Me

I would quote one of my favorite Jesuits, Robert Southwell, in his poem "The Nativity of Christ." "Behold the father is his daughter's son, / The bird that built the nest is hatch'd therein." Only a deeply spiritual person could ever come up with those words. Robert is expressing his shock before the mystery of the Incarnation. My God, *God has become a baby.*

Holy Poet-Martyr St. Robert Southwell, 1985
Illustration for Jesuit Community Christmas card, Manhasset, Long Island

I love his poetry so much because he is such a pure soul. There's no artifice. He could see with the eyes of a child but also an extremely masterful intellect and use of words. They still teach his poem "The Burning Babe" in schools in England. I don't know that I could say it any better than Robert Southwell.

In the "The Nativity of Christ" he says, "God is my gift, Himself He freely gave me, / God's gift am I, and none but God shall have me." It's a beautiful vision of the human vocation—"God's gift am I"— not unlike Irenaeus: by virtue of the Incarnation, we dare to affirm something about us: "The glory of God is the human person fully alive." Do you see a kinship between Southwell's and Hopkins's poetry?

Oh yes. I wrote an article on Southwell many years ago, "A Child, My Choyce," which touches on the strong resonances between them. Hopkins was aware of Southwell, one of the few Jesuit poets who preceded him. In the article, I bring in the famous semiologist Roland Barthes, who says in his essay on Ignatius that the Spiritual Exercises really creates a distinct school of writing, because Ignatius has you activate the imagination when you're praying. The poetry of Southwell and Hopkins totally confirms that beautiful insight for me.

Really this takes us back to *Jesus of Galilee*. What did he feel? What did he know? What did he see? What impact did the experience of being rejected by his own people have on his heart?

Yes, even with Jesus, perhaps especially with Jesus, Ignatius would want us to activate all the powers of imagination to know him, as it were, to walk with him, to love him as a whole person, from the inside. It's much like your icon of Lazarus, the intense focus on the face, the knowing look in his eyes, having died and come back while now grasping something of the other side.

Yes, and Lazarus's life was immediately threatened, it says in the Gospel of John. As I men-

163

tioned earlier, after he was raised from the dead, they wanted to kill both him and Jesus.

We began our conversations, Fr. Bill, with the story of your heart collapse, which happened in 2012. You said that experience was much on your mind when you did Lazarus. It's been twelve years since that remarkable event, a near-death experience in your life.

And I'm still not back.

You've still got one foot on the other side.

A little bit. That's why I could do Lazarus the way I did him. I've never gotten back to the way I was before that time, fully on Earth. In a sense it's how we all live right now, part here, part there. During the AIDs ministry, the young men who were dying would often tell me that their relatives or someone they loved who had passed was visiting them and "coaching" them into the process of coming home, of letting go. Almost any hospice doctor or nurse will tell you exactly the same thing.

During that time, I saw many Broadway shows, but none affected me more than Stephen Sondheim's *Into the Woods*. The words "sometimes people leave you halfway through the wood" were too close for comfort, and would just afflict my heart. I never got used to these young men dying by the thousands, but I accepted my vocation to accompany them right to the doorway.

Often, they would die before I could get back to the hospital, and when I went back in and found

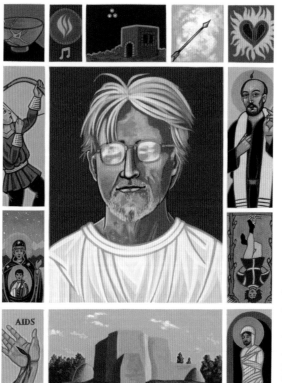

Self-Portrait with Symbols

they had gone, I'd go outside in a kind of violently forced trance, walking up and down Manhattan for miles to get my bearings. It was as if some huge part of me had left too, or wanted to, and walking was my way of pounding the earth as an assurance that I was still here. I identified with the image of the tarot card "le pendu," or "the hanged man," halfway on earth and halfway in the realm beyond life.

Every year on November 2, I place a large scrapbook filled with pictures and names of people who have passed into God beneath the Eucharist at Mass and pray for them. The psychologist Carl Jung thought of death as a wedding. Right before he died he asked a friend to drive him around his native villages, and the car was joyfully halted by several weddings. This delighted him.

Sondheim's Into the Woods *really captures this sense of walking through the world "part here, part there" and reassuring us that nobody, on either side, does so alone. "Hard to see the light now, just don't let it go. Things will come out right now. We can make it so. Someone is on your side, no one is alone." You placed the hanged man in the border of your second self-portrait painting,* Self-Portrait with Symbols, *2014, right there with St. Ignatius, the archer and the arrow, and the famous adobe church of Ranchos de Taos; there's also an image of Lazarus, still wrapped in burial cloths.*

Going back to your Lazarus *icon, much like Jesus of Galilee, it really has a narrative quality, the eyes filled with an awareness of something incom-*

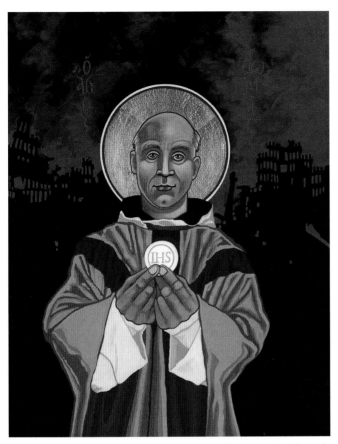

Holy Prophet Thomas Merton: Gaudete! Christus Est Natus!

municable. In a similar way, your new Merton icon expresses something that I think very few images of Merton have captured. Can you say a word about the experience of writing this icon, Holy Prophet Thomas Merton: Gaudete! Christus Est Natus!

Offering Christ to a Broken World

When I was commissioned to do a new Merton icon by the Thomas Merton Center, the Merton archives in Louisville, I found it extremely daunting, but also a blessed opportunity to find a part of Merton that I felt was often unrepresented, his priesthood. Not only his priesthood in the Roman Catholic Church, but his priesthood for and to the entire world. In the many books I consulted, I was acutely aware of his immersion in one war after another, which followed him all his

life. Like Jesus himself, Thomas was born "into this demented inn," a world afflicted by violence and continual war. Because he died December 10, 1968, I waited until Advent to begin.

In 1968, Gaudete Sunday was December 15, just five days after his death. There are only two times in the liturgical year when the vestments for Mass are rose or pink colored, the liturgical color signifying joy. These two Sundays are Gaudete Sunday, the third Sunday in Advent, and Laetare Sunday, the fourth Sunday in Lent. I chose to portray Thomas in the vestments of Gaudete Sunday, something he would have experienced that year, 1968, in heaven.

I am definitely not a Merton expert, but I know that the Eucharist is the center of the life of most every priest I have known or know now. We don't always talk about it, because it's something that is so much a part of our lives that we all hope it should be easily seen. I saw that clearly in Thomas's life.

In this icon Thomas offers Christ to a broken world. The debris of violence and war clutter the background behind him. It could be the debris of any war, the tragedy of 9/11, or the present wars in Ukraine and around the world. He emerges from that broken world, from which his life and work continue to minister and contribute to the eventual arrival of the Kingdom of God. In this icon Thomas is inviting us to bring Christ into our world, a world so desperately in need of beauty and love. We are each given absolutely unique ways to do that.

I have to say, as a longtime Merton reader and scholar, I was overcome with emotion when I first saw this icon. The warmth of his eyes, the brilliance of the vestments, the offering of Christ in the Eucharist against a background of devastation—it brings together so much of his witness, not least his meditation on the Incarnation, one of his most mature, prophetic, even apocalyptic essays, "The Time of the End Is the Time

165

of No Room." "Into this world, this demented inn, in which there is no room for him at all, Christ has come uninvited."[3]

Merton was just 53 when he died, leaving behind a legacy of dialogue and friendship with artists, scholars, and practitioners of other traditions. In a way, he did what Robert Lentz would do with icons, finding holiness among people of great cultural and religious diversity, a practice you would follow.

When I was a child in the 1950s we were not allowed to go into any church that was not Catholic, let alone any synagogue, temple, or mosque. Native American religion was considered paganism as were all Eastern religions. At the same time, Merton was beginning to scan the entire world's religions in a Spirit-led search for the similarities in our common need and common journey into God.

By age 24, when I was teaching at Regis High School, I was required to teach St. Mark's Gospel and Houston Smith's book *World Religions*. A decade later, in 1983, during the AIDS ministry, I was speaking to people of every faith and performing funerals for people of no faith and all faiths. What had happened to open the church to embrace the world instead of condemn it?

Part of it, of course, was Vatican II and the great theologians who had begun to dialogue with the reformed churches and world religions: von Balthasar with Barth, de Lubac with Buddhism, Rahner, Schillebeecxk, and even Teilhard de Chardin, with the entire cosmos. But most of all, I believe, it was Thomas Merton who gave us "permission" to engage and respect people of all faiths. Here is a man whose insatiable spiritual curiosity led him into dialogue with not only other Christian denominations but also with the world. As I mentioned, Dan Berrigan said it took him ten years to get over Merton's death. So many of my friends feel the same way about his impact in their lives.

Your first Merton icon, Holy World Evangelist Thomas Merton, *is based on a well-known photograph of him standing in front of the hermitage, wear-*

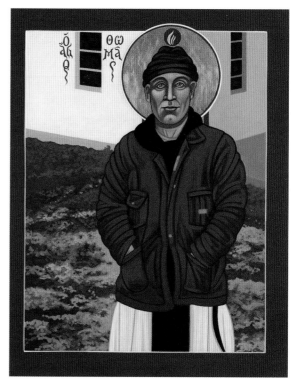

Holy World Evangelist Thomas Merton

ing his denim jacket and wool cap in the winter. I remember you calling me on the phone to ask about the photograph. Is that snow on the ground, or frost, you asked? Which would be more likely in Kentucky during winter?

Oh my gosh, I forgot about that. I remember you saw the flame above his head as a figure of Sophia, of his longing for Sophia. He was such a genius and master of many disciplines in the theological world, from the early church fathers to the Russian sophiologists—whatever it was, he could master it. His longing kept him moving, finally toward Asia, always growing. I love that about him, I love that about Picasso, about Joni. They couldn't stay in one isolated section of reality.

God's Sophia Took a Body

Your icon of Hagia Sophia Crowning the Youthful Christ *was indirectly the subject of our very first meeting, via mail, when you wrote me a letter not long after my book on Merton and Sophia was published.*

You told me you had just completed an icon inspired by a drawing of Sophia included in the book, where Sophia is crowning the boy Christ, done by Merton's friend, the Viennese artist Victor Hammer.

Yes, and I thought, Why is she not crowning the adult Christ? What is Sophia saying about the adolescent Christ? I thought it must be that passage from Luke about the boy Jesus, "He grew in wisdom and stature before God and human beings. . . ." She's crowning him as he grows in wisdom. I loved doing that icon. I wanted to make her red, because Sophia is always red in the Eastern tradition. But it's significant that she's crowing the youthful Christ, and important to ask, Why the boy Jesus?

There's also the passage from Proverbs 4, which Merton invokes in his prose poem "Hagia Sophia": "Wisdom will honor you if you embrace her / She will place on your head a fair garland / She will bestow on you a crown of glory." But for me, too, the icon evokes the "hidden years" of Jesus. It's a curious and marvelous gap in the Gospels that invites us to imagine what those years were like.

I spent a lot of time with the "hidden years" when I was working with AIDS. I wrote a poem about it, which reflects my longing to have that kind of hidden life, which I finally got when I began icons.

Sophia in your icon looks Native American to me, with the rounded cheek bones. Who is Sophia to you?

When I was at Wisdom House in Connecticut, they had a pamphlet about her, where Origen is quoted. Origen said, "God's Sophia took a body and became like every other crying child." In John's Gospel, the Word became flesh. But in Origen, Sophia, or Wisdom, took on flesh. And it makes sense to me, because in Proverbs 8, you see her playing before God during the creation. Who is she? Is she the Second Person of the Trinity before he took a body? I don't know if that is heretical, but it makes sense to me.

Hagia Sophia Crowning the Youthful Christ

Holy Quaker Martyr Mary Dyer

You told me once that when Sophia first came into your consciousness, while studying Eastern iconography and liturgy, she came not as a pleasant apparition but as a flashing red light, a warning, a kind of prophetic figure warning us especially about the planet. There is an element of fierce feminine or maternal love in her.

Something about her, I think, has to do with the protection of creation, as she is so much tied to creation imagery in the Wisdom literature. In the West, Joyce Rupp has written a lot about her, and Elizabeth Johnson, and Merton, too, of course. But as you know, the figure of Sophia is very controversial in the East. Trying to make Sophia into a divine being is anathema. What if she was and is Christ, a figure of divine-humanity, the embodiment of love in the heart of God from "before the beginning"? In the Gospel of John, Jesus speaks, I think, exactly like Sophia speaks.

As you know the last part of Merton's "Hagia Sophia" centers on Mary, the mother of Jesus, as an embodiment of "created Sophia"—which is to say, Mary is the prototype of our capacity to be receivers and bearers of Christ, God-bearers, doorways to God's Incarnation in the world. It is through her consent, says Merton, through Mary's "wise answer"—"Let it be done to me"—that "God enters without publicity into the city of rapacious men." Not incidentally, St. John of the Cross, in an Advent poem on Mary, also describes each of us as heirs of her capacity and her freedom to welcome God into the world. "Each of us is the midwife of God," he writes, "each of us."[4]

The Gates of Hell Cannot Prevail Against You

Fr. Bill, I mentioned earlier how John Dadosky was so struck by the prominence of the feminine in your work, and that even your images of holy men and boys— Joseph and Ignatius and the Child Jesus—reflect a tenderness and nurturing quality not always reflected in religious art or Christian piety. If I may, I want to ask about a number of icons that elevate feminine love and strength in the midst of great conflict. What inspired you to create Holy Quaker Martyr Mary Dyer?

St. Kateri Tekakwitha

Absolute perseverance. What happened to her symbolizes so much that's going on today, where one sect of Christianity, or rather a cult, wants to make Christianity the religion of the United States.

The Puritans left England and came to the New World for religious freedom, and then they attacked the Quakers. Mary Dyer was the last they put to death before the practice was forbidden. And, like Franz Jägerstätter, Mary Dyer had children who were still living. What a terrible and powerful witness. So, the Puritans leave religious persecution in England only to practice it against other groups. This inability to allow people to express their religious life is still happening today. Now it's roaming the halls of Congress, this gun-toting Christianity that wants to kill people for being different. It hasn't ever left us.

I shudder to think how right you are.

Tell me about your icon of St. Kateri Tekakwitha.

She was Mohawk, very quiet but strong, raised to be stoic about pain. The Iroquois, if they caught you, would torture you. So, she had to learn how not to show vulnerability or pain. She would never wear shells and the adornments that the other girls wore, and they hated her for it. She was bullied a lot. But the boys saw how strong she was and wanted to marry her.

She met the Jesuits, became a Christian, and was a very deep, contemplative person. After she died, she appeared to a Jesuit with the sun flaming behind her, almost like Guadalupe. In the icon, I wanted to symbolize the roughness of her life, with the jagged mountain surface beneath her, and then picture her transcending it, rising above it, in the way she appeared to the Jesuit after her death.

I want to ask you about The Bride: The Church, *but before you respond, I have to confess that I have a hard time connecting with this painting. First, the image of the church as a bride was never part of my Catholic piety growing up. Later it struck me that it was often used theologically to justify an all-male priesthood. But second, to portray "her" as under attack, as you do, when often it is the church, so full of clericalism, homophobia, and centered around male power, that itself is too often producing victims. Please help me understand this image, and what you mean to express by portraying the church as bride.*

This is another image, not a commission, that I really wanted to do. In 1992, the church in New Mexico was embroiled in scandal. There was a story on the CBS TV show *60 Minutes* about our bishop, Archbishop Sanchez, where they interviewed three women who said they had

relationships with him. All of a sudden, he was gone; they "disappeared" him. It was a horrible feeling for me personally and for all of us in the church in New Mexico, like everything went numb.

After that, I thought, we can no longer think of the church as the Vatican, or as St. Peter's Basilica, or as anything that can be destroyed. I began to read Henri de Lubac's book *The Splendor of the Church*, which was written when he was silenced by the church, and this image of the church as bride began to emerge.[5] And the bride, the true mystical heart of the church, is something that you can never touch.

I borrowed the image of the hands from a Fra Angelico painting, where Jesus is being attacked with sticks by hands seeming to float in mid-air. The hands are holding swords and trying to attack the bride, from within and from without. She is holding up the baby, marching forward through history, pregnant with the church, while everyone is trying to attack her. She has a radiance of protection around her, and she can never be hurt. It's the church that Jesus described when he said, "The gates of hell cannot prevail against you." To get through that terrible period I had to visualize something about the church that can never be hurt, destroyed, or "disappeared."

You say that the bride is attacked "from within and from without." By "within," I gather you mean the sexual abuse crisis and scandals surrounding church officials linked to power. Despite all of this—the swords threatening to cut her down—she walks through history unscathed, protected by the Holy Spirit, represented by the dove in your icon; by God the Father, which is the hand reaching out in the upper right corner; and the Son, the infant Jesus, the child on the medallion she holds high over her head. Your explanation, and the backstory, certainly helps me understand better, though "seeing" the church as you see, I admit, will take some work.

I can say with some certainty, and joy that I've experienced what you call the "untouchable" element of the church most palpably in Black Catholic parishes,

The Bride: The Church

where, "despite it all," an intimacy with Jesus crucified and risen and the flame of the Holy Spirit continues to burn brightly. I'm sure I felt it in the faith of my
parents, by a kind of mysterious osmosis, and in many
of the women religious who taught me as a child. I see
it every day in the commitment of many colleagues at
the university and in the theological community, religious and lay alike, who have spent much of their lives
and scholarship dedicated to the teaching of young
people, to keep the "pilot light" of faith burning in the
next generation.

Yes, the church in so many ways "has left the
building." But it doesn't mean she is lost.

The Gifts of Spiritual Conversation

*Fr. Bill, I want to mention an interview you did
recently for a radio program on The Catholic Channel
with Sr. Marie Pappas.[6] I've listened to it many times,
and there's something quite beautiful in the way that
the conversation unfolds. She begins with a shower of
praise for your work, which you found quite disarm-
ing, you later told me, having gone into the interview
very nervous and uncertain. In any case, it is clear
that she put you at ease early on, and then the real
sharing begins.*

*At one point in the conversation, you tell Sr. Marie
about being abused when you were five, and she was*

The Mother of God Overshadowed by the Holy Spirit

clearly quite moved by it. She said, "I have to tell you, when the stories were first coming out about the abuse crisis, I just sat in front of the TV and wept." While she understood from your story that your abuse didn't have anything to do with the church, still, she said, "In your art, you've witnessed to the pain of so many children and adults who do not have, as you did, a language with which to handle it." She was speaking, of course, about the "language" of your art. Her insight in that moment, speaking with evident emotion, was quite powerful and poignant to me.

Near the end of the interview, you talked about doing the Spiritual Exercises during tertianship, when nothing was moving in you for almost thirty days, until finally, on the last day, the name of Robert Lentz came to you in prayer. Sr. Marie listened quietly, and then she said, "Out of dryness, in that space of darkness, a grace was given. But not just to you, it was given to all of us. Your grace has become our grace, and our gift."

The interview, it now occurs to me, was very Ignatian, insofar as Ignatius put so much emphasis on discerning the Spirit in the give-and-take of spiritual conversations, from heart to heart. It's Sr. Thea again, "Please share your treasures with me, but I also want to share my treasures with you." It's what you did

with Thea so intensely for a year of your life in the process of writing her icon. And it's what I've experienced with you in these conversations, if I may say so.

Thank you, Chris, I very much agree. I'm always anxious about interviews, but very quickly, with Sr. Marie, I felt I had an equal partner to talk to, someone I could trust, which isn't always the case. To be welcomed and understood beyond how you might be perceived and judged by others, especially someone with a public voice in the church, is really a gift when it happens.

Recently I was having lunch with my friend Tomás, and he's now much taken with Merton. He told me the same thing that Dan Berrigan did, many years ago, that I reminded him of Merton. Instead of being quiet and taken aback, as I was with Dan, I asked him why? Tomás said we both had a loneliness that no one or nothing but God could touch. That insight alone I could accept

On the beach, Monterey, California

and agree with him. I told Tomás my experience while painting Merton was exactly that, that he had an emptiness that only God could fill. Just like G. B. Caird said about the Gospel of Luke, something like, "Jesus's only requirement for entrance into the kingdom of God was a hole or longing inside, which no one but God could fill."[7]

I'm not saying that I think I'm similar to Thomas Merton, but while working on his icon, I became aware of how many thousands of people have felt a kinship with him, for as many different reasons as there are people who love him. The point is, I think it speaks to a secret yearning that we all feel for God.

I remembered a scene from the old TV show called *Northern Exposure* where this guy on the radio says, "Well folks, it's Thanksgiving and I've got a hole inside big enough to throw a cat through." I saw that throughout my whole life, every major mistake I've made has had to do

Bill saying Mass at Robert and Monica Ellsberg's house

Epithalamium

O I am an Archer.
This is the sacred vocation
that I can stand under, that holds
onto me too.
I have run along with the
hunted Prophet Jonah year after year,
following him safely
into the heart of the
Sea Creature,
that vast water tomb
where I can rest,
long enough to surrender and
find a way
to serve You, my Lord.
Now here I am in the Zone at last.
I aim these images and the few words
I have left, into the
Heart of the Church: the Bride.
So, this is chapter eight of my
Song of Songs . . .
my Epithalamium.
One more arrow to let fly.
It says with pure speed
and perfect precision :
"Love is stronger than death, and
many waters cannot quench this
burning love."

July 1993
William Hart McNichols

with running away from this loneliness. Wanting and needing companionship, the safety of groups, just wanting to be a part of something forever. But each time I'd try, sooner or later I'd get evicted, or I'd evict or unconsciously sabotage myself. It's the truth my grandmother told my mom when I was born. And all through my life I've been running from that truth.

Again, in *Balancing Heaven and Earth*, Robert Johnson was able to put it into words for me so that I could at least begin to accept it. It was something like, "Some people are claimed by the inner life, and you will never be able to be a part of a group or even give yourself completely to another person. You must live on the slender threads God sends you, daily."

Well today, coming on 74 years, I think I've finally stopped running from that truth.

Heading Toward the Shore

Fr. Bill, I hope and pray that these conversations recorded here are just stepping stones, as it were, in a friendship that stretches "into the woods" for many, many more years. As Sr. Marie put it, "Your grace has become our grace, and our gift." I know that you will continue to create icons as long as you are able to continue in this spiritually, intellectually, emotionally, and often physically demanding work.

The first drawing we talked about was your crucifixion scene at age five. You've been creating art for nearly 70 years, and the range of your work across these decades . . .

The church in my late youth and into my young adulthood was going through an iconoclastic era. Just intuitively, I guess, my response was to become an iconographer. I've done over 330 images and icons—I just finished *St. Joseph Mirror of Patience*, which we talked about before. I always seem to go back to Joseph when the bottom feels like it's dropping out.

Sometimes people throw the word iconoclasm around with no consideration of the consequences. Ultimately it results in the monstrous

cruelty to human beings and destruction of the ancient beauty of culture, like we're seeing today in Ukraine. We have this tendency as human beings to react in extremes—it's all pure and good or it's all demonic and contemptible.

The war in Ukraine has really upset me. The ancient beauty of a culture is just getting decimated. In the Russian and French revolutions, the maiming of art did not stop with statues and paintings. That's my greatest fear for us. All this chopping off of heads, it feels like the dragon in the book of Revelation coming to devour the pregnant woman's children.

Bill and Chris, Denver, Colorado, Spring 2022

Looking back at my life I have to ask myself, Why do I believe what I believe? How, even as a child, could I filter out all the negative things that the world was sending toward me about gay people, basically that you were right in there with those considered perverse, mentally ill, pedophiles? The psychiatric term was "inverts." How did I get past that?

As an adult I am aware this separation or freedom of soul was truly a grace I lived inside without understanding. I knew what people said put me in danger, but somehow, I also knew it was not what God felt. I think it's something I would later learn from Victor Frankl, in *Man's Search for Meaning*, that when you are cornered and can't go right or left, backward or forward, the only way is to go up.

It's like what Rilke says in his letters to the young poet about writing. If it's truly your vocation, a particular gift that God has given you—that God, as it were, demands of you, irrespective of the cost—you will be incapable of not creating art. You've had that impulse and calling from the very beginning.

You remember the story I shared with you from eighth grade, when Vatican II was happening, and I was asked to make a symbol of the church as a ship? I had never heard of that image of the church as "the barque of Peter." Many years later, during the AIDS hospice years, I relied on that image to help the young men who were dying and who felt they would have to make amends with the church, yet doing so, they felt, would be a betrayal of themselves. They were terribly unsettled about it.

I'd tell them, you need to feel at peace with your relationship with God, and the best way might be for me to offer to hear your confession.

The church is a way to God, a ship to carry you during your life on earth, but it's not God. Don't worry, you're almost to the shore. And because they were so near the shore, it made no sense to get back on the ship. This greatly comforted them and allowed them the freedom of dying in peace.

As I get older, I realize that the ship is heading toward the shore. Before I die, my fondest wish is that I'll be forgiven and be able to forgive myself and everyone who has ever harmed me. I'd like to have that grace of the cross, to truly know that I, and they, and all of us, "know not what we do." And working on this book with you has opened up a place inside me to begin to do that. Maybe it is already happening?

Indeed, maybe it is. Fr. Bill, this has been an incredibly graced journey of faith and art and spiritual conversation to share with you. Thank you.

Thank you, Chris.

POSTSCRIPT

Apocalypsis *and* Veronike: *Art as Participation in the Work of God the Creator*

William Hart McNichols

The true mysticism is the belief that everything, in being what it is, is symbolic of something more.

—R. L. Nettleship

Nothing from my childhood is so ingrained in me as the art of Catholicism. The churches were like giant children's books you could walk right into, and which, in fact, seemed to shout, "Unless you become like little children, you shall not enter." That symbolic art, the world of the Gospels and of Revelation, so much a school of mysticism, has demanded that I continue to feed others through art, as I was fed, and that, I suppose, is the crux of the matter. I say "demand" because it is an order, a searing *vocatio*, a call troublesome and demanding.

The wooden ship with sails of white marked with red crosses and tilting on a green sea; the beehive swarming with bees and oozing precious honey; the wandering hart, wounded and yearning for water; the mother pelican feeding her chicks with the blood from her side; the risen phoenix, feathers still tipped with fire; the crucified Jew bleeding, bleeding everywhere; the lamb bearing the banner of the cross; the lovely, tender Madonnas of every color and race; the halos of light; the fire; the anchors; arrows; vines; lilies; bread; chalices; wishbones; blood; fish; palms; scrolls; the cribs with animals and angels; the suns, moons, and stars; the dragons; the demons who taunt; the visualization of a spiritual life at odds by its very existence with the "inhabitants of the earth," with those who would refuse to see.

Art is its own language, which now glorifies, now shocks, now horrifies, now fawns and caresses, as it incarnates things that book or word or song cannot. Art is a synthesis (though often unconsciously so) of the spiritual, physical, and intellectual. At its height, art is participation in the ongoing work of God the creator, the ongoing work of revelation. Art is adoration, is bending the knee, is worship. Art is praise of God with every stroke and movement. Art is affirming holy hope, for even to create in these apocalyptic times is to hope. Art can be terrifying prophecy, a blast of fire to awaken the sleeping, lethargic soul to repentance, to metanoia. This art born in war or persecution is the display of blessed dreams of the soul.

This is the art of *apocalypsis*: images to warn and encourage and to reach out to hold the hand of those in the struggle against the Beast. Indeed, art is waving these hand-made "anachronisms" in the face of the slick metallic Beast. And this is the *veronike* (true icon), the image of the wounded face of the suffering Christ imprinted on paper, board, muslin, or canvas. This face will not go away as long as people suffer. It cries out the injustice and death of the innocent victim. It cries out the agonies of tyranny, the prejudices of racism, of sexism, of the brutalities and cowardice of this world. This art points like an apocalyptic angel livid with an aura of fire to the judgment and the life to come. Art becomes this prophecy to warn the world or any church that whores with the world by following it in its cowardice and closing the doors to the vagrant, the outcast, the mourning, the poor, the sinners, the lepers of any age . . . all the thousand faces of shame and dishonor of the incarnate Lord Jesus.

This profound looking into the Incarnation is a contemplative work of motherhood, of waiting filled with God's seed and then giving birth through blood to life. It is a contemplative work of learning to join the dream, mind, and heart with the work of the hand; the ever-present challenge of technique and ability. And in this struggle comes a gift of humility because it is so difficult, so rare when one says in art what is really inside. And it is a gift of great joy because every so often, one can send a colorful love letter into the unspeakable suffering of a world haunted by and destined for God.

AFTERWORD

The Iconography of William Hart McNichols

Robert Lentz, OFM

For more than a dozen centuries men and women have apprenticed themselves to a master painter in order to learn the discipline of Byzantine iconography. Until recently these students have also come from the Byzantine world, but, just as the world at large has shrunk, so also has the Christian world, making the spiritual wealth of each church the patrimony of every Christian. William Hart McNichols, a Jesuit of the Latin Rite, has been my apprentice for nearly six years. We have worked together between four and six hours every week, and he has spent an additional thirty to sixty hours a week painting on his own. His line of teachers stretches through me to the monastic republic of Mount Athos. As he ends his time as my apprentice, I share my reflections on his work and its spirit.

When he came to study with me in 1990, Bill McNichols had been a Jesuit for twenty-two years. His spirituality was unique and mature. Among his more powerful mentors had been Daniel Berrigan, SJ, with whom he lived in community during the 1980s. Berrigan's prophetic voice had turned him toward our world, with its tragic injustices, but he had also seen in Berrigan a consummate artist who used his poetic craft to touch souls, and whose own soul was nourished by a hidden silent life. The seed planted by Berrigan was sufficient for the work Bill and I had to share. Rather than force a pseudo-Byzantine spirituality onto his already mature soul, I trusted that in authentic silent prayer he would find the necessary common ground to understand the spirit of Byzantine art. Such has been the case.

Bill also came to me with a professional art career behind him. Besides earning a master's degree in fine arts, he had illustrated books for almost a decade. Beginning with egg tempera, and then moving to acrylics, he has applied himself painstakingly to master the technical aspects of painting Byzantine icons. This is the work of a lifetime, but I believe he is already one of the finer painters of our day.

Almost from the beginning of his apprenticeship, Bill's work was channeled into themes commissioned by bishops, other Jesuits, and families in search of authentic spiritual art to nurture their prayer life. As every artist knows, sacrificing the freedom to choose what one paints is painful. Byzantine iconography, however, is an apostolate as well as pure art. For six years Bill has sent icons to inner-city churches, new Christian communities in Russia, Jesuit chapels, and the homes of simple families.

In spite of the constraints imposed by commissioned work, a number of themes important to Bill run through his icons. Foremost is the church as Christ's Bride and Mystical Body. He credits this emphasis to Teilhard and to Berrigan, as well as to Adrienne von Speyr, and expresses it most often through images of the Madonna and Child. The Madonna for him is archetype of the church, putting into proper perspective its all-too-evident juridical aspects. With the Madonna he also helps balance masculine and feminine energy in modern spirituality. He paints her frequently, and includes her in other icons whenever possible—pointing out her presence in the lives of various saints.

Another common theme in his work is the Holy Child—including the kenosis and vulnerability embraced by Christ in his Incarnation. The Christ Child appears with St. Clare, St. Thérèse of Lisieux, and Rutilio Grande. His vulnerability is reflected in almost every face Bill paints.

With Berrigan for his mentor, it should be no surprise that his opus includes Franz Jägerstätter, a worker priest, a martyr from Central America, a victim of the Nazi holocaust, an icon honoring those who died in Soviet concentration camps, and icons related to the AIDS epidemic. He expresses suffering in his icons in ways a Byzantine painter would not, but we live in new times when East and West will perhaps embrace and learn from one another after so many centuries of separation. As John XXIII said so well, "We are not on earth to guard a museum, but to cultivate a flourishing garden of life!"

He has painted a number of Jesuit saints and will continue to do so in the future. He loves the Society deeply and has an appreciation for the varied ways its spirituality has been expressed in the past. Through his images he shares with the rest of the church what is often overlooked in Jesuit history even by other Jesuits.

As I watch my apprentice leave, it is only natural that I wonder what direction his work will take in the future. He is by nature an artist, so I have no doubt that he will continue to create visual images, regardless of whatever other responsibilities the Society places upon him. He remains a Latin Christian, so I expect to see him continue to adapt what I have taught him, so as to be able to express what comes from his native spirituality. But whatever direction he takes, he leaves me as an accomplished iconographer, whose glory and burden is to depict the Kingdom for pilgrim eyes.

DAYS IN THE LIFE OF WILLIAM HART MCNICHOLS

〜

1949

Born July 10, Denver, Colorado, to Marjory Roberta Hart McNichols and Stephen Lucid Robert McNichols. St Joseph's Hospital, a full moon.

1953

Begins kindergarten, Christ the King Elementary, with Sisters of the Precious Blood from Dayton, Ohio. Creates one of his first drawings, *The Precious Blood Crucifixion*. Sometime around age five an incident of abuse occurs.

1956

First Communion, October 28, receives *Little Lives of the Saints* by Fr. Daniel Lord, SJ. Subjected to bullying throughout subsequent elementary school years.

1957

Bill's father, Stephen McNichols, is elected governor of Colorado, the first Catholic to hold the office.

1960

Confirmation, May 4, taking the name of St. Dominic. Begins collecting books about the saints, statues, and holy cards. Family moves into the Boettcher Mansion, now the Governor's Residence, at 8th and Logan Street, Denver. Brother

Steve has a swing band; brother Bob plays trumpet; mother Marjory plays music all the time. Steve and Bob attend Regis High School; Billy, Mary, and Margie attend St. John the Evangelist School, with Sisters of Loretto. Bullying stops during seventh and eighth grades.

1963–67

Stephen McNichols loses re-election bid, November 1963. Billy begins at Regis High School, run by the Society of Jesus; terrible bullying resumes. Hears a call to become a Jesuit, sophomore year, decreased bullying junior and senior years. Works as a groom at the dog track in Commerce City. After graduation, accepted to Colorado State University, Ft. Collins, Colorado.

1967–68

During first year of college, again hears call to enter the Jesuits. Enters St. Stanislaus Kostka Jesuit Novitiate, Florissant, Missouri, September 1968. Meets Novice Master Fr. Vincent O'Flaherty, SJ, and makes the 30-day long retreat, the Spiritual Exercises of St. Ignatius.

1969–71

Repeats the long retreat during second year of novitiate, a "major gift that has never left me." Begins to come to come to terms with homosexuality; is administered aversion (shock) therapy from a behaviorist at St. Louis University. Takes first vows, September 11, 1969; moves into Fusz Memorial Jesuit Scholastic Building. Discontinues aversion therapy. Introduced to the work of Daniel Berrigan, SJ, and the anti-war movement. Writes statement for twenty-six Jesuit scholastics who turn in draft cards.

Visits New England Province, summer 1971, moves to Brighton, Massachusetts, attends Boston College for philosophy and Boston University for art. Teaches art at Boston College High School, awarded "Teacher of the Year." Designs a chapel for the Jesuit residence in Brighton, based on the Vietnam War and the promise of resurrection; moves to the Jesuit House on Beacon Hill. Designs a chapel on the healing power of the Blood of Christ, dedicated to St. Robert Southwell, SJ.

1971–74

Begins Jesuit "Regency," age twenty-four, inaugurating the Art Department at Regis High School on the campus of Regis College (now Regis University) in Denver. Reads a first book on Lady Julian of Norwich, deepening his theology of the Precious Blood. Across these years (1968–1983), his uncle Bill (William H. McNichols) serves multiple terms as mayor of Denver.

1975–79

Begins "Theology" stage of Jesuit formation, Weston School of Theology, Cambridge, Massachusetts, taking additional classes at the Episcopal Divinity School School and Harvard Divinity School. Attends California College of Art in Oakland, summer 1976, with sister Margie; studying with artist Harry Krell "changes my art forever"; also learning techniques of book illustration. Returns to Cambridge, paints first self-portrait; meets regularly with Jungian therapist Alexandra Kubler-Merrill, and discovers the books of Robert A. Johnson. Takes classes on preaching and praying the Mass, makes ordination retreat, passes oral exams, and returns to Denver for ordination. Ordained May 25, 1979, by Denver Archbishop James Casey, at the Cathedral (now Basilica) of the Immaculate Conception. First Mass, May 27, at St. John the Evangelist Church in Denver (now Good Shepherd).

1979–80

Artist-in-Residence, Regis College, Denver. Assists with Masses and Confessions at the Cathedral.

First art exhibit, "What a Fool Believes," April 1, 1980, Regis College. Designs Sangre de Cristo Chapel for the Jesuit Community, including 1974 deposition painting of Fr. Pedro Arrupe, *Llego' Con Tres Heridas* (*I Come with Three Wounds*). Creates another chapel for Regis High School, inspired by poet Gerard Manley Hopkins, SJ. Accepted to Pratt Institute in Brooklyn.

1980–83

Moves to an apartment in Park Slope, Brooklyn, summer 1980; serves as a priest at St. Mark's Church, Sheepshead Bay, and chaplain, Coney Island Hospital. Creates a flood of drawings in the fall of 1980 and during Advent, some wrestling with gay identity. Begins classes at Pratt, including human anatomy, and begins to shop drawings to publishers. Wins contest with Paulist Press to illustrate *The Cathedral Book*, launching career as an illustrator, eventually contributing to some twenty books for Paulist Press and others. (See Fr. Bill's *Wikipedia* page for a complete bibliography.)

Asked by Dignity, New York, to celebrate weekly Masses at Xavier Church, 16th Street, Manhattan; becomes a regular celebrant with Fr. John McNeill, SJ, and a few others. Begins to learn gay history from authors John Boswell, Fr. Malcom Boyd, Fr. John McNeill, John E. Fortunato, and Heinz Heger. Gives directed Ignatian retreats, both individually and to the Sisters of St. Joseph in Baden, Pennsylvania. While visiting in Sea Isle City, NJ, has his first mystical encounter with "the Bride." Commissioned in 1981 to do a sound-and-slide show on the 800th Anniversary of St Francis's birth; meets Fr. André Cirino, OFM, and eventually joins the Third Order Franciscans, inspiring a 1984 pilgrimage to Italy and the tombs of Francis, Dominic, and Ignatius.

1983–85

Graduates from Pratt Institute, final exhibition includes fourteen watercolor and gouache paintings of Prospect Park, Brooklyn. Moves into America House Jesuit Community, Manhattan, does illustrations for *America* magazine. Asked by Dignity, August 1983, to celebrate the first Mass for Persons with HIV/AIDS, and begins AIDS hospice ministry, training with Sr. Patrice Murphy at St. Vincent's Hospital and the Gay Men's Health Crisis, a ministry that would last seven years. Illustrates and writes *Stations of the Cross of a Person with AIDS*, giving the Stations to priests of the Archdiocese of Seattle, the Archdiocese of New Jersey, and parishes around the city. Meets Fr. Daniel Berrigan, SJ. Moves from Long Island to an apartment on Bleecker Street.

1986–89

Moves into the 98th Street Jesuit Community, becomes friends with the Berrigans, Jim Douglass, Martin Sheen, Jim Reale, many others in the peace movement. Serves as a chaplain at NYU chapel, begins Healing Masses for People with AIDS at Our Lady of Guadalupe Church. Befriends Fr. Mychal Judge, OFM. Reads the anonymously published *Meditations on the Tarot*, learning about its author, Valentin Tomberg. Presides at funerals and memorials for young men and their families of every religious background. Appears on the first documentary on AIDS, "AIDS Hits Home," hosted by Dan Rather on CBS. Publishes essays and drawings in *The Advocate*, *Christopher Street Magazine*, and others. Attends first Catholic Conference on AIDS at University of Notre Dame.

1989

Jesuit tertianship, Austin, Texas. Completes last children's book, *Feliz Navidad Pablo*. Discerns apprenticeship with Robert Lentz. Death of friend Louis Swift, September 3. Arrives in Albuquerque, September 7. Begins lessons with Robert, October 4. Death of friend Bill Dobbels, December 22.

1990–96

Continues apprenticeship with Robert while beginning to receive commissions: *Our Lady of the New Advent*, from Archbishop Stafford of Denver; *Our Lady of the Sandias*; *Our Redeemer Jesus Christ Holy Silence*; a second icon of *Our Lady of the New Advent*. Serves at San Felipe Church, Old Town, Taos. Attends Russian Orthodox church of the Holy Royal Martyrs, imbibes Orthodox liturgy, learns of many Orthodox saints.

1992

Child abuse scandal breaks out, Lafayette, LA, then Albuquerque, NM. Priests once revered now seen as contemptible. When Bill nears a nervous breakdown, friend Bob Kerr nurses him back to health.

1993

Presents icon *Our Lady of the New Advent: Burning Bush* to Pope John Paul II during World Youth Day in Denver. Commissioned by Archbishop Hurley of Anchorage, Alaska, for an icon of *Our Lady of Magadan*, as a gift to the Russian Orthodox Bishop of Magadan.

1995

Travels to Anchorage, then to Magadan, October 1995. Visits Monastery of St. Sergius of Radonezh Lavra, whose monks commission *Our Lady of Pochaev* icon. Archbishop Hurley delivers the icon personally the following year.

1996

Having completed nearly 70 icons, required by Jesuit superiors to end the apprenticeship and "find a real job." Leaves Albuquerque for Boston College, July 23, while completing icon of *Holy New Martyr Nestor Savchuk*. Commissioned by BC Jesuit community to do five icons. Invited to hold a chair of theology at BC; decides to turn it down.

1997

Moves back to 98th Street Jesuit Community, Upper Westside, Manhattan, October 1997.

Flies to Denver to be present for father Stephen McNichols's death, November 25. Travels to Ireland after Christmas with Dan Berrigan and John Dear, who is making tertianship. Meets filmmaker Christopher Summa; serves Mass periodically at the Catholic Worker in New York City.

1998

Makes first pilgrimage to Medjugorje. Asked by Fr. Tim Martinez to do an icon of St. Francis receiving the stigmata for the Church of San Francisco de Asis, Ranchos de Taos, NM.

1999

Pilgrimage to Akita, Japan, April 1999, to see Our Lady of Akita, which takes place during the massacre at Columbine High School, April 20, in a suburb south of Denver. Granted permission to travel to Taos, June 1999, to complete the icon for San Francisco de Asis Church. Falls in love with the people of the community, where he will serve for fourteen years.

2000–2001

Stays in Taos while working on new commissions and serving at Ranchos de Taos Church. Assigned to serve temporarily with Fr. Tim at San Geronimo Church in Taos Pueblo, January—September 2001. Midnight Mass at Taos Pueblo, Christmas 2001. "Heaven on earth."

2002

Interviewed by *Time* magazine, May 2002; defends gay people who were being scapegoated following new reporting by the *Boston Globe* of child sexual abuse in the church; open conflict with Jesuit superiors. Death and burial of Philip Berrigan, Jonah House, Baltimore, December 6, 2002. Departure from Jesuits, Feast of Our Lady of the New Advent, December 16, 2002, after 35 years in the order.

2003–12

Continues to reside in Talpa, NM, six miles south of Taos, painting six to eight hours per day. Has a small speaking role in the 2003 film *Off the Map*, set in rural New Mexico, starring Joan Allen, Sam Elliot, and J. K. Simmons. Death of mother, Marjory Hart McNichols, August 3, 2006. Exhibit of original works, "Silence in the Storm," Millicent Rogers Museum in Taos, September 2008. Moves into a small house in Arroyo Seco with adjacent studio, 2011. Christopher Pramuk's first visit to Taos, March 2012.

Heart collapse, April 27, 2012, while hiking in Pagosa Springs, Colorado. Flown to Presbyterian Hospital in Albuquerque. Awakens from coma May 11, brought back to Taos by brother Bob McNichols. Heart surgery, June 6. During recovery, "let go" by the pastor at Ranchos de Taos. Celebrated by the city of Taos for his service to the community. Pramuk family visits, July 2012.

2013–15

Pope Francis elected, March 13, 2013. Invited to assist in sacramental ministry at St. Joseph on the Rio Grande Church, Albuquerque. Moves to Albuquerque, August 15, 2013, residing in the home of friend and fellow artist Kenn Ashe. Interviewed by theologian John Dadosky for the book *Image to Insight: The Art of William Hart McNichols*. Filmmaker Christopher Summa begins working on *The Boy Who Found Gold*. Interviewed for the film *The Berrigans: Devout and Dangerous* (2021). Fr. Mark Bosco, SJ, commissions *Viriditas: Finding God in All Things*, for Loyola University Chicago; installed September 2, 2015.

2016-19

The film *The Boy Who Found Gold* is released, premiers in Taos, June 2, 2017. Exhibit at the McNichols Center, "Light in All Darkness," Denver, September 20, 2018–January 6, 2019. *Image to Insight* awarded Best Arts Book 2019, by New Mexico-Arizona Book Awards. Celebrates fortieth anniversary of priestly ordination, May 25, 2019, at St. Joseph on the Rio Grande Church. Christopher Pramuk publishes first academic journal article and a book chapter on Fr. Bill's life and work.

2020–24

Invited by Fr. Jim Martin on pilgrimage to Israel with one hundred other pilgrims; returns to New York, March 8, just ahead of coronavirus pandemic shutdown and quarantine. Begins work on a huge cross, collaborating with master woodworker Roberto Lavadie and master framer-gilder Marcia Vargas. Pope Francis declares the Year of St. Joseph, December 8, 2020–December 8, 2021. Creates three images from the Litany of St Joseph: *Flower of Jesse, Terror of Demons, Mirror of Patience.*

Completes icons of Fr. General Pedro Arrupe, SJ, for Xavier High School, Manhattan; Hadewijch of Antwerp (Brabant) for spiritual writer Andrew Harvey; St. Henry Walpole, SJ, for Henry Pramuk, uncovering a theology of being "Splashed by the Blood"; *Our Sister Thea Bowman,* for Georgetown University; and *Holy Prophet Thomas Merton: Gaudete est Natus!* for the Merton Center at Bellarmine University. Interviewed by Sr. Marie Pappas for Catholic Radio, August 2022; contributes original works to an exhibit on the AIDS epidemic, "Eyes Wide Shut: Visual Meditations on the Plague," at the McNichols Building in Denver, summer 2023.

Gives a presentation on the spirituality of icons for the International Thomas Merton Society, June 2023. The giant cross, *The Cross of Life—The Flowering Cross,* measuring 9' x 12', is relocated from Santa Fe to St. Joseph on the Rio Grande Church, but has yet to be committed to the sanctuary. Records a year of conversations with Christopher Pramuk for their book *All My Eyes See.*

At the time of this writing, Fr. Bill continues to write icons and serve the people of God as a priest in sacramental ministry in the Albuquerque area. He is currently creating an icon *Maria Lanakila,* or *Victorious Mary,* for the people of Lahaina, Maui, and the church of that name that survived the devastating wildfires of August 2023.

BIBLIOGRAPHY/ADDITIONAL READING

Beckett, Sister Wendy, and Robert Ellsberg. *Dearest Sister Wendy: A Surprising Story of Faith and Friendship*. Maryknoll, NY: Orbis Books, 2022.

Berrigan, Daniel, and William Hart McNichols. *The Bride: Images of the Church*. Maryknoll, NY: Orbis Books, 2000.

The Boy Who Found Gold. Directed by Christopher Summa. Dramaticus Films, 2016.

Dadosky, John, and William Hart McNichols. *Image to Insight: The Art of William Hart McNichols*. Albuquerque: University of New Mexico Press, 2018.

Dear, John, and William Hart McNichols. *You Will Be My Witnesses: Saints, Prophets and Martyrs*. Maryknoll, NY: Orbis Books, 2006.

Eichenberg, Fritz. *Works of Mercy*. Maryknoll, NY: Orbis Books, 1992.

Lentz, Robert, and Edwina Gately. *Christ in the Margins*. Maryknoll, NY: Orbis Books, 2014.

McKenna, Megan, and William Hart McNichols. *Mary, Mother of All Nations*. Maryknoll, NY: Orbis Books, 2000.

McNichols, William Hart, and Kathy Hendricks. *Heavenly Friends: An Introduction to the Beauty of Icons*. Twenty-Third Publications, 2019.

O'Laughlin, Michael. *Hidden Mercy: AIDS, Catholics, and the Untold Stories of Compassion in the Face of Fear*. Minneapolis: Broadleaf, 2021.

———. *Plague: Untold Stories of AIDS and the Catholic Church*. America Media.

Pappas, Sr. Marie. "Pathways of Learning." Catholic Channel, Sirius XM Radio, August 21, 2022.

Pramuk, Christopher. *The Artist Alive: Explorations in Music, Art and Theology*. Winona, MN: Anselm Academic, 2019.

———. "What You Gaze Upon You Become: The Iconography of William Hart McNichols." ARTS: *The Arts in Religious and Theological Studies*, 31, no. 1 (2019): 65-83.

Starr, Mirabai, and William Hart McNichols. *Mother of God, Similar to Fire*. Maryknoll, NY: Orbis Books, 2016.

Tueth, Michael. "Icons: An Invitation to Love." *America* 219:9 (April 23, 2018), 40–41.

NOTES

Introduction
Opening the Eyes of the Heart

1. Daniel Berrigan and William Hart McNichols, *The Bride: Images of the Church* (Maryknoll, NY: Orbis Books, 2000); John Dear and William Hart McNichols, *You Will Be My Witnesses: Saints, Prophets and Martyrs* (Maryknoll, NY: Orbis Books, 2006); Mirabai Starr and William Hart McNichols, *Mother of God, Similar to Fire* (Maryknoll, NY: Orbis Books, 2016); John Dadosky and William Hart McNichols, *Image to Insight: The Art of William Hart McNichols* (Albuquerque: University of New Mexico Press, 2018); Megan McKenna and William Hart McNichols, *Mary, Mother of All Nations* (Maryknoll, NY: Orbis Books, 2000); William Hart McNichols and Kathy Hendricks, *Heavenly Friends: An Introduction to the Beauty of Icons* (New London, CT: Twenty-Third Publications, 2019); *The Boy Who Found Gold*, dir. Christopher Summa (Dramaticus Films, 2016); *Plague: Untold Stories of AIDS and the Catholic Church*, America Media, episode 3; Michael O'Laughlin, *Hidden Mercy: AIDS, Catholics, and the Untold Stories of Compassion in the Face of Fear* (Minneapolis: Broadleaf, 2021).

2. Sister Wendy Beckett and Robert Ellsberg, *Dearest Sister Wendy: A Surprising Story of Faith and Friendship* (Maryknoll, NY: Orbis Books, 2022), 257–58.

3. Michael Tueth, "Icons: An Invitation to Love," *America* 219:9 (April 23, 2018), 40–41.

4. William Hart McNichols, "*Apocalypsis* and *Veronike*: Art as Participation in the Work of God the Creator" (unpublished). See "Postscript," 175–76 in this volume.

5. In addition to the studies by other authors noted above, I have previously explored Fr. Bill's iconography in a number of publications. See Christopher Pramuk, "What You Gaze upon You Become: The Iconography of William Hart McNichols," *ARTS: The Arts in Religious and Theological Studies* 31, no. 1 (2019): 65–83; Christopher Pramuk, *The Artist Alive: Explorations in Music, Art, and Theology* (Winona, MN: Anselm Academic, 2019), 212–44.

6. Fritz Eichenberg, *Works of Mercy* (Maryknoll, NY: Orbis Books, 1992), 98–104, at 98.

7. Roy P. Basler, cited in Carl Sandburg, *Abraham Lincoln: The Prairie Years and the War Years*, one volume ed. (Norwalk, CT: Easton Press, 1954), viii.

8. Gamaliel Bradford, cited in Sandburg, *Abraham Lincoln*, viii.

9. O'Laughlin, *Hidden Mercy*, 174.

10. Paul Angle, cited in Sandburg, *Abraham Lincoln*, viii.

11. In 1959, the Boettcher family mansion was offered as a gift to the State of Colorado to become the governor's residence. The family moved in when Bill was eleven, at the start of seventh grade. They lived there a year and a half, moving back to their home in east Denver when his father lost his bid for re-election in November 1963.

12. McNichols and Starr, *Mother of God, Similar to Fire*, 11.

13. McNichols and Starr, *Mother of God, Similar to Fire*, 9.

14. McNichols and Starr, *Mother of God, Similar to Fire*, back cover.

15. See Robert Lentz and Edwina Gately, *Christ in the Margins* (Maryknoll, NY: Orbis Books, 2014).

16. Founded in 1923 as part of Goethe University in Frankfurt, Germany, the Frankfurt School of Critical Theory sought to understand key social and economic forces in society—capitalism, technology, mass culture, consumerism—utilizing ideals from Marxism and other social scientific perspectives. Its leading proponents included Max Horkheimer, Theodor Adorno, Herbert Marcuse, Erich Fromm, Walter Benjamin, and, in later years, Jürgen Habermas.

17. See especially Walter Benjamin's classic essay, "The Work of Art in the Age of Mechanical Reproduction" (1935), as well as his unfinished masterpiece, *The Arcades Project* (1927–1940), which he called "the theater of all my struggles and ideas." The former is reproduced in Walter Benjamin, *Illuminations*, ed. Hannah Arendt (London: Fontana, 1968), 214–18; the latter in Walter Benjamin, *The Arcades Project*, trans. Howard Eiland and Kevin McLaughlin (Boston: Harvard University Press, 2002).

18. Interview with Stuart Jeffries, author of *Grand Hotel Abyss: The Lives of the Frankfurt School*, *Vox* (Dec. 26, 2017), https://www.vox.com/conversations/2016/12/27/14038406/donald-trump-frankfurt-school-brexit-critical-theory.

19. I borrow the phrase from German theologian Johann Baptist Metz, who uses it describe the spirituality of Jesus, who "did not teach an ascending mysticism of closed eyes, but rather a God-mysticism with an increased readiness for perceiving, a mysticism of open eyes, which sees more and not less." See Johann Baptist Metz, *A Passion for God: The Mystical-Political Dimension of Christianity*, trans. J. Matthew Ashley (New York: Paulist Press, 1998), 163.

20. Metz, *A Passion for God*, 163.

21. To offer just one of many possible examples, today the ancient town of Bethlehem, a city of about 22,000 residents, is surrounded on three sides by a concrete security wall, eight meters high, littered with graffiti. In one place the graffiti gives way to an icon of the Virgin Mary, known by locals as *Our Lady Who Brings Down Walls*. The man who wrote the icon is Ian Knowles, a British theologian and founder of the Bethlehem Icon Center, where Palestinians and students from around the world are learning the ancient art of icon writing and finding their own lives illuminated by newfound hope. During the season of Advent tens of thousands of pilgrims come to contemplate and pray before *Our Lady Who Brings Down Walls*. Knowles explains why: "When you've got mothers whose children have been killed, where do you go? Here, the Christian community goes to their heavenly mother. So this image is a place where those people can come with their pain, and find some glimmer of hope." Cited in "The Icon Painters of Bethlehem," BBC World Service, Heart and Soul Radio Program (Dec. 24, 2017), https://www.bbc.co.uk/programmes/w3cswcyx.

22. Phil Ochs, *Farewells and Fantasies*, Elektra, liner notes. Filmmaker Godfrey Reggio, whose classic *Qatsi* trilogy registered an unsettling visual-aural protest against the technological milieu that colonizes planetary life in our times, put it this way: "Beauty is a form of provocation, and my particular provocation is that I want to show the beauty of the beast. What this is, is an attempt at the hour of death to rise above yourself, and to see yourself in another context, and this context is the technological order." See Pramuk, *The Artist Alive*, 87–115.

23. Paul Evdokimov, *Woman and the Salvation of the World*, trans. Anthony P. Gythiel (Crestwood, NY: St. Vladimir's Seminary, 1994 [orig. pub. 1949]), 128. During the German occupation of Paris, Evdokimov's family hid people who had been targeted for arrest; after the war they ran a hostel for displaced persons and political refugees.

24. Evdokimov, *Woman and the Salvation of the World*, 129–30.

25. Edward Kaplan, "Introduction," in Abraham Joshua Heschel, *The Ineffable Name of God: Man* (New York: Continuum, 2005), 7–18, at 15.

26. Sergius Bulgakov, *Icons and the Name of God*, trans. Boris Jakim (Grand Rapids, MI: Eerdmans, 2012), 25–26, 36.

27. In comparison to Western doctrine, heavily shaped by Augustine's doctrine of original sin, in Eastern Orthodoxy the Incarnation supports a highly exalted view of human nature such that human beings, like Christ, have the capacity to "become divine," as it were, a process referred to as divinization, *theōsis*, or deification. In the famous formulation of St. Athanasius, "He became human so that we might become divine." Iconography seeks to make visible this mystery of divinized humanity.

28. Henri J. M. Nouwen, *Behold the Beauty of the Lord: Praying with Icons* (Notre Dame, IN: Ave Maria, 2007), 24.

29. See Bulgakov, *Icons and the Name of God*, 26.

30. "Gnosticism" is a term with ancient Christian provenance that views salvation or participation in the divine realm as an escape from the limits and moral corruption of the body and the embodied human community in history. While condemned as heretical to Christian orthodoxy, various forms of Gnosticism, which hinges on body/spirit dualism, have lived alongside and within Christian thought from the beginning.

31. Aristotle Papanikolaou, endorsement of Bulgakov, *Icons and the Name of God*, back cover.

32. Mirabai Starr, "Foreword," in Dadosky, *Image to Insight*, x (emphasis added). In her meditation on Fr. Bill's icon *Our Lady of the Apocalypse*, Starr writes:

"Queen of the Universe, / in the midst of terrible danger / you labor to give birth to the Prince of Peace. / In the face of violence and warfare / you stand on the moon of mercy" (*Mother of God, Similar to Fire*, 24–25).

33. Starr, "Foreword," *Image to Insight*, ix.

34. Dadosky, *Image to Insight*, 137.

35. For all its hazards, one of the more astonishing benefits of the technological milieu is that works of art from around the world that might otherwise never be seen are easily accessible via the Internet. In addition to the works presented in this book, all of Fr. Bill's icons, sacred images, as well as many paintings, drawings, and illustrations, can be viewed at his website, http://frbillmcnichols-sacredimages.com, where they are organized thematically into a series of galleries.

36. Cited in Starr, "Foreword," *Image to Insight*, ix.

37. John J. L. Mood, *Rilke on Love and Other Difficulties: Translations and Considerations* (New York: W. W. Norton, 1975), 34–35.

38. See Christopher Pramuk, *Sophia: The Hidden Christ of Thomas Merton* (Collegeville, MN: Michael Glazier/Liturgical Press, 2009); and Christopher Pramuk, *At Play in Creation: Merton's Awakening to the Feminine Divine* (Collegeville, MN: Liturgical Press, 2015).

39. Rowan Williams, *A Silent Action: Engagements with Thomas Merton* (Louisville, KY: Fons Vitae, 2011), 50.

40. Wendy M. Wright, "A Wide and Fleshly Love: Images, Imagination, and the Study of Christian Spirituality," in *Minding the Spirit: The Study of Christian Spirituality*, ed. Elizabeth A. Dreyer, and Mark S. Burrows (Baltimore, MD: Johns Hopkins University Press, 2005), 316–33 (emphasis added).

41. Abraham Joshua Heschel, *Man's Quest for God: Studies in Prayer and Symbolism* (New York: Scribner's, 1954), 39–40.

42. Robert Henri, *The Art Spirit* (New York: Basic Books, 2007 [orig. 1923]), 144.

43. Paraphrasing Walt Whitman, in "Song of Myself": "Do I contradict myself? / Very well then I contradict myself, / (I am large, I contain multitudes).'"

44. Henri, *The Art Spirit*, 9.

45. N. T. Wright, *Surprised by Hope* (New York: HarperCollins, 1989), 222–24.

46. This sense of "taking instruction" is powerfully, almost painfully expressed for me in Fr. Bill's 1982 painting *Write What You See and Send It to the Seven Churches: The Apocalypse 1:11*, based on the Apocalypse of St. John the Divine, patron of iconographers. Though technically not a self-portrait—Bill asked a friend to model for the painting—to my eyes it is one of his most self-revelatory works, truest to his deepest nature, and how he experiences his vocation. Bill borrows the phrase "slender threads" from Jungian analyst Robert A. Johnson's memoir, *Balancing Heaven and Earth* (San Francisco: HarperOne, 2009).

47. Hopkins's poem "Ash-Boughs" begins with the beautiful lines: "Not of all my eyes see, wandering on the world, / Is anything a milk to the mind so, so sighs deep / Poetry to it, as a tree whose boughs break in the sky." See Gerard Manley Hopkins, *The Poems of Gerard Manley Hopkins*, ed. W. H. Gardner and H. H. Mackenzie, 4th ed. (New York: Oxford University, 1967), 314.

48. In Ignatian spirituality, the imagination is critical to cultivating the spiritual senses. Not to be confused with fantasy, where images are utilized in a way that is more or less untethered from the concrete data of human experience, for Ignatius, the imagination is a holistic, cumulative faculty that assembles all the elements of our concrete experience and memories into a whole. To "contemplate" a scene in the Gospels, for example, one seeks to enter fully into the scene through the imagination so as to feel oneself immersed in what is happening. As Ignatius counsels in the Spiritual Exercises: "It is profitable to use the imagination and to apply the five senses [to the scene], just as if I were there. I will see, listen, smell, and taste, I will embrace and kiss the places where the persons walk or sit. Then, reflecting upon myself, I will draw some profit from this." The imagination, in other words, includes the intellect and the empirical data of sensory experience but goes beyond these to affirm the transcendent or depth dimensions of experience. "For, what fills and satisfies the soul, consists, not in knowing much, but in our understanding the realities profoundly and in savoring them interiorly." See *Ignatius of Loyola: Spiritual Exercises and Selected Works*, ed. George E. Ganss (New York: Paulist Press, 1991), 60 and 121, respectively.

49. Henri, *The Art Spirit*, 11.

1. Vision to Share

1. Matthew Shepard (1976–1998) was a 21-year-old college student living in Laramie, Wyoming, who, on October 6, 1998, was tortured and left to die in an open field by two attackers because he was gay. Beaten severely and strung up on a fence post, he was found eighteen hours later by a cyclist who had initially mistaken his body for a scarecrow. He died three days

later. Completed in the year 2000, Fr. Bill dedicated his image *The Passion of Matthew Shepard* to "the Memory of the 1,470 Gay and Lesbian Youth Who Commit Suicide in the U.S. Each Year and to the Countless Others Who are Injured or Murdered." For his mother's account of her son's life and death, see Judy Shepard, *The Meaning of Matthew* (New York: Hudson Street Press, 2009).

2. Dianna Ortiz (1958–2021) was a Roman Catholic religious sister of the Ursuline order. On November 2, 1989, while serving as a missionary in Guatemala, she was abducted by members of the Guatemalan military, tortured, and raped repeatedly under questioning. It was later confirmed that an American military adviser was among her captors. She managed to escape while being transported to the U.S. embassy, and would later participate with others in protests demanding the release of CIA papers detailing her capture and U.S. government support of the Guatemalan military. After decades of human rights activism, she died of cancer in 2021. See Sister Dianna Ortiz with Patricia Davis, *The Blindfold's Eyes: My Journey from Torture to Truth* (Maryknoll, NY: Orbis Books, 2004).

2. The Unseen World Is Real

1. Servant of God Sr. Thea Bowman (1937–1990) was a Black Catholic religious sister in the order of the Franciscan Sisters of Perpetual Adoration, a teacher, musician, and scholar, whose many contributions to the U.S. Catholic Church and elevation of the spiritual gifts of African American Catholics to the church are still being realized today. See Maurice Nutt, *Thea Bowman: Faithful and Free* (Collegeville, MN: Liturgical Press, 2019); Charlene Smith and John Feister, *Thea's Song: The Life of Thea Bowman* (Maryknoll, NY: Orbis Books, 2012).

3. God in All Things

1. The Sisters of Loretto, a Catholic women's religious order founded in Kentucky in 1812, has a long history of service in the Rocky Mountain West, and a storied witness of activism in the Denver area. Sr. Mary Luke Tobin SL, a Denver native, was one of fifteen women invited to be an auditor at Vatican II. A friend of Thomas Merton, after his death she co-founded the International Thomas Merton Society, and like many of her fellow Loretto sisters in Colorado, she was a constant presence in demonstrations for peace, racial justice, and nuclear disarmament.

2. Fr. Pedro Arrupe (1907–1991) was a Spanish Basque priest who served as the Superior General, or worldwide leader, of the Society of Jesus from 1965 to 1983, presiding over a critical period of change in the post-Vatican II church and in the Jesuits. A survivor of the atomic bombing of Hiroshima, Japan, where he was posted as a young Jesuit during the war, and best known for his emphasis on the link between faith and justice, Arrupe has been called a "second founder" of the Society of Jesus. Fr. Bill's work includes several paintings and icons of Arrupe.

4. The Zen of Seeing

1. The Enneagram is a popular model of nine distinct but interrelated personality types, sometimes used in various contexts of religious formation or in discussions of spirituality as an aid toward self-awareness and in understanding the dynamics of interpersonal relationships between different personality types at play in families, workplaces, or in religious communities. It would not have been uncommon to find the Enneagram used in particular stages of Jesuit formation or used by other religious orders in the early 1970s and even today. The Enneagram Institute describes Type Four as the Individualist: "The Sensitive, Introspective Type: Expressive, Dramatic, Self-Absorbed, and Temperamental." It is commonly attributed to artists.

2. Fr. Michael Sheeran came to Regis University in 1975 as assistant professor of history and political science, and served as president from 1993 to 2012. Just months after his inauguration, in August 1993, Pope John Paul II and President Bill Clinton met on the grounds of the Regis University campus in north Denver. John Paul II had come to Denver for World Youth Day, and it was during this event that Fr. Bill presented the pope with his icon *Our Lady of the New Advent: The Burning Bush*, which had been commissioned for the occasion by Archbishop Francis Stafford.

5. Unless You Become Like a Child

1. Founded in 1969 in San Diego by Fr. Pat Nidorf as a support group for gay Catholics, within five years, Dignity had grown to over thirty chapters around the United States. For a fascinating history of the organization, its leadership, and growth, including the publication of landmark books on homosexuality and the

church that were influential in Fr. Bill's own spiritual journey, see https://www.dignityusa.org/history.

2. Fr. Jim Janda (his friends called him JJ) was a poet and author of numerous children's books and a play on the life of Julian of Norwich, a Jesuit priest for twenty-five years, and a priest in the Diocese of Salt Lake City until his death in 2010. A dear friend of Fr. Bill—they collaborated on eight books together—he was remembered warmly by Jesuit Fr. John Staudenmeier as follows in a blog post after his death. "I can't remember ever visiting with Jim without feeling bathed in wisdom and tenderness, and in his awareness of how deep grief runs in human beings, right there along with whimsy."

3. Born Josef de Veuster (1840–1889), St. Damien of Moloka'i was a Roman Catholic priest from Belgium and member of the Congregation of the Sacred Hearts of Jesus and Mary. From 1873 until his death in 1889, he ministered on the island of Moloka'i, in the Kingdom of Hawai'i, to people with leprosy, or Hansen's disease, eventually dying of the disease himself. He was canonized in 2009, and May 10 is his feast day.

4. Journalist Michael O'Laughlin's book *Hidden Mercy: AIDS, Catholics, and the Untold Stories of Compassion in the Face of Fear* (Minneapolis: Broadleaf, 2021), details the stories of those in the Catholic community who chose compassion "at great personal cost" during the AIDS crisis of the 1980s and 1990s. A summation of O'Laughlin's exhaustive research and interviews conducted for the landmark podcast *Plague: Untold Stories of AIDS and the Catholic Church*, Fr. Bill's ministry and art are featured throughout the book, as well as Sr. Patrice Murphy, Sr. Carol Baltosiewich, and other "legendary" women religious, alongside secular organizations, who responded with compassion and courageous public advocacy to the marginalization of people living, and dying, with HIV-AIDS.

5. O'Laughlin, *Hidden Mercy*, 51, 82–83.

6. Saint Ignatius Retreat House in Manhasset, Long Island, served as a retreat center and "Catholic Sanctuary" in New York for seventy-five years. Featuring a majestic Tudor-style mansion on a thirty-three–acre estate, the main house was completed in 1920 and donated to the Jesuits in 1937. The property was closed in 2012, sold, and demolished by the buyers in 2013 to make way for a housing development.

7. William F. Lynch, SJ, was a Jesuit priest and a prominent American literary theorist, theologian, and philosopher. Among his nine books were *Christ and Apollo*, *Images of Hope*, and *The Integrating Mind*. Though Fr. Bill never met him, Bill Lynch is a beloved

figure to us both and an enduring topic in our conversations. See chap. 6 n. 1.

8. See O'Laughlin, *Hidden Mercy*, 240–41. As the firstborn son to a family of Italian nobility, Aloysius de Gonzaga (1568–1591) was set to become a soldier and heir to his father's title and status of marquis. Against his father's wishes and his family's persistent attempts to dissuade him, the young Aloysius renounced his inheritance, adopted an ascetic lifestyle, and entered the Society of Jesus at age seventeen. When a plague broke out in Rome in 1591, the Jesuits opened a hospital, where Aloysius washed and fed the victims. Like Damien of Moloka'i, he eventually contracted and died from the disease of those he cared for. His feast day is June 21, the date of his death. Michael O'Laughlin closes his final chapter, "AIDS Crucifixion," titled after Bill's drawing, telling the reader why he wears an Aloysius medal. "As a gay Catholic, it makes me feel connected to the pioneers who came before me, to people like Father Bill" (241).

9. A contemporary of Gonzaga and Robert Bellarmine, Bernardino Realino (1530–1616) renounced a successful career as a lawyer and judge when a sermon by a Jesuit preacher so moved him that he changed course, made a week-long retreat, and entered the Society of Jesus in 1564, at age thirty-four. Much of his ministry as a Jesuit was dedicated to pastoral care, serving as a novice master in Naples, founding a Jesuit house in Lecce, preaching at parish missions across Italy, ministering to diocesan priests, and caring for the poor and sick. It was a vision of Mary that compelled him to enter the Jesuits while on retreat; some years later, as Bill alludes to here, on Christmas Eve, while hearing confessions in the freezing cold, the Child Jesus appeared to him, warming Bernardino with his love for him. He was canonized in 1947, and his feast day is July 2.

10. See chap. 1 n. 1 for Matthew Shepard. Rachel Carson and Elijah McLain are referenced in later conversations about the icons.

6. Arrows into the Heart of the Church

1. Though Fr. William F. Lynch, SJ, is not well-known outside Jesuit and academic theological circles, for both Bill and me he is a revered teacher. As Bill shared the story of his experience at Pine Ridge, I thought of Lynch's brilliant 1965 book, *Images of Hope: Imagination as Healer of the Hopeless* (Baltimore: Helicon Press, 1965), based on his own struggles with severe depression and his years working as a counselor in mental health institutions. Two insights from the book

are especially relevant to Fr. Bill's story of Pine Ridge and his ministry to this day. The first is made plain in the book's title, Lynch's argument that hope is linked inextricably to imagination. If despair cannot imagine a way out, then hope "is the fundamental knowledge and feeling that there is a way out of difficulty . . . that there are ways out of illness." Hope "is a sense of *the possible*, that what I hope for may be difficult, but I *can* have it—it is possible" (32). In short, to break free of despair, we need images that kindle the flickering pilot light and feed our dying dreams of what is yet possible. Lynch's second key insight is that hope is a communal endeavor, that there is *no hope without help*: "Hope not only imagines. It imagines *with*. . . . Hope cannot be achieved alone. It must in some way or other be an act of community, whether the community be a church or a nation or just two people struggling together to produce liberation in each other" (23–24). When our hopes are drowning, it is often the faith, hope, and love of others—living and dead—that lift and sustain us. Hope "is always relative to the idea of help," says Lynch. "It looks to the outside world. There are no absolute heroes" (31).

2. Maria Teresa Goretti (1890–1902), one of the youngest saints to be canonized by the Catholic Church, was an Italian peasant who was murdered after refusing the sexual advances of twenty-year-old Allesandro Serenelli, with whom her family shared a home. Taken to the hospital after being stabbed fourteen times, she died twenty-four hours later, having expressed forgiveness for her attacker. Maria was canonized in 1950, and her feast day is July 6.

3. In a chapter entitled "A Tangible Love," Michael O'Laughlin relates a story that after one of Fr. Bill's Healing Masses, a young man named David, whose partner, also named Bill, was dying, approached Fr. Bill at the back of the church, and said to him, "I think my partner is in his last stages and I'd like to ask you for some kind of message." O'Laughlin describes what happens next: "Father Bill listened to David's request, and then he prayed. His mind transported him back home to the Southwest, where he remembered a custom in cemeteries in which friends and family of the deceased placed candles inside wax paper bags. Lights to guide their loved ones home. Father Bill was moved by the memory, and he told David, 'When you go home tonight, tell Bill that the Blessed Virgin Mary is setting up luminaria to guide him home.' Back home, David climbed into bed next to his partner. He whispered Fr. Bill's message, promising him he wouldn't be alone on the next journey.

A few hours later, Bill died. David envisioned the candles, the luminaria, guiding Bill home, making it easier for him to find his way to peace" (*Hidden Mercy*, 175–76). Some thirty years later, when Fr. Bill heard David's story and others, many told for the first time on O'Laughlin's podcast, he broke down crying. As O'Laughlin notes, for every story like David's, "there are surely dozens more, individuals who were comforted by Fr. Bill's art or spiritual wisdom. We will never know the intimate details." See *Plague: Untold Stories of AIDS and the Catholic Church*, episode 3, "The cost of AIDS ministry to a gay priest," *America Media* (aired Dec. 20, 2019).

4. Fr. James Martin, SJ (b. 1960), a longtime friend of Fr. Bill, is perhaps the most public face of the Society of Jesus in the United States today, excluding Pope Francis, the first-ever Jesuit pope. The author of numerous best-selling books—*My Life with the Saints*, *The Jesuit Guide to (Almost) Everything*, *Jesus: A Pilgrimage*, and many others—Fr. Jim's outreach to the LGBTQ community after the 2016 Pulse Nightclub shooting in Orlando, and his subsequent 2017 book, *Building a Bridge*, has drawn both widespread support and vocal condemnation from within the Catholic community in the United States. Though Fr. Jim's advocacy for LGBTQ persons has been explicitly supported by Pope Francis and his message well received by a great many Catholics—his Facebook page has nearly 650,000 members—Fr. Jim continues to be the subject of personal attacks for his outreach to and defense of the LGBTQ community, and on a number of occasions, for his association with Fr. Bill.

7. Midwives to the Second Birth

1. William Josef Dobbels, SJ, *An Epistle of Comfort*, illustrations by William Hart McNichols (New York: Sheed & Ward, 1990).

2. On Jim Janda, see chap. 5 n. 2.

3. From the Hebrew *shakhan*—to be present or dwell as in a sanctuary or tent—the Shekhinah emerges in rabbinic literature as "an image of the female aspect of God caring for her people in exile." See Melissa Raphael, *The Female Face of God in Auschwitz: A Jewish Feminist Theology of the Holocaust* (New York: Routledge, 2003), 82. Israel's God is "an accompanying God whose face or presence, as Shekhinah, 'She-Who-Dwells-Among-Us,' goes with Israel, in mourning, into her deepest exile, even if Israel cannot see her in the terrible crush" (6). For further exploration of Raphael's theology in

dialogue with the Christian Wisdom-Sophia tradition and other contemporary expressions of the feminine divine, see Christopher Pramuk, "Making Sanctuary for the Divine: Exploring Melissa Raphael's Holocaust Theology," *Studies in Christian-Jewish Relations* 1 (2017): 1–16; and Christopher Pramuk, *At Play in Creation: Merton's Awakening to the Feminine Divine* (Collegeville, MN: Liturgical Press, 2015), esp. chaps. 7 and 9.

4. Mirabai Starr, "Foreword," in John Dadosky and William Hart McNichols, *Image to Insight: The Art of William Hart McNichols* (Albuquerque: University of New Mexico Press, 2018), x.

5. On William Lynch, see chap. 6 n. 1.

8. The Flowering Wounds

1. Malcolm X, *The Autobiography of Malcolm X, told to Alex Haley* (New York: Ballantine, 1964), 347; James Cone, *Martin and Malcolm and America: A Dream or a Nightmare* (Maryknoll, NY: Orbis Books, 1992).

2. See Michael Eric Dyson, *Come Hell or High Water: Hurricane Katrina and the Color of Disaster* (London: Civitas, 2007).

3. See J. Janda, *The Legend of the Holy Child of Atocha*, with illustrations by William Hart McNichols (Mahwah, NJ: Paulist Press, 1986).

4. Melissa Raphael, *The Female Face of God in Auschwitz: A Jewish Feminist Theology of the Holocaust* (New York: Routledge, 2003). See chap. 7 n. 3.

5. Abraham Joshua Heschel, *God in Search of Man* (New York: Farrar, Straus and Cudahy, 1955), 117. "The beginning of our happiness lies in the understanding that life without wonder is not worth living. What we lack is not a will to believe but a will to wonder."

6. Johann Baptist Metz, *A Passion for God: The Mystical-Political Dimension of Christianity*, trans. J. Matthew Ashley (New York: Paulist Press, 1998), 163. Metz employs the phrase "a mysticism of open eyes" to describe the spirituality of Jesus, imbibed from his Jewish heritage. See Introduction, n. 19.

9. Images That Return Our Love

1. See Robert Lentz and Edwina Gately, *Christ in the Margins* (Maryknoll, NY: Orbis Books, 2014).

2. John G. Neihardt, *Black Elk Speaks* (Lincoln, NE: University of Nebraska Press, 1988).

3. Mirabai Starr, "Foreword," in John Dadosky and William Hart McNichols. *Image to Insight: The Art of William Hart McNichols* (Albuquerque: University of New Mexico Press, 2018), x. See chap. 7 n. 4.

4. Unpublished; see "Postscript," 175–76 in this volume.

5. Paul Evdokimov, *The Art of the Icon*: A *Theology of Beauty* (New York: Oakwood Press, 1989).

6. Henri J. M. Nouwen, *Behold the Beauty of the Lord: Praying with Icons* (Notre Dame, IN: Ave Maria, 2007), 24.

7. Jim Forest, *Praying with Icons* (Maryknoll, NY: Orbis Books, 2008).

8. Mirabai Starr and William Hart McNichols, *Mother of God, Similar to Fire* (Maryknoll, NY: Orbis Books, 2016), back cover.

9. For Matthew Shepard, see chap. 1 n. 1.

10. Splashed by the Blood

1. Lester B. Brown, *Two Spirit People: American Indian Lesbian Women and Gay Men* (New York: Routledge, 1997).

2. Will Roscoe, *Changing Ones: Third and Fourth Genders in Native North America* (New York: Palgrave Macmillan, 2000).

3. Amanda Ripley, "Inside the Church's Closet," *Time*, May 12, 2002.

4. Michael O'Laughlin, *Hidden Mercy: AIDS, Catholics, and the Untold Stories of Compassion in the Face of Fear* (Minneapolis: Broadleaf, 2021), 237.

5. The print issue of May 20, 2002, had a cover image of Spider-Man, with the headline "Spider-Man Rules," anticipating the release of the first installment of the Marvel Enterprises Spider-Man film franchise.

6. Gerard Manley Hopkins, *Gerard Manley Hopkins: The Major Works*, ed. Catherine Phillips (New York: Oxford University Press, 2009).

7. Christopher Pramuk, *At Play in Creation: Merton's Awakening to the Feminine Divine* (Collegeville, MN: Liturgical Press, 2015).

8. John Dadosky and William Hart McNichols, *Image to Insight: The Art of William Hart McNichols* (Albuquerque: University of New Mexico Press, 2018), 85.

9. *Oppenheimer*, dir. Christopher Nolan (Universal, 2023).

10. On Daniel and Philip Berrigan, see Jim Forest, *At Play in the Lion's Den: A Biography and Memoir of Daniel Berrigan* (Maryknoll, NY: Orbis Books, 2017); *The Berrigans: Devout and Dangerous*, dir. Susan Hagedorn (Seedworks, 2021).

11. Thomas Merton, "Hagia Sophia," in *Emblems of a Season of Fury* (New York: New Directions, 1963),

61–69. For a close study of Merton's prose poem and the Wisdom-Sophia tradition, see Christopher Pramuk, *At Play in Creation: Merton's Awakening to the Feminine Divine* (Collegeville, MN: Liturgical Press, 2015); Christopher Pramuk, *Sophia: The Hidden Christ of Thomas Merton* (Collegeville, MN: Liturgical/Michael Glazier, 2009).

12. Thomas Merton, *Conjectures of a Guilty Bystander* (Garden City, NY: Doubleday, 1966), 157.

13. Our son Henry was born to a Haitian mother in the city of Port-au-Prince and brought to an orphanage at three days old. We initiated adoption proceedings during the summer of 2009, and he was brought to the United States on January 24, 2010, just before his first birthday, following the devastating earthquake in that country on January 12, 2010. His sister Sophia, from the same orphanage but not biologically related, was six years old, having lost both of her parents at age three or four. Lauri and I also have two biological children, Isabell, then eleven, and Grace, then six. While there has been a lot of joy in our lives as a family since the adoptions, the "pain body" of Haiti has affected us all.

14. For Matthew Shepard and his mother, Judy, see chap. 1 n. 1.

15. See Christopher Pramuk, "At the Foot of the Black Cross in America," *Jesuit Higher Education: A Journal* 12, no. 1 (June 2023): 9–15.

11. What You Gaze Upon You Become

1. See Adrienne von Speyr, *Book of All Saints* (San Francisco: Ignatius Press, 2017).

2. On Thea Bowman, see chap. 2 n. 1.

3. James Martin, *Come Forth: The Promise of Jesus's Greatest Miracle* (San Francisco: HarperOne, 2023).

4. Rachel Carson, *Silent Spring* (Boston: Houghton Mifflin, 1962).

5. See Roseanne Murphy, *Martyr of the Amazon: The Life of Sister Dorothy Stang* (Maryknoll, NY: Orbis Books, 2022); Binka Le Breton, *The Greatest Gift: The Courageous Life and Martyrdom of Sister Dorothy Stang* (New York: Doubleday, 2008).

6. See Dorothy Day, *The Long Loneliness* (New York: HarperCollins, 1997); Robert Ellsberg, ed., *Dorothy Day: Selected Writings* (Maryknoll, NY: Orbis Books, 2005); Jim Forest, *All Is Grace: A Biography of Dorothy Day* (Maryknoll, NY: Orbis Books, 2011).

7. See Robert A. Johnson with Jerry M. Ruhl, *Balancing Heaven and Earth: A Memoir of Visions, Dreams and Realizations* (San Francisco: HarperOne, 2009).

8. Maura O'Halloran, *Pure Heart, Enlightened Mind: The Zen Journal and Letters of Maura "Soshin" O'Halloran* (New York: Riverhead, 1995).

9. Louis Massignon, *The Passion of Al-Hallaj, Mystic and Martyr of Islam, Vols. 1–4*, trans. Herbert Mason (Princeton, NJ: Princeton University Press, 2019).

10. For Merton's most prominent uses of the phrase *le point vierge*, see Thomas Merton, *Conjectures of a Guilty Bystander* (Garden City, NY: Doubleday, 1966), 118, 132, 140–42, 156–58. See also *"le point vierge,"* in *The Thomas Merton Encyclopedia* (Maryknoll, NY: Orbis Books, 2002), 363–64.

11. Susannah Heschel, *The Aryan Jesus: Christian Theologians and the Bible in Nazi Germany* (Princeton, NJ: Princeton University Press, 2010).

12. James W. Douglass, *Lightning East to West: Jesus, Gandhi, and the Nuclear Age* (Eugene, OR: Wipf & Stock, 2006).

13. Sister Wendy Beckett and Robert Ellsberg, *Dearest Sister Wendy: A Surprising Story of Faith and Friendship* (Maryknoll, NY: Orbis Books, 2022), 259–60.

14. Henri J. M. Nouwen, *Behold the Beauty of the Lord: Praying with Icons* (Notre Dame, IN: Ave Maria, 2007), 24.

15. Beckett and Ellsberg, *Dearest Sister Wendy*, 257–58.

16. William F. Lynch, *Images of Hope: Imagination as Healer of the Hopeless* (South Bend, IN: University of Notre Dame Press, 1974).

17. Simon Kent Fung, "Dear Alana," Tenderfoot TV (2023), available to stream at www.dearalana.com. Other sources in Catholic media include: https://www.americamagazine.org/faith/2023/09/01/dear-alana-podcast-245990 (O'Laughlin); https://www.ncronline.org/opinion/ncr-voices/sometimes-lgbtq-issues-are-literally-life-and-death (Heidi Schlumpf); https://www.ncronline.org/news/young-womans-suicide-puts-focus-churchs-counseling-lgbt-catholics (Julig); https://www.ncronline.org/culture/dear-alana-hit-no-1-apple-podcasts-are-church-leaders-listening .

12. Then We Shall See Face to Face

1. See Melissa Raphael, *The Female Face of God in Auschwitz: A Jewish Feminist Theology of the Holocaust* (New York: Routledge, 2003), 130.

2. Gregory Hillis, *Man of Dialogue: Thomas Merton's Catholic Vision* (Collegeville, MN: Liturgical Press, 2021).

3. Thomas Merton, "The Time of the End Is the

Time of No Room," *Raids on the Unspeakable* (New York: New Directions, 1966), 65–75, at 73.

4. See St. John of the Cross, "If You Want," in *The Collected Works of John of the Cross*, trans. Kieran Kavanaugh and Otilio Rodriguez (Washington, DC: ICS Publications, 1991).

5. Henri de Lubac, *The Splendor of the Church* (San Francisco: Ignatius Press, 1986).

6. "Interview with Fr. Bill McNichols, *The Boy Who Found Gold*," Pathways of Learning, The Catholic Channel, August 2022. Available at https://www.youtube.com/watch?v=NnnY3dO9i_k.

7. G. B. Caird, *The Gospel of St. Luke*, Westminster Pelican New Testament Commentaries (Louisville, KY: Westminster John Knox Press, 1978).